A Treasury for
Word Lovers

The Professional Writing Series

This volume is one of a series published by ISI Press®. The series is designed to improve the communication skills of professional men and women, as well as students embarking upon professional careers.

Books published in this series:

Communication Skills for the Foreign-Born Professional
    by GREGORY A. BARNES

The Art of Abstracting
    by EDWARD T. CREMMINS

How to Write and Publish a Scientific Paper
    by ROBERT A. DAY

A Treasury for Word Lovers
    by MORTON S. FREEMAN

Presenting Science to the Public
    by BARBARA GASTEL

How to Write and Publish Papers in the Medical Sciences
    by EDWARD J. HUTH

How to Write and Publish Engineering Papers and Reports
    by HERBERT B. MICHAELSON

A Treasury for Word Lovers

by MORTON S. FREEMAN

Foreword by
EDWIN NEWMAN

iSi PRESS®

Philadelphia

Published by

iSi PRESS® A Subsidiary of the
Institute for Scientific Information®
3501 Market St., University City Science Center, Philadelphia, PA 19104 U.S.A.

Library of Congress Cataloging in Publication Data

Freeman, Morton S.
  A treasury for word lovers.

  (The Professional writing series)
  Includes index.
  1. English language—Usage—Dictionaries.
I. Title.   II. Series.
PE1628.F67   1983   423.1   83-12610
ISBN 0-89495-026-6
ISBN 0-89495-027-4 (pbk.)

Printed in the United States of America

To my children's children—
Lauren Rose, Cara, and Jill
Arin and Sammy

Foreword

In the last few months, I have—without organized effort and merely by being alive and moderately alert—heard and seen the following:

The publisher of the so-called Hitler diaries, a television news correspondent reported, "failed to convincingly authenticate them." Even with the infinitive unsplit, it is the unconvincing authentication that must be guarded against.

Two men, according to another television newsman, were "self-confessed Cuban agents." Maybe they self-confessed to keep someone else from doing it for them.

A racing car, its driver said, was not merely totaled but completely totaled, which evidently is worse.

The Navy put an expensive sectional sofa into a destroyer's wardroom not to make the officers more comfortable but for "habitability improvement."

"Alteration in comfort," a term used in some medical circles instead of pain.

"Leadershipping." It is possible to take courses in leadershipping. Their sponsors hope that businessmen and businesswomen will sign up.

"I am not skilled in linguistics." This reply was made by the head of a government agency who farmed out, to a private company, at a cost of $23,000, the drafting of a letter. He had been asked why he had not written the letter himself.

"Input-Output User Access Facilities." In the days before computers, these were known as Work Windows.

"Tortuous," a perfectly good word, but the speaker, a television sports broadcaster, meant "torturous."

"A detergent so unique it is patented." There are no degrees of uniqueness, even in television commercials.

"Nobody can help you do that better than us." Another television commercial.

By a bank, "principle" for the principal in principal and interest.

From a Supreme Court Justice's opinion: ". . . to say more would belabor the obvious." He meant "labor." To belabor the obvious is to hit it, which hardly seems judicial conduct.

From a local television news anchorman: "The vessel sunk."

From one of America's leading newspapers, a small miracle: "Self-made brick shanties." Squatters live in these in Caracas, Venezuela. Apparently the shanties erected themselves.

The following words, among many others, misspelled on television and in the press: publicly, scorcher, accidentally, martial, deficit, cathedral, pompom, missiles, parquet, severance.

Why do I bring all of this up? To suggest—this is a gross understatement—that the English language is not being well served by many of those who use it. They, as the saying goes, need help. So does English. Mr. Freeman's book supplies that help, directly, practically, and entertainingly.

EDWIN NEWMAN

Preface

. . . here and there a touch of good grammar for picturesqueness.

—MARK TWAIN

A Treasury for Word Lovers has been compiled from my experience as an English teacher and as the Director of Publications for the American Law Institute-American Bar Association (ALI-ABA). Primarily in the latter capacity I have been called upon to answer questions, almost daily, regarding grammar, word usage, punctuation, capitalization, the use of numbers, and kindred matters that affect one's style of writing.

Resolving these problems is a ticklish task because the English language has not stood still, and what was learned in the classroom of yesterday might be obsolete today. Hence some explanations of current usage, particularly, will not be readily accepted by those readers who had tender knuckles rapped and young minds indoctrinated with inflexible rules of grammar. However, it is assumed that all readers desire to express themselves correctly and effectively both in speech and in writing. To this end the accent on formal writing—that which is expected on a high literate level—predominates throughout this book. Knowing the strictest requirements of formal English does not, however, demand continuous usage of orthodox forms. One may always back down. But without that knowledge, it is impossible to go up.

Formal writing, since it is grammatically pure and precise, is most suitable to documents, scholarly papers, and textbooks. The language tends to be stilted, for it hews strictly to the letter and does not admit the lively, free-flowing rhythm and phraseology that characterize informal writing. Whether to speak and write formally or informally depends, of course, on the intended audience. One's style of communication should be as appropriate as the clothing worn at a black-tie affair or at a family picnic.

For those who would desire to learn the words and expressions of cultured people, it is suggested that this work be used as a point of reference. Strict adherence to old stodgy forms may be rejected in favor of contemporary usage; for example,

"He did not use to do that" rather than the grammatically precise "He *used not* to do that" or "The decree was to reinstate him" rather than the obsolescent subjunctive formula "The decree was that he *be* reinstated."

Every effort has been made to present the material simply and to make its reading pleasurable. The essays have been arranged alphabetically by a key word or by subject matter, with cross references of related words or concepts. To ease and expedite understanding, examples have been preferred to exposition. Basic rules have been set out only where they would not interfere with the work's practical approach. By no means is this a grammar book.

Anyone who loves words or who seeks a better command of them should find a perusal of this work useful and rewarding. (Is a person with a queasy stomach *nauseous* or *nauseated*? Why can a parent *convince* his son that the lawn needs mowing yet be unable to *persuade* him to mow it?) And those bothered by punctuation problems will also find something of value. (Does this need a semicolon? Is that comma necessary? When does material within parentheses begin with a capital letter and end with a mark of punctuation?) The English language bristles with spelling quandaries. Why, for example, is *-ible* the suffix in *deductible* but *-able* in *excludable*? And when is the noun-ending *-ance* preferred to *-ence,* or the verb ending *-ize* to *-ise*? ("Do not criticize when others compromise.") And is the plural form of *attorney general* "attorneys general" or "attorney generals"? Did the "editor in chiefs" meet or were they "editors in chief"? These questions, and others germane to the issue of good grammar, are discussed and exemplified in these pages.

My intention has been to present information that will resolve the perplexing problems one might encounter when writing for educated people. Often the mention of colloquialisms and slang was incidental on the way to a full explication of certain points.

There are, of course, many levels of English. This work was designed for those whose use of English would label them Word Lovers.

Morton S. Freeman

A, AN

A Sound Rule

The choice between *a* and *an* is determined by the initial sound of the word modified. Words beginning with a consonant, except a silent *h* or a vowel that sounds like a consonant, are modified by *a:* *a* tall man, *a* pretty painting; *a* hotel, *a* historic document; *a* unit, *a* European. Words beginning with a vowel sound or a silent *h* take *an:* *an* oyster, *an* earthen jug; *an* hour, *an* honor. Using *an* before a sounded, or aspirated, *h* (*an* historical monument, *an* humble person, *an* habitual response) is out of step with contemporary usage. The common form is *a.*

The use of *a* or *an* before letters follows the same rule—their sound: "He wrote *an n*, *an r*, *a v*, and *a u*. This means that *an* may modify a consonant and *a*, a vowel. Likewise with abbreviations and symbols: *an* FBI case, *a* NATO project, *a* UFO sighting, *an* H. R. bill.

The articles *a* and *an*, although singular forms, idiomatically may combine with *many*, a word that implies a plural: "Many *a* one has tried." "Many *an* hour has gone for nought." But neither *a* nor *an* should be used in negative comparisons. In "No easier *a* task; no brighter *an* hour," they are superfluous.

A LOT OF

A Lot Is More than Enough

It has been said that America's favorite colloquial expression is *a lot of*, meaning "a considerably large number of persons or things." The phrase is not peculiar to any one group but appears on every level of usage. Saying "We had *a lot of* fun today" or "We have *a lot* to do now" is, according to established practice, today's accepted style; saying *much fun today* or *a great deal to do now*, although precise, sounds stilted. This is equally so with "He has *lots of* (for *many*) books on archeology" and "I was sick, but I feel *lots* (for *much*) better now."

In formal writing, nevertheless, in which these variations are unacceptable, *lot* should be used only in its conventional senses, such as "a measured portion of land." It is not an approved substitute for *much, many,* or *a great deal of.* In more formal language, one would say "I feel *much* (not *a lot*) better now."

The objection of economy-minded stylists to *a lot of* is wordiness. Substituting *many* saves two words. Nevertheless, if *a lot* is used, it should be spelled as two words: *a lot,* not *alot.*

ABOUT

See WORDS OF APPROXIMATION

ABOVE

Above All

The word *above* raises no problem when it serves as a preposition ("*above* the doorway"), but it does when it acts as an adverb or adjective.

It sounds pedantic or legalistic when used adverbially to mean "stated earlier," as in "the project reported *above*" or "the *above*-described schedule." Usually it is best to avoid such phrases entirely and to repeat a name or word so that the reader need not retrace steps to see what was referred to. But if this cannot be done smoothly, then wording such as the following should be used: "the example mentioned before," "the preceding description," or "the foregoing schedule"; or, even better, "these considerations," "this fact," "that theory," or "this point." A practical objection to a phrase like "the rule cited *above*" or "the *above*-discussed matter" is that in print or typescript the rule or the matter might appear on a previous page and not actually be above the sentence being read.

Formal style does not recognize *above* as an adjective "the *above* principle" or as a noun "see the *above*."

ABRIDGMENT

See SUMMARY AND RELATED WORDS

ABSOLUTE EXPRESSIONS

See SUPERLATIVES

ACCIDENT, MISHAP

Accidents Will Happen

Although in general the word *accident* has come to mean an unfortunate or disastrous happening, it has no inherent attribute of undesirability. An accident is something that happens without known cause or deliberate intention. It is an unforeseen chance occurrence. It may be a stroke of good fortune ("By *accident* I met my uncle just after losing my wallet") or an unfortunate happening ("The *accident* destroyed his car").

A synonym, but not an equivalent, is *mishap*. Unlike the word *accident,* a *mishap* always refers to something unpleasant; one cannot have a "fortunate mishap." The misfortune that *mishap* suggests, however, is not serious. It is a minor accident. A calamity, such as a train derailment or a collision between two airplanes, would not be a mishap. It would be an accident.

ACRONYM

See PHILOLOGY

ACROSTIC

See PHILOLOGY

AD INFINITUM

See FOREIGN WORDS

ADAPT, ADEPT, ADOPT

Adept at Adoption

It should be remembered that *adopt,* which means "to take as one's own," needs a direct object: "The committee *adopted* the chairman's recommendation." *Adapt,* defined as "making suitable for a purpose" or "to fit for a new use," also may take a direct object: "Zucker *adapted* the Broadway play for the screen," but it is more often used intransitively, followed by *to* or *for. Adapt to* has the sense of "adjust to," and *adapt for,* "made (over) for." "The maid *adapted* well *to* her new position." "The novel was *adapted for* stage presentation."

Within *adapt* is the word *apt,* which means "suitable" or "appropriate." Confusingly similar to *adapt* is the word *adept.* It means "highly skilled." If a preposition follows *adept,* it is either *in* or *at;* but *in* is preferred: "He is *adept in* preparing computer programs." A person *adept* in something may be said to be apt in it. For example, "Wayne is *adept* in gardening" may be rephrased, "Wayne is *apt* in gardening" although *adept* is the usual term.

ADDICT, DEVOTEE

Love and Devotion

The chief difference between an *addict* and a *devotee* (pronounced dehv-oh-*tee*) is that the former is physically dependent upon something or habitually attached to it, whereas the latter is merely an ardent enthusiast. That which an addict is attached to (the addiction) is usually socially undesirable and harmful, such as the taking of drugs, whereas a devotee is a follower of something regarded as beneficial, like symphony concerts. One may be addicted to low company or cheating or lying. A devotee, on the other hand, may be involved in promoting justice or in helping orphans or in some other laudable activity. One may, of course, become devoted to more ordinary pursuits like crocheting or playing bridge.

Addicted to and *subject to* come into comparison in that they both pertain to conditions or activities difficult or impossible to control. *Addicted to* means catering to a weakness. *Subject to* implies what is liable to occur: "John is *subject to* (*liable to*) migraines." The phrase may also mean "conditional upon," as in "Here is the curriculum, *subject to* the dean's approval." The phrase need not be used only of people: "The Caribbean Sea is *subject to* late summer hurricanes." *Addicted to* is used chiefly in the passive voice and must be followed by a noun: "He is *addicted to* goofers."

ADDUCE, DEDUCE, DEDUCT

The Deuce You Say

Adduce (spelled with two *d*'s) means "to present as an argument" or "to cite," as one does who adduces reason in his behalf. What should not be confused with it is *deduce*, which means "to infer," "to derive as a conclusion from something assumed or known," as one who deduces from flimsy excuses that a person is lying. It is therefore incorrect to say "We must *adduce* from your statement that you are not interested." The right word is *deduce*.

The meanings of *deduce* and *deduct* are different, even though one may reach a deduction through a process of deducing. To *deduct* is "to subtract," as in "*Deduct* your selling costs from the retail price to learn your net profit." Yet both *deduce* and *deduct* come from the Latin *deducere*, "to lead away," "to infer logically." *Deduct* stems directly from its past participle *deductus*. A *deduction*, therefore, has two senses: either the drawing of a conclusion from a general principle (an inference) or a taking away (the lowering of a figure by subtraction).

ADJECTIVES, TYPES OF

Position Is Everything

The adjective, a part of speech that describes or limits nouns or pronouns, has four possible positions in a sentence, each of which has an identifying name.

The most common adjective, the *attributive adjective*, is usually placed before the noun it qualifies: "The *young* man is a *brilliant* student." When it follows the noun, the phrasing, although proper, sounds contrived: "Pavlova was a ballerina *supreme*."

An *appositive adjective* explains or identifies the preceding noun. Because it follows the noun, its position is unnatural and its effect, stilted: "His criticism, *intelligent* and *constructive,* was deeply appreciated." "Many books, *new and used,* were on display."

A *predicate adjective,* which describes its subject, is placed at the end of a sentence or clause to complete the meaning of the verb. This adjective follows a stated or implied linking verb, such as *seem* or *become* ("Valenza's version seemed *credible*") or verbs pertaining to the senses ("The food smelled *good*").

An *objective complement* follows and describes the direct object of a predicate verb, as in "He considers the *plan* (direct object) *excellent*" (objective complement) and "Such criticism made *him* (direct object) *angry*" (objective complement).

(Words that can be either adjectives or adverbs are discussed under FLAT ADVERBS and RIGHT, WRONG.)

ADEPT

See ADAPT, ADEPT, ADOPT

ADMIT

Free Admission

Admit is a word that admits of many definitions. Most commonly it means "to allow to enter," as in "He was *admitted* into the room." It also means "to acknowledge" ("We *admit* that she is right") and "to allow as valid" ("The man *admits* the justification of his neighbor's claim").

A witness, in correct usage, admits having seen the accused, not *to* having seen him, even though the added *to* is commonly heard. The phrase *admit of* is employed only with abstractions. The subject of *admit of* is an impersonal noun; therefore, a person does not *admit of*: "His problem *admits of* several different solutions." "Her behavior will not *admit of* any other interpretation." Here the sense of *admit of* is "leaving room for."

Another example of the use of *admit* and *admit of* is in "The gate *admits* the employees (affords them entrance), but the size of their cars will not *admit of* (allow or permit) easy passage."

ADOPT

See **ADAPT, ADEPT, ADOPT**

ADVERBIAL PHRASES AND CLAUSES

It's a Follow-Through

A fundamental rule concerning introductory adverbial phrases or clauses is that they modify all verbs in the following independent clause. Just as *usually* in "*Usually* he golfs and swims during his vacation" means he *usually* golfs and *usually* swims during his vacation, so, too, the adverbial clause in "*When he goes on vacation,* he golfs and swims" modifies both *golfs* and *swims.*

The construction to guard against is the compound predicate in which the second verb and the introductory phrase are incompatible, for the results can be ludicrous. For example, "In 1980 Wallace served in the State Department and returned to his farm a year later" says that Wallace went back to his farm both in 1980 and in 1981. What is said in "During the first semester, the dean lectured daily and retired the following semester" is that the dean retired during the first semester and the second semester as well. Although the thoughts meant to be expressed are clear, grammatically the sentences need unraveling. The simplest solution is to restrict the introductory phrase to a single thought "During 1980 Wallace served in the State Department. In the following year he returned to his farm." Or one fact might be subordinated: "Having served during 1980 in the State Department, Wallace in 1981 returned to his farm."

ADVERBS

See **FLAT ADVERBS** and **RIGHT, WRONG** for a discussion of words that can be used as either adjectives or adverbs. Further discussion of adverbs appears under **HOWEVER** and **INTRODUCTORY EXPRESSIONS.**

ADVERSE, AVERSE, ADVERT, AVERT

Your Turn

From two similarly spelled Latin words, several English words derive. Their spelling and phonetic resemblance can lead to much confusion. The first is *adversus,* "turned toward," past participle of *advertere.* The English words it has spawned are *adverse* and *advert.* The second is *aversus,* "turned away," past participle of *avertere,* from which the words *averse* and *avert* originated.

Both *adverse* and *averse* connote opposition, but they are not synonyms. *Adverse* means "opposed, contrary, or unfavorable," as in adverse rulings or adverse criticism. *Averse,* defined as "reluctant or unwilling," denotes a distaste or dislike for something and a tendency to avoid or spurn it (averse to crowds; averse to travel; averse to lectures; averse to study). It may involve an emotional feeling (averse to telling a lie). *Adverse* implies a mental state that may not necessarily suggest dislike or disgust. It more aptly describes ideas and judgments. A person's position may be adverse (opposite) to another's. A law may be adverse (run counter) to the beliefs of some people. Although both *adverse* and *averse* are followed by the preposition *to* in the preceding examples, *from* may occasionally follow *averse.* *Adverse* always takes *to.*

Avert means "to turn away; to prevent; to ward off." A person may avert an accident by jumping into a safety zone or, by deflecting a flying object, avert being struck on the head.

Advert and *refer* are synonymous terms. What one adverts to is referred to, and *to* ordinarily is needed in either case. Since *advert* is a bookish word, *refer* is usually a better choice.

ADVICE, ADVISE

Some Free Advice

In general language *advise* is loosely, and inappropriately, used to mean "inform." Strictly speaking, a person is not advised that a package has arrived. He is notified. An accountant does not advise a secretary to file his reports; he tells her.

The meaning of *advise* is "to counsel"; to "warn"; "to give advice"—that is, to suggest that a course of action be followed.

A doctor advises a patient on matters of health. A flagman advises a motorist of dangerous road conditions. Obviously the sentence "My wife *advised* me she will go shopping today" is poorly worded. Only in rather formal announcements, from which a feeling of seriousness is expected, is *advise*, in the sense "to give information," acceptable ("The President *advised* his staff that he will resign." "The administration spokesman *advised* the reporters that war is imminent"). Except for that latitude, *advise* is a pompous substitute for *say, inform, tell,* and other ordinary verbs.

The noun *advice* means "counsel, guidance, a recommended opinion." Statements and announcements devoid of recommendations or opinions are not advice. For example, in "The present *advice* is that the office will be closed next Monday," *advice* is wrongly used.

A sister word that is also often treated loosely is *advisedly.* What is done advisedly is done deliberately, after considering the possible consequences. Intentional acts are done purposely, but not necessarily advisedly—that is, according to advice or a plan. A teacher who intentionally cuffs an unruly student was probably not advised to do so.

Such phrases as "we wish to advise" or "we beg to advise" are both old-fashioned and unnecessary. They should be treated like deadwood—removed and discarded. Saying "Please be advised that four truckloads were shipped yesterday" may be restated, pointedly: "Four truckloads were shipped yesterday."

The spelling *adviser* is generally preferred to *advisor. Advisory* is spelled only one way.

AFFECT, EFFECT

It's the Effect That Counts

Affect, except for its technical use as a noun in psychology, is a verb meaning "to have an influence on" or "to produce a change in" ("Economic dislocation affects our standards of living." "Cold weather affects older people"). It also means "to assume" or "to make a show of" ("The actor *affected* a guilty look"). *Effect* as a verb means "to bring about," "to produce," "to accomplish" ("The expert promptly *effected* changes in our office procedure"). But it is most commonly employed as a noun, meaning "a result, outcome, or consequence" (After he dyed his hair, the *effect* on his appearance was startling").

Two unrelated matters warrant attention. One, *affect* often wrongly displaces more precise words. In "The uncle's illness *affected* Franklin's departure," *delayed* would be more appropriate. In "Marlene was *affected* by the loss of her dog," Marlene was *saddened*. Two, the verb *effect* lends itself more to the passive voice than to the active: "The change in government *was effected* by violence."

Although the meanings of *affect* and *effect* are clear, their spellings are sometimes confused, a problem that can be resolved by remembering that something must *affect* something to have an *effect* on it. In this sequence *a* comes before *e*, just as it does in the alphabet: "We all will be *affected* by the *effect* of a lopsided federal budget."

AFFINITY

A Deep Feeling

The word in issue is *affinity*. In Latin, *affinitas,* its ancestor, means "bordering on, related by marriage." Its English offspring, *affinity,* has evolved to mean "a natural liking for, or attraction to, a person or thing."

In the sentence "Robert Tolson has an *affinity* for chess but not for geometry," some purists would insist that *affinity* was wrongly used because, according to them, "a natural liking for" refers only to people and not to unfeeling objects nor to a propensity for doing or being something, an interpretation that has not been widely adopted, however. Only time will tell whether it will survive; the chances are against it. The replacement in the example that they would recommend is *aptitude, knack,* or *ability.*

The prepositions that *affinity* takes are *with* and *between* (not *for*) because they point to a mutual relationship: "They have an *affinity* of long standing *between* them—a delight in English words!"

AFFIXES

In a Fix

From the Latin word *figere*, "to fasten," has evolved the English word with the same meaning—*fix*. The term used in grammar, *affix*, is *fix* prefaced by *af*, which means "to." The doubling of the *f*, to avoid the *d* in *ad-* (a prefix for "to"), is designed to make pronunciation easier. An affix is a prefix, a suffix, or a combining form attached to a root to form a new word, which then acquires a meaning different from that of the original base.

Letters attached to the beginning of a word that create a new meaning are called a *prefix* (Latin *pre-*, "before"). A prefix may dramatically turn the sense of a word completely around (*emphatic, unemphatic*). An attachment of letters to the end of a word that changes the function of the word is a *suffix* (*theory, theorize*). The prefix *suf-* in suffix means "under," and it replaces *sub-* for the same reason just given regarding the word *affix*. A combining form is a word element (*micro-*, "small"—*microcosm, microbiology; tele-*, "distant"—*television, teleprompter; psycho-*, "mind"—*psychiatry, psychoanalysis*) that combines with other word elements to form a compound or a new word.

Suffering Suffixes

The rules governing the addition of suffixes are bothersome. Some suffixes fit easily; unfortunately, many do not. Perhaps the most difficult question to answer, before adding an *-ing* or *-ed* suffix, is whether to double a final consonant. The rule to follow is this: When a final consonant is preceded by a single vowel, the consonant is doubled when the suffix is added to a two-or-more-syllable word in which the final syllable is stressed. Examples are *admit, admitting; begin, beginning; control, controlled.* Examples of words in which the final consonant is not doubled because the accent does not fall on the last syllable are *benefit, benefited; travel, traveling; worship, worshiping.* If the final syllable has an almost equal stress with another, the final syllable is usually doubled: *handicap, handicapped; outfit, outfitted; sandbag, sandbagging.* The best advice is to double if the end is stressed.

Words ending in *ee* and *oo* add suffixes without change: *see, seeing; glee, gleeful; woo, wooed, wooing; flee, fleeing.* Words ending in *c* add a *k* for clarity before a suffix beginning with *e, i,* or *y: mimic, mimicked; picnic, picnicking; traffic, trafficking; panic, panicky.*

The suffix *-endous* serves only three words in the English language—*tremendous, horrendous, stupendous*—hence sharing a place of distinction with *-ceed,* which also is the ending for only three words, *exceed, succeed,* and *proceed.* Of course, *-sede* is even more exclusive. It is the ending for only one word: *supersede.*

AFFLICT, INFLICT

The Bread of Affliction

Both *afflict* and *inflict* connote something unwelcome. This is understandable, since their Latin root means "to strike to the ground."

Today *afflict* means "to trouble" or "to lay on bodily or to cause mental pain." It suggests distress so severe as to cause prolonged suffering: "He was *afflicted* with an unknown stomach ailment." "God *afflicted* Job with many tribulations."

Similarly, *inflict* means "to lay on" or "to impose." Like *afflict,* it refers to something unwanted and burdensome that may be damaging or painful: "The colonel *inflicted* severe punishment upon the sergeant." "The coroner determined that the mortal wound was *inflicted* by a carving knife."

The distinction between these words is that the object of *afflict* is an actual person or thing, whereas the object of *inflict* is inanimate: God afflicted Job, but He inflicted tribulations. *Afflict* takes the preposition *with; inflict* takes *upon.*

AFRAID, AGGRAVATE, BLAME

Don't Bug Me

"I'm aggravated that I can't blame anything on my brother, but I'm scared of him." This statement, although not uncommon, contains three informal expressions: one so firmly entrenched in the language as to be considered standard English by some authorities; one that has been continually denounced, but with little effect on its widespread usage; and one that has received no approval from any respected source.

The word in popular usage that has withstood the onslaught of grammarians is *aggravate*. Derived from the Latin *aggravare* (from *gravis*, "heavy,"), it means "to make worse," "to make more of a burden," or "to intensify"—all pertaining to disagreeable conditions but not to people. *Aggravate* is correctly used in "Smoking can *aggravate* a sore throat" or in "Untended wounds are bound to become *aggravated*." In everyday speech *to aggravate* has come to mean "to make angry," "to irritate," or, in the vernacular, "to make someone mad." This is what is meant by "Don't *aggravate* Mr. Panchoni." In formal style a person who is angered is said to be *irritated, vexed, bothered, exasperated, annoyed,* or *provoked.*

The expression *blame on,* as in blaming an accident on someone, although widely used, is inaccurate. It should be the other way around—some one should be blamed for the accident. Logically only people, not things, situations, or circumstances, can be assessed with blame. Therefore, it is correct to say (although perhaps futile to argue it): "We *blame her* for the accident," not "We *blame* the *accident* on her." In standard English the verb *blame* takes *for* when a preposition is needed. *On* is used only after the noun *blame:* "Let's put the *blame on* Mame."

The phrase *scared of* is a colloquialism best replaced by *afraid of,* which implies habitual fear: "I'm *afraid of* my brother." "Many people are *afraid of* snakes, of the dark, of loud noises." To be scared or frightened, on the other hand, is to experience a sudden but temporary unnerving condition: "We were *scared* (or *frightened*) by the sudden stopping of the elevator between floors." Both these passive forms, unlike the idiomatic *afraid of,* take *by;* for example, "Alice is *frightened by* squirrels" not *of* squirrels. Since *frighten* is a transitive verb, it needs an object. One may say, "Dogs *frighten* her" (active voice) or "She *is frightened* by dogs" (passive voice), but not "She *frightens easily*" when she sees dogs."

An afterthought. The expression "She's *afraid* he's right" is an informal—and incorrect—way of saying "She *fears* that he's right." And "I'm afraid not" is folksy for "I *think* not." The use of *afraid* should be restricted to reflect a real cause for fear, fright, or alarm.

AFTERMATH

After Math Comes Geometry

The *-math* in *aftermath* means "mowing." Hence an aftermath literally comes after the first mowing—the mowing of a second crop of grass in the same season: "The yield of the *aftermath* was disappointing this year."

No longer does *aftermath* enjoy its original agricultural meaning, however. Its use today is only figurative, "a consequence or result," as in "The aeronautical exposition had a pleasant *aftermath;* several students enrolled in flight school." This usage—to designate something that follows something else—is deplored by many authorities, for *aftermath* refers not just to a result but to a disastrous result. For example, in both "Homeless families are bound to be an *aftermath* of an earthquake" and in "An epidemic of crime may be the *aftermath* of war," *aftermath* is used properly, since both the events and the consequences are lamentable. Therefore, strictly speaking, sleeping late on New Year's Day is not an *aftermath* of the previous night's festivities: only the hangover is!

AGGRAVATE

See **AFRAID, AGGRAVATE, BLAME**

AL-, ALL

All Together Now

Words beginning with *al-* and expressions beginning with *all,* because of their similar sounds, are sometimes written incorrectly. One may safely say "This pie has twelve ingredients *all together,*" since *all together* sounds like a single word; but it is wrong to write it that way. If there are only twelve ingredients, the word to use is *altogether,* meaning "wholly, entirely, or completely"—the equivalent of "in all." The term *all together* means "all at the same place," "in a group," or "in concert," as in "The legislators have assembled *all together* in the rotunda to greet the newly elected governor."

Another *al/all* twosome that sometimes is a source of confusion is *already* and *all ready.* The former, the adverb *already,* means "earlier," "previously," or "by this time." The latter refers to a state of readiness—that is, everyone or everything is ready. To determine which word to use, one should omit the al- or the all and note the effect on the sense of the sentence. The all in "all" expressions can be omitted without impairing meaning. For example, just as in "The faculty left all together," the sentence without all retains its logic, as it does in "The faculty is all ready." But this is not so with already in "Tim has already painted the barn." The truncated ready is meaningless. "Tim has ready painted the barn" is nonsense.

Two matters worthy of notice. First, already is used with verbs in the perfect tense, not in the simple past: "Jeanne has already cleaned the tables," not "Jeanne already cleaned the tables." (This does not apply to words signifying continued action, such as knew or realized: "The patient knew the prognosis already.") Second, for the sake of economy, "all" words may be excised without occasioning a loss in emphasis. Certainly the all's are unnecessary in "The actors are all together and all ready to perform."

All right is a correct term. Alright is nonexistent in acceptable usage.

ALIBI

See MISUSED WORDS

ALIEN, FOREIGN

Alienated Foreigners

A person who has immigrated to another country may be called a foreigner or an alien. Although both terms are accurate designations, they are not synonymous.

An *alien*, according to its Latin root, *alienus*, is a stranger, "one who belongs to another." Today the word *alien* denotes "a person who owes political allegiance to another country"; in short, a resident in a country of which he is not a citizen. By extension, the word has come to mean "strange or different," as in "*Alien* customs are sometimes hard to understand." When the adjective *alien* needs a preposition, it takes *from* or *to*, but *to* is more common: "Lubitsh's style of dancing is *alien to* ours."

Its verb form *alienate,* which bears a strong connotation of "estrangement," requires the preposition *from:* "The Civil War *alienated* brothers *from* brothers."

Foreigner, a term derived from the Latin *foras,* meaning "out-of-doors," referred to a person who was kept outside and not admitted to the fireside. It now refers to any outsider. Hence a traveler in a country other than his own is a foreigner. Americans, too (surprised?), are foreigners while visiting abroad. Figuratively *foreign* describes anything "outside" native practices or discussion: foreign dishes, foreign languages, foreign dress. Although the word *foreign* bears no pejorative overtones, nevertheless it has an alien flavor for some people. The opposite of a *foreigner* is a *denizen,* "one who lives within"; therefore, a resident.

ALLEGEDLY, REPORTEDLY

Reporter-at-Large

Two words that seem to be the exclusive property of journalists are *allegedly* and *reportedly. Allegedly* refers to what has been stated or declared without proof and is thus open to controversy, as in "The defendant *allegedly* threatened the victim a week previous to the shooting." *Reportedly* is a comparative newcomer to the dictionary, partly because its use strains the grammatical mind. One wonders, for example, in "Fourteen picnickers *reportedly* became ill from food poisoning," how the picnickers could become "*reportedly* ill."

Word authorities are slowly recognizing both terms, but in serious writing they are preferably avoided. In other kinds of works their economy overcomes any minor prejudices against their use.

An adverb that instills a sense of conviction into a statement is *assertedly.* Something asserted may be unsubstantiated, but it is set forth boldly and positively as true.

ALLUSION, ILLUSION, DELUSION

Passing Fantasies

Allusion, illusion, and *delusion* are sometimes confused because of phonetic similarity. Yet they are not synonymous, although *illusion* and *delusion* have a sense in common—the impression that something is so when it is not.

An *allusion* is an indirect, passing, or casual reference. It also may be described as a hint or suggestive phrase: "The President's inaugural address contained several *allusions* to his predecessor." "In his book, the author makes many *allusions* to works written before 1900." Allusions that are not too obscure, that are recognizable without much difficulty (for instance, an allusion to the Boston Tea Party or to a passage from *Hamlet*), give the reader a feeling of satisfaction, for his memory enriches the sense of the writing.

An *illusion* is a false idea or impression that arises from things that look natural but are not. They are deceptive appearances or are things misperceived: "I was sure I had seen a flying saucer, but it was only an *illusion.*" The illusion may even be known to be false but welcomed nonetheless. One enjoys the illusions created by magicians, for example. Indeed, a magician is frequently called an "illusionist."

The word *delusion,* which suggests self-deception, refers to an idea clearly perceived to be unfounded by everyone except the person deluded. Efforts to dispel delusions usually are of no avail, and the person suffering from them may be disposed to act in a way that is harmful to himself or to others.

ALMOST, MOST

Almost, but Not Entirely

The sentence "Most anyone knows what to do in such an emergency" does not fool the enlightened. They know that it should begin "*Almost* anyone knows." It is good that one can almost always (not *most always*) sense when not to use *most* for *almost,* for guidelines on the proper use of *almost* are few.

Almost is an adverb meaning "nearly, not quite, slightly less than": "The dinner is *almost* ready." "I am *almost* finished." It, not *most,* should modify *all* or *any:* "The professor has met *almost* (not *most*) *all* the students." "*Almost* (not *Most*) *any* person can draw pictures in sand." *Almost* may also be used to qualify indefinite pronouns, those compounded with adjectives—*anyone, everyone, anything, everything: "Almost anything* here is too expensive to consider." "He told me that *almost everyone* I would meet in Gettysburg would know Bill."

Most is commonly used as an adjective ("Most horses shy away from snakes") and as a mark of the superlative degree before adjectives and adverbs. This latter use requires a comparison of more than two items: "Robert was the *most brilliant* student in last year's class" (superlative adjective). "The actors can be heard *most clearly* from the balcony" (superlative adverb).

In some sentences *most,* with a little recasting, may replace *almost* without impairing the meaning. For example, *"Almost* everyone at the meeting is a member" in effect says *"Most* of the people at the meeting are members."

ALPHABETS

Rose Etta All the Alphabet Soupa!

The Roman alphabet, which is used in English and in the Romance languages (French, Spanish, Italian, Portuguese, Rumanian), was not invented by the Romans. It was developed by the people of many nations, stemming primarily from the Phoenicians and the Hebrews—neighbors with similar languages. The Greeks made a major addition; they added vowels. The word *alphabet* consists of the first two letters of old Hebrew: *aleph* and *bet.* The first two letters of the Greek alphabet resemble them: *alpha* and *beta.*

The term *Romance* in Romance language refers not to romantic passions but to the language derived from the Romans, which was Latin. The Romans were not the first people to commit their language to writing. The earliest writings are believed to be those of the Sumerians, who invented *cuneiform writing,* and of the Egyptians, who worked with *hieroglyphics.* These writings were pictographs, pictorial symbols representing ideas.

According to Klein's *Etymological Dictionary,* cuneiform was a name given by the seventeenth-century explorer Englebert Kampfer to the characters of the ancient inscriptions of Assyria and Persia. The writing was made by pressing a stylus—a reed with a triangular tip (*cuneus* in Latin means wedge-shaped)— into wet clay, which was then baked in the sun and which, when hardened, became tablets.

The writing symbols of the Egyptians were carved in, or painted on, stone. These symbols were all made by the hands of priests. (In Greek *hiero* meant "sacred" and *glyph*, "to carve.") Later writers (called scribes) wrote on papyrus, sheets made from a plant that grew along the banks of the Nile. The invention of sheets was a big step forward over stone tablets because sheets could be rolled up as documents and easily transported. From *papyrus* comes the English word *paper*.

The deciphering of hieroglyphics on the Rosetta Stone, a piece of basalt, was the work of Thomas Young and Jean François Champollion. The stone was found near a town called Rosetta by a soldier from Napoleon Bonaparte's army, which was then invading Egypt. Archaeologists determined that the inscriptions were in two languages and three scripts: hieroglyphics, demotic, and Greek. The inclusion of Greek, a key to the translation of hieroglyphics, unlocked the mystery of the Eygptian language.

ALTER EGO

See **FOREIGN WORDS**

ALTERNATE, ALTERNATIVE

One or the Other

Alternate means "an action by turns or step-by-step." It is not a synonym of *alternative*, which means "one or the other." If, for example, an architect receives alternate proposals, he receives them one after the other or each in turn. If he receives alternative proposals, it means that he has two proposals of which he is to select one.

A question sometimes raised is whether an alternative is any choice or the second of two possibilities. Since *alter*, the Latin word from which *alternative* was derived, means "other of two," an alternative, logically, is another choice. In general usage, however, the choice may be of either possibility. Today, therefore, it is proper to speak of an *alternative* or *alternatives*. If the plural form is used, a plural verb and the conjunction *and* must follow: "The alternatives *are* swimming *and* (not *or*) golfing." The singular *alternative* takes a singular verb and needs the conjunction *or* to divide the choices: "The alternative *is* swimming *or* (not *and*) golfing."

Additionally, the idea that only two choices are implied by the word *alternatives* has long been discountenanced except in the most formal writing. *Alternatives,* loosely speaking, may be of any number: "The armed services offer four *alternatives*—the Army, the Navy, the Air Force, and the Marines."

Although *alternative* and *choice* are equivalents, their connotations are not identical. A choice may be made, or not made, of a person's free will from available possibilities, but an alternative usually implies that a choice must be made. Inherent in *alternative* is a sense of compulsion: "The *alternative* to not paying tuition is dropping out of school."

ALTHOUGH, THOUGH

Though What!

A question sometimes posed is whether *although* is to be preferred to *though*. When those words serve as a conjunction (*though* is a shortened form of *although*), the answer is no. The words are interchangeable except for the obvious constructions in which only *though* must serve, as in *even though* or *as though*. At the beginning of a sentence, *although* is generally more desirable; on the other hand, when *though* is used as an adverb, it is usually found at the end. In fact, only the adverb *though,* and never the conjunction *although,* may end a sentence: "He said he would help; he didn't *though.*" Some writers restrict the use of adverbial *though* to informal contexts. In formal style, they would choose either *however* or *nevertheless.*

ALUMNA, ALUMNUS

See GRADUATE

AMATEUR

Beginner's Luck

A person starting in a field may be called a beginner, a novice, a neophyte, or a tyro; but he is not necessarily an amateur.

An *amateur* engages in an activity as a pastime, pursuing an avocation—art, photography, dancing—because he loves it, without thought of financial reward. The *ama* in *amateur* derives from the Latin *amare*, which many high school graduates can still conjugate: *amo, amas, amat* ("I love," "you love," "he or she loves"). Today an amateur is so called mainly to distinguish him from a professional, a person paid for his services; but the designation does not imply lack of ability or experience. Some amateurs, especially in sports, even excel some professionals. An amateur who "goes professional" does not ipso facto improve his abilities, just his finances. Nevertheless, in informal usage where precision in meaning gives way to the loose give and-take of everyday language, *amateur* suggests an inexperienced person: "James is an *amateur* typist; he has had only two lessons." *Amateur* is pronounced *am*-u-tur, not am-u-*chur*.

A *beginner*, a person new to a field, impliedly lacks experience. The synonym *novice*, from the Latin *novus* ("new"), also denotes one not yet proficient in a field or activity: "Arthur is a *novice* at roasting chestnuts; he just bought his grill." *Novice* also signifies someone admitted to a religious community for probationary training, although the word *novitiate* is preferred.

A *tyro*, from the Latin for "recruit," aptly connotes a beginner's awkwardness because of inexperience: "Frank was a real *tyro* those weeks at boot camp, acting the tough guy to conceal the clumsy, frightened kid he was inside." Military recruits, although not so titled, are tyros in the literal sense.

A *neophyte* is someone entering a field for which he has had some training, but little experience. A young lawyer, recently admitted to the bar, is a neophyte, as is a newly ordained clergyman. They both are newly planted, from the Greek *neos*, "new," and *phyton*, "plant."

AMBIGUOUS, EQUIVOCAL

Forked Tongues Are as Sharp as Knives

Something *equivocal* or *ambiguous* is unclear. Both words describe what is questionable, especially expressions that admit of several interpretations. To this extent, the terms are synonymous. But from this point on they differ in several ways.

First, the fine distinction between them lies in the speaker's or writer's purpose. *Equivocal* statements are deliberately worded to create two possible meanings; they are purposely evasive. The word (pronounced ee-*kwihv*-oh-kuhl) arrived in English as a combination of the Latin *aequus,* "equal," and *vocis,* genitive of *vox,* "voice." Hence a person who is equivocal speaks with "two voices." An ambiguous statement is also open to several interpretations, in that it has more than one meaning, but through inadvertence: "His speech was so *ambiguous* that no one knew for sure whether he had commended or criticized the vice president's decision." In "Martin wants nothing more than wealth," one may ask whether wealth is all he wants, or whether he wants wealth more than he does other things.

Second, *ambiguous* (from the Latin *ambi-*, "around," and *agere,* "to drive or to go") refers only to verbal statements, never to actions. *Equivocal* applies to words, too, but it also may describe action, quality, or state: "The draft board decided he was a person of *equivocal* loyalty." "His response was *equivocal;* I don't think he's ready to commit himself."

As a euphemism, the verb to *equivocate* has come to mean "to dissemble" or "to lie," a natural evolution, since an equivocal statement is camouflaged. One who equivocates does not do so by accident. He intends to deceive: "Come straight to the point, and don't *equivocate.*"

Unequivocal, the antonym of *equivocal,* means "clear." That which is unequivocal has only one possible interpretation: "The boss's 'You're fired' was *unequivocal.*"

AMBIVALENCE

Torn Two Ways

Ambivalence, defined as "uncertainty as to the approach or tack to take," indicates irresoluteness or indecision: "The senior partner was disturbed by the junior's *ambivalence* in choosing between research and sales." Its use in that sense, however, is loose and not recommended. A person who cannot decide between two choices, rather than being ambivalent, is undecided: "Audrey cannot *decide* whether to vacation (not is *ambivalent about vacationing*) in the country or at the seashore."

The word *ambivalence* is a coinage of Sigmund Freud. It refers to two mixed or conflicting emotions experienced simultaneously: love and hate; attraction and repulsion. Derived from the Latin *ambi-*, "both," and *valere*, "to be strong," *ambivalence*, unlike *indecision*, connotes powerful, yet troublesome, feelings. Although it may be responsible for one's inability to decide, it has nothing inherently to do with decisions or choices. It may accurately describe a child's contradictory emotions, such as obedience to, and rebellion against, a parent or teacher. And many people doubtless recall Othello's agony of ambivalence, which eventually led him to murder Desdemona. On a less tragic level, one can say, "She felt *ambivalent* about his manner, admiring and yet resenting his extreme self-confidence." Of course, the classic example of *ambivalent* is "watching your mother-in-law drive over the cliff in your brand new Cadillac."

AMONG, BETWEEN

Just Between Us

Different theories have been advanced to explain the common but incorrect phrasing *between you and I*. One theory is that in the minds of some people, *me* is too emphatic and too egotistical, whereas *I*, when combined with a noun or another pronoun, sounds softer: "It was just *between* you and I." *I*, however, is grammatically indefensible. *Between* is a preposition, and the object of a preposition is always in the objective case; therefore, *between you and me*. Perhaps the most persuasive theory is that to the untutored mind *between you and I* has to be correct because it sounds as though it ought to be.

Between is ordinarily used to express a relationship between two persons or objects. "The money was divided *between* Tom and Harry." *Among* implies more than two: "The money was divided *among* Tom, Harry, and Billie." *Between* is nevertheless properly used of more than two things when they relate to many other things individually and generally: "The Constitution regulates trade *between* the states." "An economic treaty *between* five European nations was signed this morning." When no close relationship exists and the items are considered collectively, *among* is required: a style of dress prevalent *among* the wealthy;

papers distributed *among* the students; rampant fear *among* the soldiers.

It is illogical, and incorrect, to say *between each.* A person may choose between two items—*between* the blue book and the red, for example—but cannot choose "between each one." Two items are needed for something to come between. A baseball pitcher does not rest *between each* inning. He rests *between* innings. The governing rule is that neither *each* nor *every* should follow *between* and then precede a singular noun. As further examples: "A person does not meditate for a while *between each* busy day" but *between busy days* or *after every busy day.* "The library is situated *between* Fourth and Fifth *streets,*" not *between* Fourth and Fifth *street.* A single noun following *between* must be plural.

When two items are specified, the idiom is *between … and.* Although one may say "He must choose him *or* me," if *between* is used, *or* must be changed to *and.* It is incorrect to say "He must choose *between* him *or* me." It is also wrong to say "It must be between 90 *to* 100 degrees." Numbers, including dates, following *between* should be connected by *and* rather than *or* or a dash: "He was the governor between 1974 *and* 1980," not "*between* 1974–1980." To repeat, the proper combination is *between … and.*

AMPERSAND

And That's How It Is

A question sometimes asked is whether an ampersand (&), the ligature of *et,* is permissible in formal writing. The answer is that it should not replace *and* (for which it stands) unless it is a part of an established name. Many companies now use an ampersand in their name to save space. If *and company* concludes a company's name (as indicated on the letterhead), that style should be followed, for the company's preference, naturally, should be honored. If the preference is unknown, *and* should be spelled out.

In a company name such as Harnett, Levy, Green *and Company,* no comma is placed before *and.* And no comma ever precedes an *ampersand:* Ralston, Gibbons & Company.

AMUSE, BEMUSE

The Musement Park

Judging by its use, *bemuse*, in the opinion of some writers, is synonymous with *amuse*. But that opinion is unjustified. Although both verbs have the same ancestor, *muse*, their current meanings are unrelated. To *muse* means to become absorbed in thought; to *amuse*, to divert thought in a way that cheers and entertains; to *bemuse*, to throw thoughts into disorder, to bewilder, to daze. The sentence "The jury was *bemused* by counsel's oratory," therefore, does not suggest, as some might assume, that the jury enjoyed counsel's address. The members of the jury were not entertained; they were, to say the least, puzzled.

Long ago, when *amuse* did not enjoy its present meaning, it was virtually synonymous with *bemuse*. At that time, *amuse*, a derivative of the Old French *amuser*, meant "to stupefy." It subsequently acquired its happier sense. *Bemuse*, on the other hand, has continued to connote confusion. A bemused person is still so lost in confusing thoughts as to be muddled, stupefied, obfuscated. Clearly it is better to be amused.

ANAGRAM

See PHILOLOGY

AND, OR

No If's, And's, or But's

In serious writing, sentences like "Try *and* visit Prentice today" and "Go *and* see Amanda soon" are not acceptable. The error is the misusing of *and* to conjoin two finite verbs when the second should be an infinitive: *to visit* and *to see*. Although in colloquial speech *and* is widely used to emphasize the idea of result, in precise usage the *and* should be changed to *to*, since only one thought is implied.

What is more common is the misuse of *and* for *or*. This laxity is generally the sign of an insensitive ear. In "We intend to promote a new color *such as* magenta *and* aquamarine" and in "Rachel prefers a citrus fruit *such as* oranges *and* grapefruit," *or* should replace *and,* for a color cannot be both magenta *and* aquamarine nor can a citrus fruit be both oranges *and* grapefruit.

Sometimes the converse is seen—*or* incorrectly displacing *and.* This appears in "The appointment offers no perquisites *or* no raises," which implies that the position will tender one benefit or the other: either there will be no perquisites or there will be no raises, but at least one may be expected. If rewritten, "This position offers no perquisites *and* no raises," one will know not to hope for either one.

ANTECEDENTS

Don't Be So Possessive

The antecedent of a personal pronoun should not be a noun in the possessive case. For example, in the sentence "In Samuel Johnson's *Anecdotes,* he discusses many personal incidents," *he* has no antecedent. The writer intended to refer to Samuel Johnson; that august name, however, in its possessive form is an adjective modifying *Anecdotes.* The sentence should be reworded: "In his *Anecdotes,* Samuel Johnson discusses many personal incidents."

Another rule governing the use of pronouns is that they should follow, not precede, their antecedents in accordance with the literal meaning of the word *antecedent:* Latin *ante-* and *cedere,* "to go before." But this principle is not immutable; it may be bypassed if no confusion results. For example, "If he finishes the entire job, I will congratulate Harvey myself" is clear, even though the as yet unidentified *he* precedes *Harvey.*

The word *same* or the combination *the same* is no substitute for *it:* "We have completed the drawing and are mailing *same* today" is best rephrased "… mailing *it* today."

Personal pronouns should not have vague antecedents, and repeating them in parentheses to explain who or what is meant is poor style. The sentences "He told Joe that he (Joe) would have to leave" and "Gibbs asked his supervisor whether he (Gibbs) deserved a vacation" should therefore be recast. The last example might read: "The supervisor was asked by Gibbs whether he deserved a vacation."

A questionable rule, observed by some writers but purposely ignored by others, concerns the use of *whose* and *which* in possessive reference to inanimate nouns. Which sentence, for example, is preferable: "The prospectus, the numerous segments *of which* will certainly be analyzed by many committees, is now available" or "The prospectus *whose* numerous segments will …"? In textual reports the *of* phrase preponderates, but *whose* is making steady inroads. Many particular writers avoid the heavier *of which* phraseology when possible. They consider *whose* the possessive case of both *who* and *which.*

ANY

Any Way Is Better than None

"We'll go *anyway* in *any way* we can." These *any* words raise a question of spelling—whether or not to spell them as one word. When the meaning is "in any event," "anyhow," or "regardless," the single word *anyway,* is called for: "Steuben can't leave now *anyway.*" "*Anyway,* I will take the course." The stress is on *any.* If the stress is about equal, two words are required, and the sense is "any *one* way," as in "*Any way* you do it will suit" and in "This matter was not handled in *any way* that was satisfactory." A test to determine the spelling is to see whether *whatever* can sensibly replace *any;* if it can, *any way* should be spelled as two words: "*Whatever* (or *Any*) way he tries, he will not succeed."

The pronoun *anyone* (the stress is on *any*) is written solid: "*Anyone* is welcome." When the emphasis shifts to *one,* the spelling changes to a two-word phrase, meaning "any single person or thing": "*Any one* of the guests may come in now." "We will accept *any one* of those applicants." *Anybody,* a synonym of "anyone," is always spelled as one word unless it refers to a corpse: "Although they searched, the firemen did not find *any body* among the charred ruins."

There is no consensus on the spelling of *anymore.* Although the traditional spelling *any more* is still preferred in formal writing, the one-word *anymore* is steadily attracting adherents: "We do not attend those classes *anymore.*" No matter which school of thought is followed—*any more* or *anymore*—it should, except in a question, be used only in a negative sense and at the end of a thought: "They do not see each other *any more.*"

Two *any* expressions that careful writers guard against are *any place* and *anytime*. On a formal level there is no place for *any place:* "We could not find it *anywhere*" (not *any place*). *Any time* is spelled as in this sentence. The one-word *anytime* is non-existent in the English language. The ubiquitous "No Parking Anytime" sign should be reworded: "No Parking Any Time" or, strictly, "No Parking *at* Any Time."

APOSTROPHE

See PUNCTUATION—APOSTROPHE

APPRAISE, APPRISE

Appraiseworthy

When *appraise* and *apprise* are wrongly used, one for the other, it is usually *appraise* for *apprise,* as in "We will *appraise* him of all the details." "To inform" or "to notify" is to *apprise* (or its variant spelling *apprize*). However, since *apprise* is an uncommon word and sounds starchy, the simpler word *tell* makes a better choice. If *apprise* is used anyway, it should be followed by *of,* as in "A radio announcement *apprised* the union *of* the legislature's plan."

Appraise means "to estimate the worth of." The value set by auctioneers is called an *appraisal.* Here it is used in the narrow sense of a professional judging the worth of a salable item. In its general sense, *appraise* means to analyze: "The columnists will *appraise* the political trend long before voting day." The expression "appraise the value of" is redundant—"the value of" should be dropped.

A synonym for *appraise,* but not an exact one, is *evaluate.* Its meaning is "to fix the value or amount of." Therefore, a person who says he will evaluate the value of a property repeats himself. Another word with a similar meaning is *assess,* "to make a valuation of." Most often this verb is used of property valued for the purpose of taxation.

APPREHEND, COMPREHEND

Understand and Fear Not

Both *apprehend* and *comprehend* refer to mental perception in somewhat varying degrees. *Apprehend* has a further but unrelated meaning: "to arrest"; "to take prisoner."

As a synonym of *understand, apprehend* means "to come to know," "to lay hold of with the understanding," or "to perceive the main drift." It also means "to anticipate with anxiety" or "to dread." In this sense its adjective form, *apprehensive,* is more common: "Maureen is *apprehensive* about her husband's operation." The noun *apprehension,* except for its sense of capturing, denotes a fearful expectation of the future.

For a person to know something, he must first apprehend it—catch or grasp its meaning. If he lays hold of it completely, he *comprehends* it, that is, attains a full understanding: "A child may *apprehend* what an older person is saying, yet not *comprehend* it." "Fred Powlen *apprehends* what the expert says but does not *comprehend* his detailed mathematical formulas." To apprehend is to bite into something; to comprehend, to digest it.

APPROXIMATE

See **WORDS OF APPROXIMATION**

APROPOS, MALAPROPOS

Using the Appropriate Word

Apropos (pronounced ap-roh-*poh*) is a combination of the French words *a,* "to," and *propos,* "purpose." The word means "to the purpose" or, like an English word with a similar sound, "appropriate."

Some authorities warn, however, that those words should not be equated. They contend that *appropriate* means "fitting" and that *apropos* means "pertinent." Other authorities, and the consensus is on their side, disagree, arguing that *apropos* in general application means "by the way" or "with respect to something."

Apropos is usually written as a solid word (although it need not be) followed by *of:* "This matter is *apropos of* the discussion held yesterday."

Its negative form, *malapropos* (from the French *mal a propos*), is a good but seldom used English word. It means "unsuitable," "out of place," or "inappropriate." The term *malapropism,* "a humorous misuse of a word," entered the language through R. B. Sheridan's comedy *The Rivals,* in which Lydia Malaprop consistently used ludicrously wrong words. An example is "an allegory (meaning "an alligator") on the banks of the Nile" or "Sure, if I reprehend anything in this world, it is the use of my oracular tongue, and a nice derangement of epitaphs!"

AROUND

See WORDS OF APPROXIMATION

ARTIFICIAL

It's Not Nice To Fool Mother Nature

That which does not originate in nature has probably been created or manufactured by man. Many English words describe the quality of being man-made, but each differs from the others in implications and in range of applications. They all have a sense in common, however—a contrast to natural substances.

Artificial applies to anything that is not natural. For example, in law a human being is a *natural person.* But a corporation, organized under, and licensed by, statute, is an *artificial person.* Outside the law, whatever is imitative of, but not derived from, nature is artificial—artificial flowers, artificial limbs, artificial coloring. Cold air from the North is natural; cold air from an air-conditioner is artificial. The flight of birds through the air is natural; the flight of man is not. As applied to persons, *artificial* suggests affectation.

That which is *synthetic* is "produced by artificial processes, either from relatively simple substances or from naturally occurring, sometimes complex, substances." The term more simply describes compounds formed by chemical reaction. Familiar synthetic products include nylon, which has almost entirely replaced silk in the manufacture of stockings, and oleomargarine, which substitutes for butter. The current meaning of *synthetic* corresponds to its Greek roots—*syn* and *thithenai,* "to put together."

Imitation was at one time equated with *counterfeit.* Today the words are seldom interchanged. A counterfeit is an imitation made with an intent to defraud, whereas an imitation, although also a copy of a genuine article, is made openly to serve when the real or legitimate article is too expensive or is unavailable. Indeed, people concerned with possible loss or theft will frequently wear imitation jewelry rather than genuine pieces.

Factitious also means "artificial," that is, not natural or genuine; but it is chiefly applied to intangible matters like emotions, situations, and reasons—in other words, to things that develop from customs or habits, not from nature. What is *factitious* may be said to be engineered, "trumped up," or contrived.

Spurious means "counterfeit, false, or not genuine." Derived from a Latin word meaning "illegitimate," spurious applies to whatever lacks authenticity: "The district attorney established that the document offered in evidence was *spurious.*" A similar-sounding word, *specious,* should not be confused with it. The ancestor of *specious* was the Latin word *speciosus,* which means "beautiful, handsome, good-looking." The current meaning of *specious* has been turned around: "seemingly fair, attractive, sound, or true, but actually not so." What is *specious,* therefore, is deceptive. A specious comment, for example, is pleasant, but insincere; a specious argument, though apparently convincing, is in reality fallacious; and a specious offer of assistance seems legitimate but is not. One speaks of specious statements, but spurious jewels.

AS, LIKE

A Likely Story

Except for its use as a verb ("I *like* candy") and as an adjective ("on *like* occasions"), *like* is a preposition that compares nouns, pronouns, and noun phrases. It means "similar to" or "similarly to" and is used correctly when it can replace either of these meanings: "Ralph looks *like* (is similar to) his father." "She sings *like* (similarly to) a bird." Since prepositions take an object, the following noun or pronoun must be in the objective, not the nominative, case: *like him and me,* not *like he and I.*

As, a conjunction, introduces *clauses* of comparison, which, like all clauses, must contain a verb: "Carlton does *as* he *pleases.*" "They are not so busy *as* they *were* last week." "I wish I could dance *as* he *does.*" The key to correct usage, then, is to use *as* if a verb follows the noun or pronoun, but *like* if there is no verb. Or, to put it another way, the word to use, when there is a noun only, is *like;* if a verb follows, then *as* should replace *like.*

Another common misuse of *like* is in comparing that which does not permit comparison. In *"Like* her predecessor, stamp collecting is her hobby," stamp collecting, of course, is not *like* her predecessor. The sentence should be rephrased: *"Like* her predecessor, *she* collects stamps as a hobby."

Like as Not

Although educated people know that the preposition *like* often mistakenly displaces the conjunction *as* ("Juan throws the bull *like* a toreador should"), what is seldom discussed is the opposite situation—the misuse of *as* for *like.*

When clauses are being compared, the subordinating conjunction *as* should introduce the subordinate clause. When objects or persons are being compared, the word to use is *like,* a preposition. Therefore, in "De Vries, *as* Eastburn and Devine before him, failed the examination," *like* is required, as it also is in "Whereas Mr. Diaz is the chef and supervises three bakers, *as* any baker he occasionally enjoys doing the baking himself."

Although the misuse of *as* for *like* is not common, even professional writers, as anyone else, sometimes become confused—as in this sentence. What probably causes this kind of blunder is an excessive fear of misusing *like* for *as*—which leads to faulty overcorrectness. But that is like jumping back from the fire into the frying pan.

AS FAR AS, SO FAR AS

As Far as Possible

The phrase *as far as* expresses distance: "This is *as far as* we can go." "The farm extended *as far as* the eye could see." Limitation, especially of one's knowledge, is expressed by *so far* as: "*So far as* we know, they will not be coming." This phrase suggests a doubtful or varying fact. In the sentence "*As far as* investments *are concerned,* we will consult Bruce," the complete formula must be used. Not "*As far as* investments, we will consult Bruce."

AS FOLLOWS

Follow Along

Is it possible that both "is as follows" and "are as follows" are correct? They are. The singular form *follows* is regularly used to introduce a list of items, whether the subject and its verb are singular or plural. Therefore, both of the following sentences are correct: "The analysis *is as follows*" and "The analyses *are as follows.*" Idiom simply disregards convention here, making the number of the preceding elements immaterial. One explanation offered to justify this oddity is that *as follows* is an impersonal construction, *it* being the understood subject. *As follows,* therefore, really stands for *as it follows.*

Those writers who use *as follow* after a plural subject to maintain a plural sense ignore idiom and jolt the equilibrium of some readers. This approach—as in "The figures offered today *are as follow*"—has, as it were, a small following. The established phraseology *as follows* is best used even in the face of a sequence of multiple items: "...*are as follows:* $50 to Allen; $100 to Rachel; $150 to Lester."

AS TO

As Two, As Three

As to *as to,* it may be said that those words are employed correctly only as they appear here—at the beginning of a sentence. In that position they emphasize the following word or thought: "*As to* Captain Thorne, he can steer a ship down a narrow stream."

In all other positions, a writer should carefully consider whether the phrase serves usefully. Ordinarily it does not. For instance, *as to* should not be used with *whether.* "Reginald expressed doubt *as to whether* the company could survive much longer" should be recast "Reginald expressed doubt *whether....*"

Similarly needless is *as to* with *what, how,* or *why.* In "The question *as to why* he is so obstreperous is one for psychiatrists," *as to* is unnecessary and should be omitted. Also to be condemned is the displacing by *as to* of the precise single prepositions *of* and *about:* "What is your impression *as to* (*of*) this matter?" "We know nothing *as to* (*about*) the company's finances."

ASCERTAIN, INQUIRE

Snoopy Always Inquires

To *inquire* is to seek information. To *ascertain* is to learn, to make certain—to find out by careful study, experiment, or investigation. One seeking to ascertain sets out to determine precise facts. Inquiry is the means; ascertainment, the end.

A synonym for the noun *inquiry* is *query*. Both a *query* and an *inquiry* are questions. *Inquiry* has the additional meaning of examining a matter closely in search of information (as in "Clearly we must call such a series of questions an *inquiry*") and its verb form, with *into*, "to investigate" (as in "The committee chairman said that we should inquire *into* the charges leveled against some of its members"). When *inquiry* means "request for information," it is usually followed by *about* or *after*.

The spelling *enquire* or *enquiry* is primarily British. The stress in *inquire* is on the first syllable. *Inquiry* may be pronounced ihn-*kwier*-ee or *ihn*-kwih-rih.

ASSUME, PRESUME

Don't Be Presumptuous

Assume and *presume* are related words, generally synonymous in the sense of taking something for granted. They are interchangeable in some contexts but not in all.

The Latin ancestors of *assume* (*assumere*, "to take to oneself") and *presume* (*praesumere*, "to take beforehand") indicate their similarity in meaning. The chief distinction between them is whether there is a basis for what is being taken for granted.

A person who assumes something to be true accepts it arbitrarily; that is, he supposes it is so without any evidence: "Because she *assumed* that she would not be invited, she did not buy a gift." "You *assume* he knows nothing, but he has known about your predicament for several days."

One presumes by believing—on the basis of example, experience, or logic—that something is a fact: "Since they are living together, I *presume* they're married." A presumption is accompanied by a firm conviction of likelihood; an assumption, by an inclination to believe.

Stanley's well-known "Dr. Livingstone, I presume?" uttered by the *New York Herald* correspondent upon meeting Livingstone in 1871 in the heart of Africa, indicated Stanley's belief that, in view of the circumstances, the explorer he found must indeed be the good doctor he sought.

A further common meaning of *presume* is "taking too much for granted." One who arrogates to himself an authority that is not his or who encroaches upon another's right has presumed to take excessive liberties. He is then said to be presumptuous.

ASSURE, ENSURE, INSURE

That's for Sure

Two verbs that mean "to make certain" are the phonetically similar *insure* and *ensure*. One may correctly say, "Paying attention to details will *insure* (or *ensure*) a better survey." Alexis de Tocqueville in 1830 chose *ensure*: "The special information which lawyers derive from their studies *ensures* them a separate station in society...." *Ensure* is preferable because its only meaning is "to make sure or certain" (also a meaning of *insure*), but *insure*, primarily, means "to safeguard or indemnify against a loss" ("We will *insure* our art collection").

Some long-established life insurance companies, mostly in England and Canada, use the word *assurance* in their names: Canada Life Assurance Co., Equitable Life Assurance Society. These companies might reason that although they are insuring, their policyholders need assurance of an eventual payment, which, since death is a certainty, can be made with assurance.

The faulty use of *assure* for *ensure* is somewhat common, probably more from carelessness than ignorance. "We bolted the doors to *assure* privacy," for example, should be reworded "to *ensure* privacy." *Assure* means "to impart trust," the making of a person so confident as to set his mind at ease: "We will *assure* our uncle of an early arrival." "The orchestra was *assured* that their instruments would be waiting for them."

ASTONISH, SURPRISE

Surprise

Astonish and *surprise* are not exact synonyms. One is surprised by a change in weather, for example, not astonished by it. The traditional meaning of *surprise* is "taken unaware," and its effect is no more than a mild reaction to what was unexpected. One who is astonished reacts much more intensely.

Astonish is born of *surprise*; that is, it refers to a surprise so great as to be incredible. Derived from the Latin *attono*, meaning "to strike by thunder" or "to stun," it now means "to strike with sudden bewilderment or wonder." Astonishment leaves one dazed or speechless or, figuratively, thunderstruck. The closest synonym for *astonish*, though a somewhat stronger term, is *astound*, which implies a paralyzing numbness or state of surprised shock.

An oft-repeated, probably apocryphal, tale about Dr. Samuel Johnson, the English lexicographer, illustrates the distinction between *surprise* and *astonish*. Dr. Johnson's wife, upon finding him kissing the second-floor maid, exclaimed, "I am surprised," to which Dr. Johnson replied: "No, Madam; I am surprised. You are astonished."

AUTHENTIC, AUTHORITATIVE, GENUINE

The Real McCoy

Authentic and *genuine* are distant synonyms whose meanings occasionally overlap. They do, however, have distinctive uses.

The sense of both *authentic* and *genuine* is of reliability, trustworthiness. That which accords with known information is authentic; that is, according to the Latin *authenticus*, it is verifiable. Used particularly of documents and works of art, *authentic* implies that the material or matter is true, holds to the facts, is not fictitious, and is not a copy. "The family owns an *authentic* Duncan Phyfe table." " 'All that glisters is not gold' is an *authentic* quotation of Shakespeare's."

Genuine (pronounced *jehn*-yoo-ihn, not jehn-yoo-*ine*) has within it the Latin *gen* from *genero*, "give birth to." It therefore pertains to something originally begotten. It belongs to the stock represented and is true to its own claims. It is not spurious: "The Hope diamond is *genuine*, since it meets mineralogical tests. It is a true diamond." Although a report may not be genuine, in that it was not written by the name ascribed to it, its contents may be authentic; that is, all its information is accurate and verifiable.

Authoritative (sometimes misspelled *authoritive*) means "sanctioned by authority or entitled to credence." In a more popular sense, that which is authoritative carries the weight of authority and merits acceptance: "The Durants have written an *authoritative* text on Greece."

In short, a *genuine* text is one written by the author whose name appears on the title page; an *authentic* text is one that corresponds to the known facts; an *authoritative* text is one written by an expert or specialist—by one who is an acknowledged authority on the subject.

AVERAGE, MEAN, MEDIAN

It's Mean

As a practical matter, the words *average* and *mean* are synonymous. The answer arrived at when a mean is determined is the same as an average figure. But the converse does not always follow, and the method of computation differs.

The average of a group is the sum of all components divided by the number of components. This means, to put it differently, that an average figure is determined by adding a series of quantities and then dividing by the number of quantities in the series. For example, the average of the sum of 1, 3, 5, 11, and 15 (the total is 35) is 7—35 divided by 5.

The *mean* is also the midpoint, but it is found by adding the two extreme figures in a series and dividing by two. The term is ordinarily used with temperature statistics. A day with a maximum temperature of 60°F and a minimum 30°F has a mean of 45°. In the sequence 4, 6, 10, 20, the mean is 12 (4 + 20 divided by 2), but the average is 10.

The *median* is also a middle point, for it has as many members above it as below it. This means that in a series half are on one side and half on the other. If, for example, the median weight of the people in a room is 150 pounds, as many people weigh more than 150 pounds as weigh less. In the series 10, 11, 12, 13, 14, the *median* is 12, the *mean* is 12, and the *average* is 12.

When *average* is used nonstatistically, it should not be equated with *ordinary, common,* or *typical,* terms that serve as better descriptives than *average* for a person: "He is an *ordinary* (or a *common*) (rather than an *average*) person."

AVERSE

See ADVERSE, AVERSE, ADVERT, AVERT

AVERT, AVOID

Turn About Is Fair Play

The words *avert* and *avoid* are not interchangeable. The sense of *avert* is "to keep from happening," as in "Nothing could have *averted* the collapse of the mine shaft once the supports fell." "After the credibility of the character witness was impugned, not even Clarence Darrow could have *averted* a conviction." *Avert* literally denotes a "turning from." A dictionary definition is "to turn away or aside; to ward off; to prevent." One may avert (*prevent* or *ward off*) a disaster or, if coy, avert (*turn aside*) one's eyes.

To *avoid* means "to keep away from" or "to keep clear of" anything that may cause trouble or annoyance. Frequently it suggests danger or a threat. One tries to avoid driving in heavy fog or avoid poison ivy. A debtor hides from or avoids his creditors, and a shy person shuns or avoids people.

Although *divert* and *avert* have different applications, they have similar definitions: "to turn aside." The primary sense of *divert*, however, is "to deflect"—to turn aside from an original path or course: "The stream has been *diverted* to irrigate the far fields." Another sense is to turn the mind from its present thought, by distracting or entertaining: "The child's attention was *diverted* by loud music from an adjoining room." *Diversion* is the noun form.

A pompous word sometimes confused with *avert* is *advert*, which means "to refer," as in "The lecturer will *advert* briefly to his previous book." In ordinary usage it is best replaced by *refer*. If *advert* is used anyway, it should be followed by *to*.

AWFULLY

It's Awful Wrong

Almost everyone who uses the word *awfully* to mean "very" or "exceedingly," as in "The comedian was *awfully* funny" or in "It was an *awfully* rainy Wednesday," knows it is an informal expression the moment it is said. *Awfully* is the adverbial form of *awful*, whose basic meaning is either "commanding reverential fear or profound respect (awe)" or "solemnly impressive." Shakespeare used it in *King Henry IV* when the Chief Justice said; "To pluck down justice from your *awful* bench." The adjective form *awful*, in everyday usage, has come to mean "bad" or "something that is disagreeably beyond imagination."

What bothers purists most about this colloquialism is its use as an intensive. In this use, not only is the meaning of *awful* ignored but its part of speech is also misused. For example, in "The bus came *awful* near to hitting us" and in "We were *awful* close to winning when it started to rain," a modifier of the adjectives *near* and *close* must be an adverb, of which *awfully*, not *awful*, is one. But this is not to say that a change of form will substantially improve the sentence; it will simply frame it better.

B

BACK FORMATIONS

A Verb to the Wise

In word usage, a back formation usually is a verb developed from a noun. It is not the same as an abbreviated version of a longer word (*phone* for *telephone* or *exam* for *examination*) but the construction of a new verb, like *beg* from the noun *beggar*, or *televise* from the noun *television*.

Many verbs so formed have been fully accepted and are now standard; for example, *edit* from *editor, typewrite* from *typewriter, diagnose* from *diagnosis*, and *donate* from *donation*. Obviously not all back formations are bad. Yet careful attention should be directed to them, for some undesirable ones not only have crept into spoken language but also have penetrated formal writing. Two such words, rejected by most careful writers, are *burgle* from *burglar* and *orate* from *oration*. Adjectives also have given rise to verbs. Some in widespread use, like *enthuse* from *enthusiastic* and *peeve* from *peevish*, are still considered informal; they, however, are slowly gaining legitimacy.

Those back formations designed to sound in vogue, such as "Barbara *hosted* a gala affair," are deplorable. Converting the noun *author* into a verb (although some dictionaries consider it standard) is equally gauche. Saying "Saverino authored the book" is as silly as saying that he poeted a poem. Saverino, who *wrote* the book, was its author, just as Barbara was a host. Some formations do not lend themselves to shortcuts; they have to go the long way.

BAD, BADLY

It's a Greeting, Not a Question

When asked "How are you?" a person who feels ill may wonder whether to say "I feel *bad*" or "I feel *badly*." The natural

40

inclination, since adverbs modify verbs, is to say "I feel badly." Certainly it is correct to say "He dances badly"; no one would say "He dances bad."

But the verb *feel*, in some ways, is not like the verb *dance*. As used here, *feel* is a linking, or copulative, verb. Such a verb has the unique function of tying the complement to the subject of a sentence. It is a verb of *being*, as opposed to a verb of action or a verb that asserts something. Hence when a person refers to ailing health, he should say, "I feel *bad*," not *badly*. The sentence implies no real action; and *bad*, as a predicative adjective, describes the subject "I." The verb serves simply as an equal sign: I = bad, or "I am bad."

Common copulative verbs are *be, act, appear, become, get, grow, lie, prove, remain, seem, shine, turn,* and verbs pertaining to the senses—*look, smell, sound, taste,* and *touch.* Whether a verb in a sentence is a copulative can be determined by substituting for it a form of the verb "to be." If the exchange does not seriously alter the sense, the verb is a copula. For example, "I *feel* bad" could be "I *am* (or *was*) bad"; "His look *grew* (*is* or *was*) scornful"; "The dessert *tastes* (*is* or *was*) sweet"; "The violin and the guitar *sound* (*are* or *were*) flat."

Some verbs, like *feel*, may serve both as a verb of being and as a verb of action. In "When it is dark, I always *feel* my way cautiously," *feel*, referring to tactile sensations, is a verb of action and is accordingly modified by an adverb.

In sum, "I feel bad" refers to health, although in strict formal style "I feel ill" is to be preferred. "I feel badly" means that one's sense of touch has been impaired.

BAIT, BATE

Baits and Other Lures

The homophones *baited* and *bated* can be easily confused. A mnemonic device to distinguish them is to think of *fishbait*, associatng the *i* in "fish" with the *i* in "bait."

Derived from the Scandinavian, *bait* literally means "to make to bite." As a noun, it is currently defined as "food or a lure used to catch fish or trap animals." As a verb, it means "to supply a fishhook or a trap with bait." But anything designed to entice is *bait*. Prostitutes bait men, for example, when they slyly expose themselves. *Bait* also has other less frequently used meanings, such as "to harass or persecute."

The verb *bate*, which means "to diminish or to take away," developed as a shortened form of *abate*. Anything restrained or moderated is *bated*; but as an adjective, *bated* usually pertains to the lessened force of one's breath. This latter use stems directly from the famous phrase "with bated breath" in Shakespeare's *Merchant of Venice*. The expression is so common, however, that it has become tiresome. Why, one may ask, must a person always wait with bated breath? Can he not simply hold his breath or shorten or lessen it?

In any event, it is good to remember that breath is not *baited*; rather it is, if the hackneyed phrase must be used, *bated*.

BALANCE, REMAINDER

Slightly Unbalanced

The word *balance,* in its proper usage, can be thought of in terms of a balance scale, which has two plates (Latin *bi-* and *lanx,* "plate"). Something is in balance if the weight is the same on both sides. And that is how the word *balance* should be used when a comparison is being made, particularly of the difference between two amounts. For example, a bank account that shows a balance indicates an amount available to be withdrawn. Or when half of a hundred dollar loan has been repaid, the balance is what is still due—the other half. In formal English *balance* should be used in this sense only, and not as an equivalent of *rest* or *remainder,* either of which would be more suitable in "We have the *balance* of the day free" (*rest* has a shade of preference). The *remainder,* strictly speaking, refers to what is left after a part of something is removed. If five is subtracted from ten, the remainder is five.

Another word used differently on various levels of English is *loan*. Formerly it was a verb employed only in financial transactions, especially in banking: "The bank *loaned* him the money." But today it is commonplace in any context, not merely in banking. Formal English, however, accepts only *lend* (its principal parts being *lend, lent, lent*). Their corresponding noun form is *loan*. The words are correctly used in "We will *lend* him the book," "We *lent* the company our newest material," and "She gave me a *loan*."

Balances and loans suggest money—a collective noun. Its plural forms, *moneys* and *monies*, refer to the media of exchange of various countries or to a particular form of currency within a country. The preferred spelling is *moneys*.

BARBARISMS

See TYPES OF ERRORS

BARELY

See HARDLY.

BASED ON

Home Base

It is grammatically dangerous to begin a sentence with the phrase *based on*. This compound participle, unlike an absolute participle, such as *speaking of, allowing for,* or *according to,* has not made the transition to prepositional status. Therefore, "*Allowing for* the weather, we will leave tomorrow" is properly worded, but not "*Based on* weather conditions, we will leave tomorrow." The effect of *allowing for* (or *owing to,* or *generally speaking,* or other expressions like them)—now regarded as prepositional constructions—falls on the entire following independent clause, not merely on its subject. Those participles that still function solely as verbals, of which *based on* is one, must modify the first noun in the main clause. To do this with *based on* is a difficult, if not an impossible, task. Hence the advice not to introduce a sentence with it. Rather than using *based on,* as in "*Based on* your report, we should close three units promptly," the simplest grammatical maneuver is to switch to *given* or *considering*.

BATE

See BAIT, BATE

BEGIN

In the Beginning Was the Word

To begin with, fancy words like *commence, inaugurate,* and *initiate* should not displace *begin*. Writers who prefer the high-blown seldom use *begin* and even less frequently its unadorned synonym *start*. Yet, though *begin* is not always the most precise choice, one never errs in using it.

The proper surroundings for *commence* is a dignified setting, for the word belongs with formal activities: to commence a memorial service; to commence an action at law. But in everyday beginnings, it is inappropriate. And its noun, *commencement,* is best saved for graduation.

Inaugurate describes elaborate formality and accompanying ceremony. It is in keeping with important, stately occasions, such as the induction into office of a high official or other events of historical portent. The President of the United States or the chancellor of a university is inaugurated. The ancestor of *inaugurate* is the Latin *inauguare,* which means "to take omens from the flight of birds." Before the Romans undertook anything important, their prophets or soothsayers would first observe and interpret the omens to see whether they were favorable. To *inaugurate* also means "to initiate," as in "The bombing of Hiroshima *inaugurated* a new era in warfare."

To *initiate* is to begin, which suggests the setting into action of a new project or venture, often something experimental: initiate a change in fashion; initiate a new curriculum. It emphasizes, by connotation, the initial steps, the act of entering in: to initiate negotiations; to initiate a desert irrigation project. It may also mean to instruct in new principles or to induct into a society by special rites or ceremonies.

In some instances *start* is more suitable than *begin*. *Start* implies a suddenness, a quick beginning at an exact moment; it suggests a definiteness not inherent in *begin*: to start a race; to start a machine; to start a quarrel. *Begin,* a gentler word, heralds an easing into the actual happening—like the slipping of a canoe into a lake. One does not start but begins a course of study, a correspondence, or a meal. The exact moment of the beginning is unimportant.

BEMUSE

See AMUSE, BEMUSE

BESIDES

Side by Side

The word *besides,* spelled with two *s*'s, is both a preposition and an adverb. As a preposition it is most often used to mean "in addition to," as in "*Besides* a piano, he owns a flute and a saxaphone." "*Besides* the show there was a cocktail hour." It also may mean "except for" or "other than": "No one was there *besides* us monitors."

When *besides* serves as an adverb, it means "in addition" or "also" ("We ran and swam *besides*"). When it functions as a conjunctive adverb, it means "moreover" or "furthermore" ("Professor Austin lectures almost daily; *besides* he is writing a treatise on etymology.")

Spelled without a final *s,* the word *beside* is a preposition meaning "by the side of" or "next to," as in "The television console stands *beside* the Palladian window" or in "My father is sitting *beside* my aunt." It also is used in comparisons: "My car looks dilapidated *beside* yours." *Beside* has also come to mean "apart or disjoined from," as in "That argument is *beside* the point" or in "Mancini was *beside* himself with rage."

BETWEEN

See AMONG, BETWEEN

BEWILDER

See CONFUSION, DEGREES OF

BI-, SEMI-

Verbal Bi- Ways

Everyone agrees that *biannual* means twice a year, but everyone does not agree that *bimonthly* means only twice a month or that *biweekly* means only twice a week. Popular usage, supported by many dictionaries, accepts two irreconcilable meanings for *bimonthly* ("occurring every two months" and "occurring twice a month") and for *biweekly* ("occurring every two weeks" and "occurring twice a week"). Obviously a term given two conflicting definitions can be a rich source of confusion. For the sake of clarity, each word should represent one meaning: *bimonthly*, every two months; *biweekly*, every two weeks. *Semimonthly* would continue to refer to what occurs twice a month; and *semiweekly,* to what takes place twice a week.

Until this usage is adopted, ambiguity is best avoided by spelling out what is meant, even at the expense of a few extra words—every two months, twice a month, every other month; every two weeks, twice a week, every other week. For instance, saying that paychecks will be delivered twice a month and the bulletin every two weeks makes the time of their delivery perfectly clear.

Biannual means "occurring twice a year." Its synonym, *semiannual*, meaning "half-yearly," is a more ordinary word and therefore preferable. The slight difference in meaning between them is that *semiannual* suggests six-month intervals (the prefix *semi-* means "half," implying a somewhat even division), whereas *biannual* (governed by its prefix *bi-*) simply means "two." Hence *biannual* refers to two happenings at any unspecific time during a year.

The word meaning "every two years" is *biennial.*

BILLION

See MILLION

BLAME

See AFRAID, AGGRAVATE, BLAME

BOTH

Row, Row, Row Your Both

Whether to use *of* after *both,* as in "Both *of* our houses are available," depends on the writer's preference. Although unnecessary, it adds emphasis in some sentences and improves rhythm in others. These are legitimate reasons to use it, but ordinarily its omission is preferable. With a pronoun, *of* is always required—"*Both of* them arrived safely." One may not say "Both them...."

Both may function as many parts of speech. It is an adjective (both books), a pronoun (both are here), and a conjunction (both he and I will go). Its most frequent misuse is as a correlative conjunction, in which it pairs with *and.* Orderly construction requires that *both...and,* be followed by parallel elements, the same grammatical form. That is, if a noun, preposition, or clause follows *both,* a noun, preposition, or clause, as the case may be, must follow *and.* The following sentence, for example, is not parallel: "His name is difficult *both* to spell *and* pronounce." A *to* should immediately precede *pronounce*— "*both* to spell and *to* pronounce." In "We will see him *in both* Washington and *in* St. Louis," the second *in* should be deleted or *both* repositioned, "...*both in* Washington *and in* St. Louis."

The pairing of *both* with *and* is not subject to exception. For example, in "*Both* the teachers *as well as* the students were invited to the ceremony," *as well as* is incorrect unless *both* is deleted: "*Both* the teachers *and* the students..." or "The teachers *as well as* the students...." Further, since *both* is limited to two, it may not refer to three or more. It is incorrect to say, "He has traveled throughout *both* New York, Pennsylvania, and California" or "He is well known in *both* France and Holland *as well as* in Belgium." The easy remedy, here again, is to delete *both.*

Both seems to invite redundancies. In "We *both* agree to leave early," *both* is superfluous. It is unnecessary in "They are *both* alike" and in "They *both* came together." Also in "Those boxes are *both* equally large" and in "*Both* his parents were pleased and amused." It serves no purpose in "The twins were *both* here" or in "They *both* go hand in hand." A good prescription is to review *both* carefully before using. Many sentences are both neater and healthier without it.

BOURGEOIS, PROLETARIAT

One Burgher To Go

The middle class may be fast disappearing, but one who is still a part of it may be termed a bourgeois (a *bourgeoise* is a female *bourgeois*). The collective noun *bourgeoisie* identifies the class as a whole—primarily tradesmen: "The dress of the French *bourgeoisie* distinguishes them from the aristocracy." In a plural construction, it denotes the members of the class: "Certain *bourgeoisie* still support the monarch's policies." *Bourgeois* is the spelling of the adjective form: bourgeois values, bourgeois respectability. *Bourgeois* is pronounced either boor-*zhwah* or *boor-*zhwah; *bourgeoisie*, boor-zhwah-*zee*.

Bourgeoisie was derived from the Old French *burgeis,* which in turn came from the Teutonic *burg,* a medieval fortress. It later came to mean a walled town and eventually any town. Today *burg* is an English suffix meaning "city": Williamsburg, Harrisburg, St. Petersburg.

The word *burgher,* spelled with an *h,* evolved from the same source, but along a German, rather than a French, path. A burgher was a freeman of a city (or burgh) who received his income from business profits. He was differentiated from the landed gentry on the one hand and from the wage earner on the other. He was, in other words, an early *bourgeois*. Rodin's "Burghers of Calais" has helped make this word familiar to many people.

Proletariat refers to the unpropertied class, those who depend on daily employment for their livelihood. In ancient Rome it was the lowest class of citizenry, consisting of those who were regarded as contributing nothing to the state except offspring (*proletarius,* "begetter of children").

BRACKETS

See PUNCTUATION—PARENTHESES AND BRACKETS

BROAD, WIDE

Take a Wide Berth

Broad and *wide,* since they both indicate horizontal extent, are often interchangeable: a broad or wide road, a broad or wide stream. But in some senses their meanings differ, and they afford different emphases in different contexts.

Wide commonly stresses the distance that separates limits: a wide doorway, a wide opening, a wide driveway. It is also the term used with units of measurement: "Each board is 20 inches wide." *Broad* is concerned with what lies between the limits or what connects them: broad blade, broad chest, broad shoulders. Describing an area of land, for example, as *a wide field* stresses the distance from one side of the field to the other; *a broad field* connotes its vast expanse.

Broad, and not *wide,* suggests inclusiveness or obviousness, as in a broad view, a broad statement, a broad outline, or a broad hint. A *broad* difference, for example, is an obvious one; a *wide* difference, although it may also be obvious, stresses the dissimilarity.

Some idiomatic expressions do not strictly follow these distinctions. One has a broad back but wide hands; a broad smile but a wide mouth; a broad brow but wide eyes. Trousers may be wide; certainly the world is wide. But the enemy fires broadside, whether at night or in broad daylight.

BURGLAR, ROBBER, THIEF

Who Steals My Purse. . .

Lawyers who do not practice criminal law may, like anyone else, be guilty of misusing the terms *thief, burglar,* and *robber*— designations for criminals who take what is not theirs.

A *thief* steals; that is, he takes another's property dishonestly, without violence or threat of violence and usually in secret. Its surreptitiousness is emphasized by a broader meaning of *steal,* a nonpejorative sense that designates any secret or unobserved taking: "My grandson *steals* into the kitchen and heads straight to the cookie jar." "I *stole* a kiss."

A *robber* feloniously seizes another's possessions by violence or threat of violence. To *rob* is to take, with criminal intent, personal property of another from his person or in his presence. One robs someone *of* something, but steals *from* someone. Robbery at gunpoint is called a *holdup*.

A *burglar*, according to the common law, makes a forcible entry into a dwelling at night with intent to steal. Although a robber *robs* and a thief *steals*, no verb explains what a burglar does. *Burgle*, a back formation from *burglary*, was coined to fill this need but is frowned upon in all but informal contexts. (W. S. Gilbert used a form of it in *The Pirates of Penzance:* "When the enterprising burglar's not a-burgling.") *Burglarize*, though generally labeled colloquial, is fast establishing itself. Certainly English is no poorer for it, for it steals nothing from the language.

BUT

But-Ins

As with people, words should not butt in where they do not belong. Yet this is a common fault of *but.* "We have no doubt *but that* Vance will arrive promptly" is a case in point. There the negative *no* is followed by *but that,* which implies a negative, making in effect an unfashionable double negative. The sentence needs the *but* out: "We have no doubt *that* Vance will arrive promptly."

Replacing *but that* with *but what* serves no useful purpose, for *what* is simply an awkward equivalent of *that.* "There is no doubt *but what* the play will be successful," for example, should be rephrased: "There is no doubt *that* the play will be successful." When *but what* means "except what," however, its grammatical complexion changes. It then becomes accepted idiom: "This martinet agrees to nothing *but what* he chooses arbitrarily to approve." The sentence in effect (and correctly) says, "…agrees to nothing except what he chooses arbitrarily to approve."

If *but that,* on the other hand, is not preceded by a negative, it may serve for "were it not that": "He would have been ostracized *but that* ("were it not that") he had contributed generously."

By itself *but* is either a coordinating conjunction, serving to emphasize two contrasted statements ("Cotton is cheaper, *but* wool is warmer"), or a preposition, meaning "except" ("Everyone *but* Fred knows her"). When used as a preposition, a noun or pronoun in the objective case must follow: "Nobody *but him* went." As a conjunction, *but* may begin sentences—"He wants to go. *But* his physician refused permission." It has a lighter tone than *however* and is less formal than *yet.*

C

CALCULATE

Use the Calculator

The word *calculate* in "I *calculate* that my wife will want to go out for dinner tonight" is dialectal for "think" or "guess." In more formal writing, *calculate* should be used to mean the ascertaining by computation—a precise mathematical method, as in "The captain *calculated* that the ship would dock on Monday at 6 A.M."

Calculate and *calculus* are siblings whose progenitor was the Latin *calculus*, "a pebble." Today the English word *calculus* is both a medical term, meaning "a bony growth" (*callous*, also a derivative, is hardened skin), and a mathematical term for a method of figuring. It was from this latter use that the English word *calculate* evolved.

During the days of the Roman Empire the taximeter of cab drivers was called a hodometer. It was a contraption in which the turning of the axle released a pebble into a receptacle. At the end of the trip, the pebbles, then called *calculi*, were counted to determine, or *calculate*, the fare. No guesswork there.

CALLIGRAPHY

The Beauty of the Written Word

Although *calligraphy* is a word sometimes associated with Oriental writing, it need not be so confined. Its meaning is "elegant handwriting." The word derives from the Greek *kalos*, "beautiful," and *graphia*, "writing." Describing a penmanship as beautiful calligraphy is therefore redundant. Saying, on the other hand, that someone's calligraphy is poor is a contradiction in terms. The word meaning bad penmanship is *cacography*.

Caco- (which means "ugly") comes from the Greek *kakos.* A more common word using this prefix is *cacophony,* an ugly or discordant sound.

CAN, COULD

Can Can-Can

Whether to replace *is able to* with *can* (*"I can* [or *am able to*] climb that hill") is discretionary with the writer. Those who favor *can* prefer its economy. Those in the other camp argue that *is able to* emphasizes the idea of ability more than *can* does. Which phraseology to use, therefore, depends on what is more important—brevity or emphasis.

In many instances *can* and *could* (the past tense of *can*) are interchangeable. However, what *could* be done is not quite so certain of accomplishment as what *can* be done. Implicit in *could* is a sense of doubt: "Perhaps he *could* do better if he practiced more."

When *could* is treated as a subjunctive, it should not be preceded by *if*: "*Could* Dixon have learned the language, he would have been named consul," not "*If* Dixon *could* have learned...."

Two caveats concerning the use of *could* are worth noting. The phrase *could of* is an illiteracy, since *of* is not a verb. One can easily be led into this solecism, however, because the elided *could've,* for *could have* sounds like "could of." The contracted *couldn't,* which combines *could* and *not,* is a negating phrase. It should therefore not be used with *hardly* or *scarcely,* which imply a negative. The easy remedy, to avoid the double negative, is to omit the *not.* "She *couldn't hardly* see the hole in the needle" becomes "She *could hardly*...."

CAN, MAY, MIGHT

You May if You Can

Can denotes ability or power; *may* expresses permission. The dictionary definition of *can* is "to be able to or capable of." A person who *can* do something ostensibly has the ability to do it. A person who *may* do something has received permission to do it. Obviously these words are not interchangeable. A swimming coach properly says to a learner, "You *may* now (have permission to) swim the width of the pool if you *can*" (are able to). In current usage *can* frequently serves for both permission and ability. The swimming coach probably would say: "You *can* now swim...."

In a simple sentence *may* has the further sense of "possibility," a sense shared equally with its past tense form *might*. But *may* expresses a greater likelihood than *might* that something will occur. *Might* represents what is possible but unlikely. The probability of a happening expressed in "We *may* all attend the convention next year" is greater than that expressed in "We *might* all attend." *May* is used with the present, present perfect, and future tenses; *might*, with the past and past perfect. For example, "I say (have said, shall say) what is true so that you *may* know." "I said (had said) what is true so that you *might* know."

In the main clause of a conditional sentence, *might* is used even though the condition is implied: "The Senator *might* run again" (if he is so minded). "If the project is not further funded, it *might* have to end" (the termination is conditioned on the failure to receive more funds).

Might expresses a supposition when used in the subjunctive: "The mail clerk has been acting as though he *might* leave." "The president spoke as though he *might* vote to merge." In these latter sentences *may*, it may be said, is showing her *might*.

CAPITALIZATION

Lower or Upper—Whatever the Case May Be

As a rule of thumb, one should use capital letters sparingly, remembering that an initial capital letter makes a word appear to have the quality of a proper name. Some writers, nevertheless, are reluctant to put in lowercase what they regard as key words, for fear of deemphasizing them. This judgment, of course, is merely one of style. The four seasons and the four terms designating academic years are cases in point.

Most stylebooks recommend that the seasons of the year, unless personified ("The Spring is dancing through all the countryside") be written as follows: "The four seasons of the year are spring, summer, fall, and winter." Advertisers usually capitalize a season to make it prominent; but this is also a matter of preference.

The names of academic years, like those of the seasons, are lowercased (freshman, sophomore, junior, senior), but the names of the classes themselves in high school and college are capitalized (the Freshman Class). Academic degrees are also written in lowercase when referred to in general terms: "Josephine received her *bachelor's* degree from Creighton." "Barry expects his *doctorate* next spring." But an academic degree following the name of the holder is capitalized: David Garrett, *Doctor of Philosophy*; Joseph C. Gelberg, *Ph.D.*

Although proper topographical names are capitalized (Boston, Strait of Gibraltar, Mount Fuji), not everyone agrees on the need to capitalize accompanying generic terms, or common nouns. Most stylists capitalize them: Rocky *Mountains*; Nile *Delta*; Walden *Pond*; White Sulphur *Springs*. But not when they follow two or more proper names: spanning the Monongahela and Ohio *rivers*; vacationing between the White and Green *mountains*. The opposite is true when they precede the proper names: traveled on *Lakes* Erie and Superior; climbed *Mounts* Whitney and Ranier. The Government Printing Office *Style Manual* recommends that the terms be capitalized, whether placed before or after the proper names.

The number of a century should ordinarily be written in lowercase: "The Dred Scott decision was a *nineteenth* century landmark." The names of the points of the compass—north, east, south, west—are also kept in lowercase unless they refer to a particular section of the United States. For example, "Kansas City is *west* of Pittsburgh, but it is situated in the *Midwest*." "San Francisco is farther *west*; it is, as far as Ohioans are concerned, in the *Far West*."

The first and last words in a title, as well as every important word, are always capitalized. A slogan adopted by some editors is "Do not cap the caps," a reminder to put in lowercase conjunctions (*c*), articles (*a*), and prepositions (*p*). Despite the rule, any word of five or more letters—even prepositions, such as *before, against, after*—is preferably capitalized.

An honorary title referring to a specific person should be capitalized: "The Governor of Ohio is sitting in front of the audience." But in "Our children would like to meet a governor," *governor* is a generic term and is therefore written in lowercase.

A prefix preceding a capitalized word is not capitalized: anti-Mexican; un-American.

CASE

No Case

Words that contribute nothing to the meaning of a sentence should, like deadwood, be lopped off and hauled away. The word *case* is a case in point.

In "Who was to blame *in the case of* the derailment?" *in the case of* is a roundabout way of saying *for*. "We think that *in Ralph's case* he should retire early" needs only "We think that Ralph should retire early."

Except when variation is desired, it is best not to use *in case* for *if*, *in most cases* for *usually*, and *in all cases* for *always*: "*If I go* (rather than *In case I go*), I'll need the file" and "*Usually* (instead of *In most cases*) sessions begin promptly at noon." The expression *in any case* meaning "from any point of view" always should be avoided.

The proper use of *case* is illustrated in these sentences: "The books were shipped in a large *case*." "The docket lists three *cases* to be heard today." "*He* is in the nominative *case*." But when speaking of a happening or an occurrence, *place, example, situation, operation,* or *instance* serves better than *case*. In "Arguments may be useful in legal matters, but in other *cases* that is not so," *cases* improperly displaces *matters*. And although the phrases *that is not the case,* meaning either "not so" or "that is not correct," and *such is the case,* meaning "it is true," mislead no one, they are wordy and pretentious. In the warning "*In case of* fire pull the cord," *in case of* is idiomatic, meaning "in the event of." Which makes it a good case.

CASES OF PRONOUNS

Confound Those Pronouns

Using the proper case of a pronoun is a problem that seems to resist ready solution. If this were not so, why would so many educated people say *between you and I* instead of *between you and me*?

Another frequent misusage of a pronominal case occurs when a pronoun is in a combination, like "*We* (or *Us*) *editors* are a sorry lot." The cause for this kind of error is the presence of a noun following the initial pronoun. Many persons are not sure which pronoun to reach for. If the noun *editors* were omitted, temporarily ("We...are a sorry lot"), the need to say "*We editors are*" would become obvious, for no one would say "*Us* are a sorry lot." For those who are rule-minded, the subject of a verb is always in the nominative case. It therefore follows that the pronoun in the example, the subject of the verb *are*, must be *we* (*I, we, she, he, they*, and *who* are the subjective pronouns).

It also follows that the counterparts of these pronouns, their objective forms (*me, her, him, us, them, whom*—*it* and *you* are both subjective and objective cases) must be used in such a sentence as "Some persons think little of *us* (not *we*) *editors.*" Here again the easiest path to take is to mentally omit the appositive noun *editors*, which is bound to leave only "Some persons think little *of us.*" The alternative phrase, *of we*, would jar anyone into sensibility.

The same problem arises with compound subjects and with compound objects in which one element is a noun and the other a pronoun. The case form that the pronoun takes is the nominative if it is a part of the subject of a sentence, and the objective if it is a part of the object of a verb. For those who are uncertain which case is called for, the thing to do is to treat it as one does when a pronoun and appositive are involved—mentally omit the noun. For example, in "*Jeff Dash and he/him* should arrive soon" and in "Mr. Tate instructed Oscar and *I/me* to prepare an outline," omitting *Jeff Dash* as part of the subject and *Mr. Tate* as part of the object will leave "he/him should arrive soon" (clearly *he should*) and "instructed I/me" (also clearly *instructed me*).

I Am Thou

Recalling elementary school grammar, one will remember that the infinitive *to be* always links words in the same case— the nominative case if they are sentence subjects, the objective case if they are sentence objects. In "Susan took *him* to be the *principal,*" *him*, as the object of *took*, is in the objective case. And since the subject of *to be* takes the same case after it as before it, *principal* is likewise in the objective case. This shows up more clearly in "The FBI believed the *fugitive* to be *him*," the objective case *him* agreeing with the case of the object, *fugitive*.

When a form of *to be* is not immediately preceded by a noun or pronoun, however, the predicate pronoun is in the nominative, not the objective, case. And this raises some problems. For example, in "Who would wish to be *I?*" and in "Elaine is often taken to be *I*," the case of the pronoun is in the nominative, correctly agreeing with the case of the subject. But *I* is so prominent a pronoun and the phrasing so stilted that the rule, at least in general conversation, is regularly ignored. In fact, many respected writers would say, "Who would wish to be me?" and "Elaine is often taken to be me," even though formal English does not recognize this deviation.

The sentences "Did the thieves turn out to be they?" "Does Henry Bragg really want to be I?" "Becker was believed to be he" sound awkward. They nevertheless should be so written when grammatical accuracy is required.

All this can put a purist in a bind when a friend asks whether Jim the Slugger is at bat. One doesn't want to sound stuffy and say, "Yes, it is he," or be wrong and say, "Yes, it is him." The only safe thing the purist can do is hedge and say, "Yes, it's the Slugger, all right."

CHIEFLY, LARGELY, GREATLY, MATERIALLY

A Chief at Large

Would *largely* or *chiefly* be the better word in the sentence "It is...a matter of money"? The answer depends on the intent of the speaker. *Largely* means "generally," "to a great extent," or "in great part" ("Andrew Mahl was *largely* responsible for bankrupting the business"). *Chiefly*, a more emphatic word, is defined as "above all," "especially," or "mainly" ("His interest is *chiefly* in becoming a concert pianist." "The lecture is *chiefly* concerned with economic conditions in Japan").

An idiomatic quirk holds that the adverb *largely* loses its *-ly* after the verbs *loom* and *bulk*: "The moon *looms large* on the horizon." "That tree *bulks too large* in our small garden."

Materially and *greatly*, another pair of frequently interchanged adverbs, mean "considerably" or "to an important degree" (as in "The researchers' efforts contributed *materially* [or *greatly*] to the remarkable success of the project"). But if the assistance consists of something material, like money, *materially* is an especially appropriate word: "A federal grant *materially* aided the ballet company." Although *greatly* would be suitable here, it is less precise.

CIVIL, POLITE

Polite Civilians

The word *civil,* denoting that which complies with the tenets of decent conduct and manners, has its roots in the Latin *civis,* "a citizen." Ancient communities expected their citizens to be friendly and to restrain any tendency to rudeness or quarreling. They were, in a word, to act in a way becoming to a citizen. Today a civil person is anyone who respects others and abstains from abusive language.

The Latin past participle *politus,* meaning "polished," is the ancestor of the English word *polite.* A polite person, however, is somewhat different from one who is "polished." A *polished* person has acquired that state by having the rough edges knocked off, so that they are now smoother. A *polite* person may be innately so or may, through studied effort, have learned to comply with the rules of etiquette. *Politeness* suggests even more than that—a consideration for the comfort of others, a spontaneous, gracious behavior, and a kind way of rendering service. *Civility* is perfunctory. It is a compliance with the rules of society, with no accompanying inner warmth or feeling.

CLEAN, CLEANSE

Keep It Clean

Although the verbs *clean* and *cleanse* mean "to rid of impurities or dirt," they have distinguishable usages. *Clean* is the everyday word meaning to remove dirt, stains, or impurities. A person who is cleaning is literally applying himself to the job of removing spots, smudges, splatters, or the like.

Cleanse is used chiefly in a figurative sense, pertaining to the purifying of oneself. What has been cleansed has been made spiritually or morally pure. A person cleans the basement but cleanses himself of guilt.

Cleanly is both an adjective and an adverb. As an adjective, pronounced *klehn*-lee, it means "personally neat" and describes one who is habitually clean: "She is *cleanly* in her person and habitation." When used adverbially, it is pronounced *kleen*-lee and means "in a clean manner": "The doctor excised the mole *cleanly*."

A more common word than the adjective *cleanly* to express diligence in keeping clean is *cleanliness*: "*Cleanliness* in a hospital is of prime importance" and, according to a maxim that many children learn when first they fall into a mudpile, it is "next to godliness."

CLICHÉS

See TRITE EXPRESSIONS

COHORT

It Horts for Only a Minute

Formalists do not equate *cohort* with *co-conspirator, confederate, accessory,* or *accomplice* and therefore would not approve the use of *cohorts* in "The fugitive and his two *cohorts* were apprehended today." A *cohort*, as a matter of fact, is not a colleague, not an associate, and not a companion. No single person can be a cohort, since the word *cohort* is a collective noun. A sentence such as "My *cohort* will assist me in this matter," therefore, is faulty. Yet this misusage is so widely accepted that, at least in informal English, it must be tolerated.

In the time of the Romans, a *cohort* was one of the ten divisions of a legion. Today it is a nonmilitary term that refers to a large group or company, especially one united for a contest or struggle. To do justice to this extended sense, however, the group must be so large as to be countable only with difficulty:

"The President was unable to reach all his *cohorts* before the election day."

One who assumes that the *co* in *cohort* is a prefix as in *co-trustee* is incorrect. The word *cohort* is a solid word, written with no hyphen.

COINCIDENT, SIMULTANEOUS, SYNCHRONOUS

Simultaneous Surprises

Although *coincident* and *simultaneous* are synonyms (both mean "existing or occurring at the same time"), they are not interchangeable.

Coincident, derivatively, means "to fall together." It is now used to describe incidents that agree in place, time, or circumstance, as would be the meeting of two brothers applying unexpectedly for the same position. Two things that are in coincidence are identical in the same way. Coincidences are usually surprises; since all surprises are not coincidences, however, one must be sure that *coincident* or *coincidence* always embraces at least two happenings: "That the two should meet in Boston was a coincidence," but not "His going to Boston was a *coincidence*." "My aunt's leaving was *coincidental* with my uncle's arrival," but not "It was a *coincidence* that may aunt left early." The adverbial form for *coincident* is *coincidently*; for *coincidental*, *coincidentally*.

The key to the sense of *simultaneous*, and its adverb *simultaneously*, is its root, *simul*, meaning "at the same time." Matters that are simultaneous take place at the same time. For instance, buckshot pellets leave the barrel of a shotgun together, or simultaneously. "At the seminar on social reform, five workshops were held *simultaneously*." "The *simultaneous* arrival of the two officials made it easy for us. The gate had to be opened only once."

The less common word *synchronous* also denotes an exact concurrence in time, and it, too, is often used of events recurring at the same brief intervals. Thus the chimes of two clocks set to strike at the same moment are said to be synchronous. Synchronous also is the violin section of a symphonic orchestra, which sounds as if only one instrument were being played. *Synchronize*, derived from the Greek *syn*, "same," and *chronos*, "time," is the more familiar term: "Let's *synchronize* our watches."

To is the preposition that follows *synchronous,* as in "The grandfather clock is synchronous *to* the kitchen clock."

COLLECTIVE NOUNS

Collectibles

All words with a plural sense are not necessarily treated as plurals. The pronouns *either, neither,* and *everyone,* for example, refer to more than one object or person, but the governing construction is singular: "Neither *looks* good to me." "Everyone *was* there."

Subjects referring to quantities, rather than units, are regarded as singular nouns and therefore take singular verbs: "Three miles *is* the distance between the house and the main road." "Only 70 pounds of sugar *was* allotted to the chef." If the number of items rather than a quantity is being considered, then a plural verb is required: "More than 70 pounds of sugar *were* distributed to the needy families."

Nouns known as collective nouns refer to a group, a collection of individuals, such as is implied in the words *audience, family, class, faculty, committee, flock, crowd, team,* or *public.* A collective noun may be treated as a singular or as a plural according to the sense of the sentence; that is, if it refers to the group as a whole, it is regarded as a singular noun: "The jury *has* been sequestered." "His family *comes* from Ireland." If it refers to persons or parts separately, that is, to individual members or units, it is treated as a plural noun: "The jury *are* casting their votes now." "His family *are* hard workers." A collective noun (unless its meaning points to the contrary) is regarded as a singular word, which means that in uncertain cases the safest course is to use a singular verb: "The army at the moment *is* on maneuvers."

The number given a collective noun governs the other elements in the sentence—the pronouns and the verbs. For example, "The majority of the committee wants (*want*) its (*their*) agent stationed in Geneva."

Take a Number

One who asks "Is the word *number* singular or plural?" should not be surprised by an ambiguous reply, for it is both.

Number is a collective word representing the grouping of two or more things. Whether to regard it as singular or plural depends on its sense in the sentence. When it serves as a subject, preceded by *a*, it suggests individual units and is plural: "*A number* of requests for the book *have been* received." "A *large number* of birds *were* in that flock." When *the* precedes *number* (*the number*), referring to a total, its sense is singular: "*The number* of today's telephone calls *was* higher than all of last week's." "*The small number* of dropouts *is* gratifying." *A number* points to an indefinite amount; *the number*, to what is countable.

The word *number* by itself signifies items that are countable ("Mr. Paige has a *number* of old prints on his shelf") as distinguished from *amount*, which refers to bulk, to a measurable mass ("An enormous *amount* of sand was just delivered").

Modifying *number* with a word that contains the idea of number, such as *innumerable,* is poor style. Instead of "An *innumerable* (or A *numerous*) *number* of politicians attended the convention," one might say, if not the simple "Many politicians...," either "A countless number..." or "Numerous politicians...."

COLLIDE

See MISUSED WORDS

COLLOQUIALISMS

Change To Suit

Colloquialisms are informal expressions employed by friends, casual acquaintances, and relatives. (In ordinary usage, one talks *to* friends; in formal language it is *with*.) Colloquial speech is punctuated with colorful and lively terms, yet such language is most often used when one is relaxed or feeling folksy.

The word *colloquial* is a combination of the Latin *con-* ("together") and *loquor* ("to speak"). Clearly the word derives from speech and therefore refers to words suitable in conversation but not necessarily acceptable in serious writing. "We have *lots* of time" and "Raymond pulled a *cute* trick on Dad" would be inappropriate language in formal texts. And so would "What a *deal!*" (for *bargain*), "Raymond *cooked up* (for *thought of*) a great idea," "Elaine has a *big head*" (for *is an egotist*), and "John Turk *runs a tight ship*" (for *manages well*).

Colloquial language is not to be thought of as inferior. It simply does not belong in serious writing. But neither does formal language in a note to a six-year-old boy. Which means that all language should be appropriate to the occasion.

Colloquialisms are not localisms (expressions native to particular sections of the country). The term usually applied to words used in a limited geographical area is *provincialism*. Some such words have reached a national level of usage, but they are regarded as dialectal nevertheless. Examples are *sashay*, a Western term used in square dancing; *hornswoggle*, another Western term, meaning "to cheat"; *corn-pone*, the Southerners' word for "corn bread"; and *hooch*, the Alaskan-Indian word for "liquor." The noun *poke*, meaning "sack or bag," was a Southwestern localism that spread deeper into the South and the West.

COLON

See PUNCTUATION—COLON AND DASH

COMMA

See PUNCTUATION—COMMA

COMMENCE

See BEGIN

COMMIT, PERPETRATE

A Deed Is Forever

One may say, with grammatical correctness, "Ronald *perpetrated* a crime" or "Ronald *committed* a crime." *Perpetrate* and *commit* are exact synonyms in the sense of performing a wrongful act. But *commit* is preferred; *perpetrate* sounds stuffy. The noun *perpetrator*, however, is an economical way of saying "the person who committed" and is therefore a particularly good word: "We must find the *perpetrator* of this heinous crime."

Whereas *perpetrate* has only one meaning, *commit* has many everyday senses. For example, a student commits a poem to memory; a court commits a mental incompetent to an institution; a hostess commits a faux pas by mispronouncing the honored guest's name. In casual language, *perpetrate* is used of practical jokes: "My neighbor *perpetrated* a hoax on his wife."

Unlikely though it seems, *perpetrate* is sometimes misused for *perpetuate*, as in "This obsolete method of bookkeeping is *perpetrated* by many old-fashioned business organizations." To *perpetuate* is to make enduring, to preserve, to make everlasting: "A trust fund was created to *perpetuate* the professor's name."

COMMON, GENERAL, UNIVERSAL

How Many Are Included?

The distinctions between *common, general,* and *universal* loosely parallel those between *many, most,* and *all.* What is common is shared by many: common law, common usage, common carrier. *Common* connotes the well-known. *General* concerns what is more widely applicable, usually because it is loosely defined or is nonspecific: general welfare, general terms, general creditors. It pertains to nearly all of a group or class and is therefore widespread. *Universal,* the broadest term, does not limit itself; it knows no boundaries: universal truths, universal beliefs, universal needs. It pertains to the entire world (except in the United States, where it is sometimes used to refer to what is applicable throughout the country). Grammar teachers have distinguished these terms by saying that a *common* rule applies to a great many; a *general* rule, to the majority; a *universal* rule, to everyone.

A caveat is not to confuse *common* with *ordinary.* The sense of sharing, which is inherent in *common*—common interests in safety, fire protection, education—is not present in *ordinary.* *Ordinary* means "plain" or "commonplace," that which is usually encountered. An ordinary day at the beach is one in which nothing unexpected happened. An ordinary meal is of the usual kind. There is nothing extraordinary in what is ordinary.

COMMONPLACE

See TRITE EXPRESSIONS

COMPARE TO, WITH

Compared to What?

One compares something *to* something else or *with* something else. The kind of comparison made determines the preposition to use.

When a thing or a person is likened to another but is different in class, *compare* is followed by *to*. The comparison (which is fancied) draws attention to their similarities, representing them as the same in some way: "His punch was compared *to* the kick of a mule." "The instructor compared electric light *to* the sun." "Chris compared his girlfriend *to* Helen of Troy."

When the comparison is of things of the same kind, class, or nature, *compare* takes *with*. This comparison points to resemblances and differences, appraising or measuring the first element in relation to the second. The comparison is in detail: "The subway system of Paris is often compared *with* London's." "The writing style of Virginia Woolf may be compared *with* that of James Joyce." "We should compare this year's expenses *with* last year's."

COMPARISONS

It's a Matter of Degree

When only two persons, places, or things are being likened, the comparative form of an adjective is required: "This dictionary is *better than* that one." "He is *taller* than I am." "His painting is *more* (or *less*) beautiful than Stanley's." Comparison of more than two, to indicate the greatest degree of quality or quantity among them, is expressed by the superlative form: "He is the *best* of the four candidates." "This is the *biggest* haul we have ever made." "This is the *most* (or *least*) attractive arrangement."

When a thing is compared to a group or class of which it is a part, the comparative degree must be followed by *other* or *else* to convey that relationship. For example, "John Grubb is more aggressive than any salesman in our store" does not suggest that Grubb is one of our salesmen. Only his loud, pushy manner is being compared with that of "our salesmen," regardless of how or where he is employed. But saying "John Grubb is more aggressive than any *other* salesman in our store" labels him as one of ours. In "Nothing does so much for my wife as a new hair style," the word *else*, although unnecessary, may be used to emphasize the comparison: "Nothing *else* does so much...."

If an *-est* or *most* form is used with the superlative degree, to include the thing compared within the group, *all*, rather than *other*, must express it: "His is the grandest *of all* schemes." "This is the best *of all* such books." The caution here is not to substitute *any* for *all*. In "Your plan is the best of *any* submitted thus far," a preferred wording is "Your plan is the best of *all*...."

Impossible comparisons should be guarded against to avoid sounding foolish. For example, "His is a poor technique compared with his fellow student" compares *technique* with *fellow student*. A proper recasting would be either "...compared with *that* of his fellow student" or "...his fellow student's," in which *that* substitutes for "technique" in the one and the possessive form *student's* implies "technique" in the other. No comparison is made in "Jackson is now taking four courses compared with three last semester." What was meant was "Jackson is taking four courses, whereas last semester he took three."

Words that cannot be compared, or qualified, are discussed under **SUPERLATIVES**.

COMPENDIUM

See **SUMMARY AND RELATED WORDS**

COMPLEMENT, COMPLIMENT

All Kinds of Complements

Orthographers maintain that *complement* and *compliment* must surely be one of the most frequently misspelled twosomes in the English language. The chief culprit is *complement,* which means "to complete," "to fill out," or "to make entire," as in "A fedora hat will *complement* his attire" or, in its noun form, "The addition of another pitcher brought the team up to its full *complement.*" To *compliment* is to praise or to express admiration or approval. The spellings of these words are distinguishable by remembering that *complement* means "*to complete*" and that *complement,* like *complete,* has two *e*'s.

In grammar, the word *complement* has a special meaning. It is the element of a sentence that completes the predication of certain verbs. The complement of a transitive verb is a direct object: "He built a *house.*" A transitive verb may also have another kind of *complement,* one that completes the sense of the verb by referring to the direct object. This kind of complement is called a predicate objective or an objective complement: "The controller labeled the *charges* (direct object) *unacceptable* (objective complement)." "The men called themselves (object) *professionals.*" "The gardener dug the hole (object) *deep.*" In each case, the objective complement stands after and modifies the noun or pronoun—the direct object of the verb.

A linking verb, such as *be, seem, feel, grow, look,* or *smell,* may have a complement that is either a noun or an adjective. These complements describe the subject—"James is *an engineer*" (predicate noun); "The tree grew *straight*" (predicate adjective); "Theodore became *an architect*" (predicate noun); "It is going to turn *windy*" (predicate adjective).

COMPOSE, COMPRISE, INCLUDE

Does Comprise Surprise?

The idea of containing or embracing is suggested in the words *compose, comprise,* and *include.* These synonyms are not always interchangeable, however, for each has a distinctive sense.

Comprise means "to contain, encompass, or comprehend." A body comprises, or "is made up of," the elements of which it is composed. The elements, on the other hand, constitute, or "make up," the body: "Great Britain *comprises* England,

Wales, and Scotland." "The garden *comprises* four distinct arbors."

The trouble with *comprise* is that it is misused so regularly that its sense is often reversed. For example, "Twenty-five players *comprise* the full complement of a professional baseball team" should be stated the other way around. It is the full complement that comprises twenty-five players. Neither "He listed the elements that *comprise* the crime" nor "Three movements *comprise* Beethoven's Piano Concerto No. 2" is correct. The crime comprises the elements, and the concerto comprises the movements. The safest step to take with *comprise* is to replace it with "consists of" or "is composed of," which is what *comprise* means ("Great Britain *consists of*..." "The garden is *composed of*...") or, when appropriate, to substitute *constitute* or *form* ("Three movements *constitute* [or *form*] Beethoven's Piano Concerto No. 2")— or even *has*, a much simpler word ("The City of New York *has* [instead of *comprises*] five boroughs").

Comprise may not be used in the passive voice. Saying "The book *is comprised of* five chapters" is incorrect because the whole is not comprised *of* its parts. Perhaps *comprise*, since it starches any sentence, while lending itself to frequent misusage, is best avoided entirely.

Compose—which can usually serve felicitously for *comprise*— additionally means "to make; to form; to combine things." Although a whole comprises parts, parts compose a whole, thus forming it: "Fifty states *compose* (or *form*) the Union." Unlike *comprise, compose* may be used in the passive: "The Union *is composed of* fifty states."

Include, which refers to a part of the content and is therefore unlike *comprise* and *compose* (words that refer to the whole), is frequently misused for *comprise* (although dictionaries regard *comprise* and *include* as synonyms). Since *include* suggests that only some of the component items have been mentioned, that which follows is, or should be, a partial listing: "The faculty *includes* two Nobel prize winners." "The book *includes* three chapters on linguistics." If *comprise* were used, the sentences would mean that the faculty consisted of two persons and that the book contained only three chapters. With *include*, more is to be expected; with *comprise*, all has been said.

COMPOUND SUBJECT

Let's Get Together

It is hornbook grammar that a compound subject—whether both elements are singular or plural or one singular and one plural—takes a plural verb: "Statues and trees *adorn* their lawn." "Trees and a statue *adorn* their lawn." But when two or more parts of a compound subject—persons, objects, ideas—combine into one idea, they make a singular subject.

> Two nouns of closely allied meaning are often felt to make no more than a single notion.
>
> —Fowler,
> *A Dictionary of*
> *Modern English Usage*

"Lox and bagel *makes* a good snack." "To be wise and do well *is* not always easy." "Singing and dancing at the same time *requires* perfect coordination."

Two nouns that refer to the same person take a singular verb: "My adviser *and* friend *is* due here soon." If two persons are meant, then a plural verb is called for: "My adviser *and* my friend *are* due here soon."

Multiple subjects modified by *each, every,* and *many a* take a singular verb: "*Each boy and each girl is* to sit down promptly." "Almost *every* casino habitué *and many a* hobo *finds* himself sharing a park bench."

COMPOUND WORDS

Hyphens Fill the Gap

A question sometimes raised is, "When is a compound term hyphened and when is it spelled as two separate words?" No answer can be definitive because the practice of hyphening keeps shifting, and only inconsistencies remain. In current spelling, some compound words are regularly hyphened, others only occasionally, and still others not at all. For example, both *tax payer* and *taxpayer* are correct spellings, although *taxpayer* is favored. Yet the two-word version is sometimes preferable, often for the sake of balance and clarity, as in "The *penalty payers* and the *tax payers* were placed in separate lines." In some instances a hyphen can change the meaning. The difference between "He is a large-tax payer" and "He is a large taxpayer" is that one has the burden of a large tax and the other of excessive weight. Similarly, a *big-business man* need not be a *big businessman*.

Some of the varied combinations with *tax* are *taxpayment, taxgatherer; tax-free, tax-exempt, tax-supported; tax rate, tax shelter, tax collector.* A punster might say it is taxing to spell these words right. The spellings of other compound words are equally confusing.

Today's trend is to amalgamate associated words into one-word compounds—a transition that usually takes two steps. An example is *basket ball*, which first changed to *basket-ball* and then to *basketball. Air plane* became *air-plane* and then *airplane*, whereas other *air* words did not move at all. *Air raid, air force,* and *air express* still are two separate words.

> . . . the conversion of a hyphened word into an unhyphened single one is desirable as soon as the novelty of the combination has worn off, if there are no obstacles in the way of awkward spelling, obscurity, or the like.
>
> —Fowler,
> *A Dictionary of
> Modern English Usage*

No logical method for the spelling of compound words has been devised. Why do some dictionaries spell *boyfriend* as one word and *girl friend* as two? Why do some spell *drug store* this way when others spell it *drugstore?* Why do some hyphen *safe-deposit* and *moth-eaten*, whereas others do not? Until recently, *today* and *tomorrow* were hyphened. Currently, many spellers say that a one-word *postman* works in a two-word *post office*, but delivers a hyphened *postal-card*, and that the *bookcase* in the *book club* is *book-lined.* The only sensible thing to do is to consult a reliable dictionary.

COMPREHEND

See **APPREHEND, COMPREHEND**

COMPRISE

See **COMPOSE, COMPRISE, INCLUDE**

CON-

O Say Con You See?

The Latin prefix *cum-*, meaning "with or together," appears in many English words as *con*. For example, one who *concocts*—literally "boils together" (Latin *con-*, "together," and *coquere*, "to cook")—composes, devises, or puts things together. But not all *con* words have retained the literal sense of *with*. Some, in fact, need their own *with*; others carry *on*.

When *confer* means "to bring together," it takes *with* in the sense of "exchanging views" ("The internist will *confer with* the orthopedist"). It does not mean *talk with*, however, because mere talking is not the same as exchanging views. When its sense is bestowing an honor or granting a privilege, *confer on* is idiomatic: "Degrees were *conferred on* the candidates by the chancellor."

A student who adapts himself to the routine of a new school is said to *conform to* it. He acts in accordance with customs and obeys the rules. *Conform with*, on the other hand, has the sense of being "in harmony or agreement with": conform *with* a superior's ideas or conform new concepts *with* present strategies. *Adapt to* is a close synonym of *conform with*.

The word *concur* originally meant "to run together." It now means "to have the same opinion; to agree." One concurs *in* a decision but *with* others: "The faculty concurred *with* the principal *in* the decision to remove Latin from the curriculum.""The tax advisers concurred *with* the agent *in* the opinion that the law is unenforceable."

Confide has two distinct meanings. The first, "to have faith in" (which comes almost directly from the Latin *con-*, "with," and *fides*, "faith"), "to tell in confidence" or "to impart a secret," takes *in*: "My mother *confides in* her sister." The second, "to put into another's keeping" or "to entrust," is used transitively and takes *to*: "Before leaving, Agnes *confided* her savings *to* her best friend." In sum, as to secrets, a person confides *in* someone, but as to possessions, one confides them *to* someone.

Depending on how it is used, *convenient* also takes different prepositions. When its meaning is "accessible or suitable to one's comfort or purpose," or when a person or place follows it, *to* is called for: "The new branch store will be *convenient to* major transportation facilities." When purpose or use is suggested, it takes *for*: "This library is *convenient for* research."

There are still other "con" games: one *connives at* deception, but *connives with* an accomplice; two cities *connect by* a highway, but the bus route *connects with* Allsburg; a pleasure *consists in* enjoying opera, but a bracelet *consists of* gold and silver. Finally, *contingent* may take *on* or *upon*; but *contiguous* and *conducive* take *to* and *consistent*, *conversant*, and *contemporaneous* take *with*.

CONCISE, SUCCINCT

A Pithy Thought

Both *succinct* and *concise* suggest brevity. The only difference between those words, slight as it is, is that *concise* refers to style and *succinct* usually to content.

Succinct derives from a Latin word meaning "girded" or "tucked up." That is succinct, therefore, which is "held up as by a girdle," implying the making of something compact, tight, and well-knit. Succinct material is devoid of elaboration, conveying much with few words. "A strict and succinct style is that where you can take away nothing without loss, and that loss to be manifest"—Ben Jonson.

The word *concise*, from the Latin past participle *concisus*, "to cut up" (formed from *con* and *caedere*, "to cut"), originally meant "to cut short." Today *concise* primarily refers to a style of writing in which there is not a word to spare. Thoughts or phrases that are pared to the minimum, that express only what is necessary, are concise: "The style of Sir Ernest Gowers was *concise*; he used few adjectives and adverbs and fewer expletives."

CONFOUND

See CONFUSION, DEGREES OF

CONFUSION, DEGREES OF

Brain Strain

A person intellectually baffled, perhaps by a difficult problem or question, is *puzzled*: "Those equations have long *puzzled* me." "He was *puzzled* by the speaker's attitude." A *perplexed* person is not only puzzled but also discomfited by the intricacies of a problem. Derived from a Latin word meaning "entangled" or "interwoven," *perplex* suggests both worry and uncertainty over the complicated character of a thing: "The witness recounts it differently with each telling. Surely, the jury will be more *perplexed* than enlightened by his testimony."

An even stronger word is *bewilder*. Originally meaning "to be lost in a pathless place," it continues to suggest a loss of bearings and, with it, a loss of confidence. A bewildered person cannot trust his conflicting impressions, nor can he choose between vaguely comprehended alternatives. He is therefore temporarily unable to think clearly or reason normally: "The market's fluctuations have me utterly *bewildered*: Are we rich or poor?" "The farmer stood at the edge of Times Square, *bewildered* by the noise, the lights, and the traffic."

To *confuse* is to discomfit, to bewilder to the point of shame or embarrassment: "The child was *confused* and frightened by the fierce argument between his parents." In this sense, it is a stronger word than the other three. *Confuse* also means "to disorder," "to mix up," or "to fail to distinguish," as in "Only a CPA can unravel these *confused* accounts" or in "She is forever *confusing* speed with efficiency."

To *confound* once meant "to bring to ruin." It implied such confusion that even the elements of the problems could not be sorted. At present it suggests confusion that borders on astonishment: "The fluctations of the money market have *confounded* all the leading economists." "The suddenness of their attack *confounded* the enemy."

All these verbs are regarded as synonyms and, loosely speaking, they are. But each one suggests increasingly greater degrees of bafflement. Their climactic sequence is *puzzle, perplex, bewilder, confuse, confound.*

CONSECUTIVE, SUCCESSIVE

After You

The adjectives *consecutive* and *successive* are sister words in that they refer to time sequence. *Consecutive* refers to things that follow one behind the other in uninterrupted succession, as do the twelve months of the year in sequence. *Successive* has a similar sense. But it refers to what follows in a regular order, one behind the other, regardless of the intervals between them. This means that these matters need not be next to each other. For example, although Monday, Wednesday, and Friday are not consecutive days, they are successive. The position of one with reference to the other is implied in successive.

CONSENSUS

Come to Your Consensus

Everyone agrees that there is a consensus if everyone agrees. But everyone does not agree on how the word *consensus* should be used or even how it should be spelled.

Consensus means "general agreement or collective opinion." It is redundant, therefore, to precede it with *general* ("The *general consensus* is to cancel the affair") or to follow it with *of opinion* ("The dean sought a *consensus of opinion*"). However, in the eyes of some authorities, "consensus of opinion" is justified when the implication of *consensus* is doubtful. The added phrase *of opinion* then differentiates it from a consensus of ideas, evidence, ratings, and so forth. Some dictionaries note that the phrase "consensus of opinion," despite its redundancy, is widely accepted. But prudence should be the watchword before using it. Ordinarily it should not be done.

Possibly the most commonly misspelled word in the English language, excepting "supercede" for *supersede*, is "concensus" for *consensus*. The latter word has nothing to do with a census. Actually it is related to "sense." The prefix *con-*, which means "together," enlarges its sense to "a common sense." The progenitor of *consensus* is the Latin *consentire* ("to feel together" or "to agree"), which also spawned the word *consent*.

CONSIDER

For a Slight Consideration

The statement "I consider McGrath a good salesman" is clear enough. Strictly speaking, however, *consider* suggests deliberation, pondering—the giving of close thought, which the example does not imply. Saying "I think McGrath is a good salesman" expresses it more accurately. Although *consider* is regarded by some dictionaries as a synonym for *think, believe, feel,* and *suppose,* it should preferably be reserved to reflect objective evaluation. A person considering a matter contemplates or studies it. Originally one who considered had the benefit of astral influence. The *sider* in *consider* came from the Latin *sideris,* genitive of *sidus,* "star." When soothsayers observed the stars, they considered; that is, they were with, "con," the stars.

The several meanings of *consider* are governed by idiom. In its most frequent use, *consider* means "to regard as," "to believe to be," or "to judge." In that sense a direct object, not *as,* follows it: "We all consider her intelligent" (not "consider her *as* intelligent"). *As* follows *consider* only when it means "to discuss" or "to examine": "The report *considers* him first *as* a strategist, then *as* a tactician." *Consider* never takes a clause as its direct object: "The accountant considers the figures incorrect" (not "considers the figures *are* [or *to be*] incorrect").

CONSIST

That's What It's Made Of

The reference of *consist of* is to the elements or parts of which the whole is made up or composed— the material: "Paint *consists of* coloring matter, oil or water, and other ingredients." "Goulash *consists of* chunks of beef and potatoes and pieces of carrots and celery." *Consists in* refers to an inherent quality, to that which resides within. It defines or shows identity: "Integrity *consists in* being as good as your word." "Happiness *consists in* peace of mind." In those examples, *is* could replace *consists in.*

A synonym of *consist of,* but not *consist in,* is *contain.* To *contain* is to have within itself, as in "The Pentateuch *contains* five books." Another synonym, *compose,* refers to parts that constitute a whole. One may say, "The book *contains* (or *is composed of*) twelve chapters, a bibliography, and an index." That is what the book *consists of.*

CONSUL, COUNCILOR, COUNSELOR

Free Advice

On different occasions one might seek advice from a consul, a councilor, or a counselor. The nature of the advice may differ, as may the relationship of the inquirer to the adviser.

A *consul* is an officer in the foreign service of a country: "Algernon visited the Canadian *consul* in Paris."

A *councilor*, or *councilman*, is a member of a council, a governing board or a body of persons elected to legislate, an assembly: "The mayor met with four *councilmen* to consider the water problem." "O'Reilly was named an alternate *councilor* to the Forum of Senior Citizens."

A *counselor* is an adviser. He gives counsel, as does an attorney at law; but counselors need not be lawyers. Anyone who offers opinions or instructions is a counselor: "Many high school students seek advice from a school *counselor*." The corresponding verb form of *counselor* is "counsel": "A lawyer *counsels* his clients." "An older brother may *counsel* his younger brother."

CONTAGIOUS, INFECTIOUS

Catch It Anyway You Can

The distinction between the words *contagious* and *infectious* lies not in the kind of illness contracted but in the way that the disease is transmitted. A contagious disease is one communicable by contact. (In Latin, *tangere*, the root of *contagious*, means "to touch.") The contact need not be with the sick person; it may be with his clothing or with air he has breathed. An infectious disease is transmitted by organisms in such agencies as water, air, food, and insects. An infectious disease may, but need not, be contagious.

Although these terms are interchanged outside medical usage, they should not be confused. Even their figurative senses should be given distinctive meanings. *Contagious* implies a rapid spreading, as in "*Contagious* fear swept through the community"; *infectious* suggests an irrestible quality: "My wife's laughter is *infectious*; the moment she laughs, everyone joins in."

Although the sense of "touching" resides in both *contagious* and *contiguous*, the words are unrelated. *Contagious* in everyday usage means "catching." *Contiguous* means "adjacent."

CONTEMPORARY

Now or Then

The definition of *contemporary* "is existing or occurring at the same time." Obviously it does not refer only to the present. President Lincoln, for example, was a contemporary of General Grant, for they belonged to the same period. Mark Antony was a contemporary of Julius Caesar.

When the term *contemporary* describes time not in the present, this fact should be clearly indicated by context or direct mention. If no date has been given and none is inferable, the sense of *contemporary* is "now." This means that *contemporary*, standing alone, refers to the modern. A historian who, after discussing the Civil War, says that its effects should be weighed in the light of contemporary views (now? then?) may perplex his audience. Describing the chairs in a Revolutionary War home as contemporary is also less than precise. Were they contemporary with Paul Revere or Noguchi? This kind of sentence can easily be clarified by using *now, then, at that time, in the past,* or *at the same time.*

The words *contemporary* and *contemporaneous* in some instances are interchangeable, since both refer to what exists or occurs at the same time (Latin *con,* "with"; *tempus,* "time"). *Contemporary,* both a noun and an adjective, may be applied to people, but the adjective *contemporaneous* is used only of objects or events.

CONTEND

Nolo Contendere

The sentence "My husband *contends* that to avoid traffic, we should leave early" is more appropriately expressed, "My husband *says*...." Generally the term *contend* is best used to denote an assertion by argument or a striving in opposition—or contention. One does not contend when making an ordinary statement but simply says or makes it. Unlike *contend, say* does not imply disagreement, nor do its related words *maintain, state, assert, declare,* and *aver,* despite their different connotations. What one *maintains* (which need not be in disagreement but may be in opposition) must have been previously asserted. To *state* is to set forth formally in speech or in writing. The sense of *assert* is to state boldly, and often without evidence; that of *declare,* to state emphatically. *Aver* and *declare* are closely related in meaning—*to aver* is "to declare in a positive, dogmatic or formal manner"; *to declare,* "to make a formal, explicit statement."

CONTINUAL, CONTINUOUS

The Pros of Con

In modern usage *continuous* and *continual* are carefully distinguished. The main difference between them lies in whether the action they describe has been interrupted.

Continual means recurring at short intervals. What is continual is regularly or closely repeated; it happens again and again. The ringing of a telephone is continual, as is the action of a person who intermittently interrupts a speaker.

Continuous means "without interruption." The word implies an unending action or an unbroken extent in space while it continues. To put it differently, what is continuous has no pauses or breaks: a continuous rain, a continuous noise, a continuous pain, a continuous slope. Some machines operate continuously for a long period. Waterfalls flow continuously. ("What a faucet!" one may say. "It lets the water run *continuously* when it's turned on—but drip *continually* when it's turned off.")

CONTRAST

In Contrast

The preposition that *contrast* takes depends on whether it is a verb or a noun. The verb (pronounced kahn-*trast*) is customarily followed by *with:* "Geoffrey *contrasted* the storms in the Atlantic Ocean *with* those in the Pacific." "The decorator *contrasted* the effect of blue *with* that of yellow." As a noun, in which case the first syllable is stressed (*kahn*-trast), it offers a choice:

to or *with* ("Current economic conditions provide a decided *contrast to* [or *with*] the rosy predictions of the pollsters." "One may make a *contrast* of the king's position *to* [or *with*] that of the archduke"). The phrase *in contrast* enjoys no such latitude. It takes only *to*: "In *contrast to* the power he wields, I am a weakling." And *in comparison* is limited to *with*: "Lessey's sculptures are static in *comparison with* Rodin's."

CONVINCE, PERSUADE

Convincing Argument or Friendly Persuasion?

Although the statement "His mother had to *convince* him to return to school" may seem correct, in the opinion of many writers it is not. Idiomatically, *convince* should not be followed by an infinitive. If consequent action is to be indicated, then a construction introduced by *of* or *that* must be used: "His mother *convinced* him *that* he should return to school." This means that a person can be convinced, for example, *that* a report is accurate or convinced *of* its accuracy, but grammatically cannot be *convinced to approve* it. He may, however, be persuaded to do so, for *persuade* is not governed by the limitations imposed on *convince*. In fact, *persuade* can take any one of three constructions— *that*, *of*, or *to*. Hence, although a person may not *convince someone to*, he may *persuade someone to*.

The meanings of *convince* and *persuade*, despite their sense similarity, are not identical. *Convince* means "to satisfy by argument or evidence"; *persuade*, "to influence a person to an action or belief." In every day usage, however, those distinctions are too slight to be observed. They are regularly ignored and the words interchanged. What, one may ask, is the practical difference between "I convinced him that he should go" and "I persuaded him to go"? Strictly speaking, *convince* is a static verb used to emphasize the idea of proof by argument, the satisfying of someone of a truth or a necessity. *Persuade* is an active verb. It emphasizes the idea of winning over to a course of action. A person convinced that he ought to do something may do nothing unless persuaded to do so. A father might convince his son that the lawn needs mowing, yet be unable to persuade him to mow it. There is a practical difference between these words after all—it's in the doing.

COPULATIVE VERBS

See BAD, BADLY

CORRELATIVE CONJUNCTIONS

They Work Together

Conjunctions used in pairs (those that work in correlation with another conjunction) are called correlative or parallel conjunctions: *both... and, either ... or, neither ... nor, not only ... but also.* Like coordinating conjunctions, they connect expressions of equal grammatical rank. This means that the same kind of phrasing follows each conjunction. For example, the elements in this sentence have the same grammatical value—both are nouns: "He bought both *the coat* and *the hat*." In "He said it is either *in the warehouse* or *in the office*," prepositional phrases make a balance, as do the verbs in "The thief not only *stole* the money but also *beat up* the proprietor."

Although some authorities recommend that a writer pay more heed to the rhythm of the sentence than to its balance, the rule of parallelism is usually the best one to follow. Unbalanced sentences may not only look awkward but also sound illogical. Such sentences ordinarily can be corrected by repositioning a word or two. For instance, "The book *should neither be* revised nor reprinted" could be rephrased: "The book *should be* neither revised nor reprinted" or "The book *should neither be* revised nor *be* reprinted." In "Carol *both liked* the blue bag and the red one," the words *both liked* should be transposed. (For further discussion of *both ... and*, see **BOTH**.)

A caution worth repeating is to make certain that the same construction—noun, verb, adjective, prepositional phrase, clause—follows both conjunctions.

COST, PRICE, VALUE, WORTH

Pay the Price

Everyone who purchases something considers, to some degree, its *price, cost, value,* and *worth.* The terms *price* and *cost* are often confused, as are *value* and *worth.*

Price is a selling term. It is the amount a person is willing to sell an article for. The price is usually indicated by a figure on a ticket, a price tag. *Cost* is a buying term. It is the amount the purchaser actually pays for the article, which may be different from the figure on the ticket. *Value* is an abstract term—a ratio that an object bears to a recognized standard. The item may be superior or inferior in quality, making the price attractive or unappealing. Its *worth*, however, is subjective in that it relates to a buyer's desire or need for an item. What has great worth to some may have little or no worth to many. Bottle tops may be worth much to a collector, for example, but have no worth to almost anyone else.

The words *costly* and *expensive* are frequently interchanged. Something that is regarded as *costly* or *expensive* carries a price tag with a figure higher than one cares to pay. *Costly*, however, often pertains to the high value of an article, which, at least in the eyes of the seller, justifies the high price: "Paintings by famous artists are now so *costly* that only the very rich can afford them." If *expensive* had been substituted for *costly*, the sentence would make as much sense—still only the rich could afford them. The implication of *expensive*, however, is that the price is beyond what the object is worth. The price of something expensive is just too high.

COULD

See CAN, COULD

COUNCILOR, COUNSELOR

See CONSUL, COUNCILOR, COUNSELOR

COUNTENANCE

See FACE

COUPLE

A Couple Do Better than One

Unless two persons are considered a unit, as in "The *couple* in the far corner *looks* drunk," it is best to regard the word *couple* as a plural noun: "The *couple* who *live* next door are very friendly" and "My aunt met a *couple* who *were* the best golfers in the state of California."

What must be guarded against is inconsistency. Since the word *couple* as a collective noun may be either singular or plural, the number of the verb that *couple* governs depends on the number ascribed to *couple*. A decision in this regard should be made early to avoid awkwardness or even downright confusion. A case in point is "A Miami couple *was* awarded first prize. The couple, Mr. and Mrs. Arthur Stouffer, *were* simply overwhelmed." The phrases *couple was* and *couple were* are incompatible. The safest tack to take is to treat the word *couple* as a plural—*couple were*. Only when *couple* clearly connotes a singular, in a sentence that stands alone ("The *couple* was married last year"), should it be so considered.

Is it acceptable English to refer to a distance as being "a couple of miles" when "a few miles" is meant? The logical answer is no, since the sense of *couple* is of two things or persons related in some ways. The word, from the Latin *copula*, "a bond," is often used of two persons legally bonded in marriage. *Couple*, therefore, means "a pair," which is the equivalent of the word *two*. Nevertheless, idiom, which many times overrides logic, has decreed that *couple* may be used in the sense of several, not necessarily two. Charles Dickens, among other literary dignitaries, used the phrase "a couple of miles." That usage, except in the most formal style, has persisted and is now well established.

CREDIBLE, CREDULOUS

See INCREDIBLE, INCREDULOUS

CRY HAVOC

See RAVAGE, RAVISH

CURRICULUM VITAE

See SUMMARY AND RELATED WORDS

CUSTOM, HABIT, PRACTICE

Practice Makes Perfect

Although *custom*, *habit*, and *practice* are considered synonyms, in that each implies an established way of doing things, their meanings are divergent. Writers should therefore use them judiciously.

Custom, as applied to social or community activity, refers to the practice followed as a matter of course among the people. It is a regular or somewhat permanent mode or form of action: "It is the *custom* in Spain to close places of business in the early afternoon." "It is an American *custom* to blow horns on New Year's Eve." In many instances *custom* is the result of habit.

Habit is the unconscious tendency to repeat an action so constantly that it becomes spontaneous. Some habits are desirable (brushing one's teeth before retiring), whereas others are not (scratching one's head before speaking). Habits associated with nervousness, shyness, or boldness are socially undesirable. Acts that are deliberate—surrendering a seat to an elderly person or tipping a hat as a sign of respect—are not occasioned by habit, but are customary, accepted convention in certain cultured societies.

Practice refers to the developed behavior of a person or class. Hence *practice* and *custom* are somewhat synonymous except that *practice* applies to habitual performance, procedures that are so set as to be unvarying: "It is Alfredo's *practice* to clear his desk of all mail before leaving for the day." "Reading the daily newspaper at breakfast is a *practice* of many businessmen." When a practice of a large group becomes customary, it is called a *usage*. The behavior of individuals tends to follow this usage and is thus regulated by it.

D

DANGLING MODIFIERS

Left Dangling

All high school students are taught to avoid dangling participles, those participles that usually begin a sentence but refer to no subsequent noun, as exemplified in the following sentences: "Walking over the hill on the left, the clubhouse can be clearly seen" and "Waiting in front of the hotel, the air turned chilly." The clubhouse was not walking, and the air was not waiting. Likewise, in "When reviewing the article, an effort was made to be fair," the present participle has nothing logical to qualify. But a subject is provided, to which the dangling phrase can relate, if reworded, "When reviewing the article, *the writer* made an effort to be fair." And certainly in "Running through the woods, three fallen oaks were seen," it was not the oaks that were running. Introductory participles do not dangle if an active subject is set out in the main clause.

A similar error is to attach a participle to the wrong noun. In "Singing before a large audience, a stage prop fell on him," the grammatical sense is that a stage prop was singing. A rephrasing might be "Singing before a large audience, *he* was struck by a falling stage prop" or "While singing...."

The term *dangling participle* is so well known that the words seem to go together automatically, but other verbal phrases are potential danger spots, too. Any unattached phrase is distracting, and the sentence that contains one needs correcting.

Second to a dangling participle in misusage is the dangling prepositional-gerund. An example of this kind of error appears in "*In assembling* the necessary equipment, it is advisable to consult an experienced guide," in which no subject specifies the one assembling the equipment. A correct rephrasing would be "In assembling the necessary equipment, *one* should seek the advice of an experienced guide." The "doer" of the action implied in the gerund must be made apparent in the main clause. In "*On arriving* at the terminal, the bulletin board informed us that the bus is on time," the question to ask is, Who is arriving?—the bulletin board? Corrected versions are "On arriving at the terminal, *we* learned from the bulletin board that..." and "*When we* arrived at the terminal, the bulletin board informed us that...."

Dangling infinitive phrases are just as incorrect as other danglers; but since infinitives seldom begin sentences, their misusage is less common. These danglers, like other kinds of danglers, are corrected by rearranging the sentence so that the modifier refers to the right word; that is, the "doer" of the act is clearly made the subject of the following clause. For example, in "To grow straight, Steven must keep the plants in sunlight" the main clause (since the intended meaning was not that Steven should grow straight) should be reworded "the plants should be kept in sunlight." The infinitive phrase in "To be meaningful, the writer should rewrite the sentence" erroneously refers to the writer. It is the sentence, not the writer, that needs to be made meaningful.

Some exceptions to the above rules pertain to those modifiers that do not dangle either because they have their own subject or because they indicate a general rather than a specific action. Examples of the first kind are "The storm having subsided, we were able to leave" and "They all left for home, the class being over." The clause with the participle (the subordinate clause) is an absolute construction in that it is grammatically independent of the rest of the sentence. In the second group are modifiers, such as *strictly speaking, to be perfectly frank*, and *to say the least*, that do not apply to a word or word group but modify the entire remainder of the sentence. No specific "doer" of the action is, or need be, suggested. Such introductory words or phrases as *in brief, in sum, allowing, in fact, granting, concerning, to tell the truth*, or *owing to*, since they are independent elements, also need nothing to attach to. Other examples are found in "*Considering* everything, the partners were lucky to get their investment back" and "*Generally speaking*, the bank forecloses after the second default."

DASH

See **PUNCTUATION—COLON** and **DASH**

DEAL

Big Deal!

The noun *deal* in "We made a good *deal* today" is a colloquialism for "business transaction" or "bargain." *Deal* is also used loosely to mean either "secret or underhand arrangement" ("You can be sure that Senator White will arrange another payoff *deal*") or "treatment" ("The boss gave him a raw *deal*"). A somewhat different colloquial use makes it synonymous with "quantity, amount, or extent," as in "It was a great *deal* more (*a larger amount*) than we had expected." And, of course, the familiar question, "Whose *deal* is it?"

Although the combination *deal with* is a common expression, more precise wording is needed if the phrase is not clear in that context. For example, in "Before the Taft-Hartley Act, management generally was unwilling *to deal with* the demands of employees," was management reluctant *to negotiate with* labor? *to comply with* the demands of labor? *to give in* to the demands? or *to admit* the fairness of the demands?

To deal fairly with the matter, it must be admitted that *deal with* is not always confusing. In "The courts must *deal with* lawbreakers," for example, *deal with* means "to take action in regard to" and is a proper, albeit general, term. *Deal with* may also mean "to treat or to address as an issue" ("The report *deals with* child abuse").

DECIDED, DECISIVE

Decisions, Decisions

The words *decided* and *decisive* have one attribute in common: they both may apply to persons in the sense of "characterized by or displaying decision" ("The dean's manner is *decisive*." "His is a *decided* manner").

By and large, however, *decisive* is preferably not used of persons, especially when *decided* will do. The primary meaning of *decisive* is "bringing things to a conclusion," referring to that which decides an issue: "The haymaker was the *decisive* blow." Its synonyms are "final" and "conclusive." An attractive financial arrangement may be the decisive point in the success of a merger; a particular battle may be decisive in turning defeat into victory.

Decided means "clear-cut," "unmistakable," "unquestionable," and "resolute." It is used of persons or things. As to persons, its sense is "determined" or "showing determination." A person may affect a decided air of bravado or exhibit a decided aloofness or be a decided adherent to a philosophical view. But when used of things, it means "unmistakable" (as in "That was a *decided* error").

An even stronger word is *determinative*, which in Latin relates to the crisis of a disease. When a cause, effect, factor, or influence is determinative, it is conclusive. The result of what is determinative is immutable, fixed.

DECIMATE

And Then There Were Nine

The word *decimate* evolved from the Latin *decem*, which means "ten." It is a gruesome word, in that it describes the method of punishment given rebellious or cowardly soldiers in the Roman legions. The leaders would choose one of every ten warriors by lot to be put to death.

Today *decimate* is no longer associated with the number ten. Rather than denoting the slaughter of a tenth part of something, it has come to mean "to kill or destroy a large, or the greater part of." ("The Black Plague *decimated* the population of Europe"). When it is used in other than its original sense, it should not be employed with fractions or percentages, as in "We *decimated* over half the Egyptian moths." It likewise does not belong in contexts such as "If the smog continues, it will *decimate* the health of the inhabitants" or "Ferguson's arguments *decimated* almost all of his opponent's." Abstractions cannot be decimated.

The adverbs *totally* and *completely* should not modify *decimate* because the extermination it implies is less than total or complete. Nor should *decimate* be considered a substitute for *annihilate*, which means "to put out of existence altogether, to destroy utterly."

DEDUCE, DEDUCT

See ADDUCE, DEDUCE, DEDUCT

DEGENERATE, DETERIORATE

From Better to Worse

The verbs *degenerate* and *deteriorate* both mean "to become worse." That which degenerates or deteriorates declines in some quality or capacity, whether physical, moral, or mental.

The origins of *degenerate* convey the sense of falling from a position one had at birth (*de*, "from," *genero*, "birth"); in other words, to sink below a standard of conduct or vigor set by one's ancestors. More generally, one who has degenerated has reverted to a lower cultural or moral state, becoming, perhaps, morally degraded or sexually deviant. In this sense the Nazis degenerated into savagery. To *degenerate* may also mean to retrogress physically or intellectually. Muscles may degenerate from lack of use, or creative powers may degenerate because of continuing stress. Similarly, social drinkers may degenerate into alcoholics. John Wilkes Booth degenerated from a respected actor into a despised murderer.

Deteriorate, from the Latin comparative *deterior* (meaning "worse") does not suggest, as *degenerate* often does, a worsening of one's sense of morality or loss of virtue; it denotes a process more of impairment than of retrogression.

DELIGHTED

Delight of My Life

Although no one may be delighted to hear this, the past participle *delighted* may take the prepositions *at, in, with*, or *by*— each employed in a different sense.

Abstract terms or phrases take *delighted at*: "He is *delighted at* the opportunity to show his wares." Material objects are introduced by *delighted with*: "She is *delighted with* her new automobile." The happiness derived from an activity is expressed by *delighted in*: "Lois *delighted in* playing before so large an audience." "The boss seems to *delight in* irritating his employees."

The phrase *delighted by* correctly applies either to abstract or to concrete terms, but the emphasis then shifts from the delight felt by the person to the delight that the thing gives. For example, "He is *delighted by* the opportunity to show his wares" stresses the pleasure derived from the opportunity.

DELUSION

See ALLUSION, ILLUSION, DELUSION

DESERT, DESSERT

She Deserves Dessert

The spelling of the identically pronounced *dessert* (a sweet course at the end of a meal) and the present tense of the verb *desert* ("to leave, forsake, or abandon") should not be confused. An arid region, such as the Sahara, is a *desert*, spelled with one *s* and accented on the first syllable. A person who gets his *just deserts* (with one middle *s* and the second syllable stressed) gets what he deserves. This *deserts* comes from the Old French *deservir*, "to deserve."

DETERIORATE

See DEGENERATE, DETERIORATE

DEVOTEE

See ADDICT, DEVOTEE

DIFFERENT

Different Opinions

What preposition should *different* take? The categorical answer is *from*, since different things differ *from* each other. And yet the practical answer is not quite so simple. Although *different from* is established usage (*from* is a preposition that relates *different* to the following noun or pronoun), many authorities recommend that *different than* be used (even though *than* is a conjunction) if it avoids awkwardness and wasteful words. An example would be "It has caused him problems in ways *different than* he had ever imagined" rather than "...*different from that which* he had ever imagined," Or "They use *different* systems today *than they did in 1959*" rather than "They use *different* systems today *from those which they had in 1959*." Formal usage, nonetheless, resists the less wordy expression and holds firm with *different from*.

Even though *different than* is gaining linguistic respectability, particularly when the object is a long clause, its ceremonial entry into formal acceptance has not as yet taken place. Perhaps its use should not be criticized, but, strictly speaking, it should not be welcomed either.

Although the idiom *different to* (as in "The red tulips are *different to* those grown in Holland") is another possibility, it is accepted only in Great Britain. Its closest rival in the United States is *dissimilar to*. It may be said that a building on the block is both larger *than,* and *dissimilar to,* the others, but it can only be *different from* them.

An unrelated construction is used when differences themselves are being compared; *different than* is then the proper phrasing. For example, in "The decorators' styles *differ from* one another, but Mr. Alywyn's is more *different than* the others," *than* is governed by *more*, not by *different*.

One last thought. The expression "no different from" is generally disapproved. It is better to say, "It is *not* different from..." or "It does *not differ* from...."

DIFFERENTIATE, DISCRIMINATE, DISTINGUISH

Can You Tell The Difference?

At some time everyone is called upon to analyze or compare the characteristics of different things. When the items compared are closely related, the problem is to determine what sets them apart from each other. Several words, whose meanings are similar but not identical, may describe this process.

To *distinguish* is to mark subtle or gross distinctions, usually with reference to external qualities, that without going into specific details will establish the separate identities of the items analyzed: "How does one *distinguish* between art and illustration?" "The Australians may be *distinguished* from the British by their dialect." "Its brilliance and clarity *distinguish* crystal from glass."

To *differentiate* is to distinguish more precisely, pointing out exact dissimilarities in some detail: "The curator, by *differentiating* the various species, made understanding easy." "Without binoculars, we are unable to *differentiate* between one kind of blue bird and another."

To *discriminate* is to exercise intellectual or emotional judgment, as, for example, between proper and improper conduct or between good and bad design. One who discriminates observes or senses sharp distinctions between things and analyzes their significance. Such a person is not necessarily making unfavorable distinctions; they could just as well be favorable. But the word has been placed in a disparaging light, as though discrimination must always be in someone's disfavor. Perhaps this is due to the generally accepted doctrine that there shall be no discrimination because of race, creed, color, or country of origin.

DIGEST

See SUMMARY AND RELATED WORDS

DILEMMA

Troubled Times

Are the words *dilemma* and *problem* equivalents? Is it correct to say "The principal *dilemma* confronting us is inflation" or "Bill has a terrible *dilemma*—he doesn't know which game to watch"? The answer is no in both instances.

A *dilemma* is not just a predicament or a problem. And it is not a choice between the good and the bad or the desirable and the undesirable. It is a choice between *two unpleasant* alternatives. To have to choose between inflation and recession would be a true dilemma, as would be a forced choice between communism and fascism; but it is not a dilemma to have to choose between apple pie and chocolate custard, two palatable dishes. That the alternatives are undesirable is graphically indicated by the complete expression, "to be on the horns of a dilemma." Horns, of course, come in pairs, and no one likes to be gored by either one.

Many words in the English language, other than *dilemma*, denote an unhappy or confused state because of a difficulty that needs resolving. A person in a *quandary* is mentally perplexed (although all the solutions may be equally acceptable). A *predicament* is an unpleasant or dangerous situation. *Plight* suggests an unfortunate, trying condition. But none of them constitutes a dilemma unless the resolution is one of two courses, both of which are unsatisfactory.

DISCLOSE, REVEAL

Shocking Revelations

Reveal, perhaps because it sounds dramatic, is less often used than *disclose*. To *disclose* is "to make known" or "to expose to view." To *reveal* is to disclose suddenly, strikingly, or unexpectedly. Its sense is "to uncover," as though by lifting a veil. A magician exhibits a white rabbit, which he then thrusts into a booth; seconds later he lifts the front curtain to reveal a beautiful woman. A British curator reveals that he was once a Russian spy. One who reveals something expects the viewer or listener to be surprised or even shocked by the revelation.

The noun *revelation*, however, in the minds of some people has such a strong theological connotation ("the *revelation* of God's truth") that it is avoided in everyday usage. Derived from the Latin *revelare*, "to draw back a veil," it has not strayed far from its original meaning.

DISCOVER, INVENT

Discover What Is—Invent What Isn't

In some instances people are not sure whether something is *discovered* or *invented*. Although they would not say that Columbus invented America or that Edison discovered the gramophone, they may confuse these words in less obvious situations.

To *discover* means to find out or to learn about something already existing but previously unknown. The discoverer obtains man's first knowledge of it, accidentally or after long searching. An explorer may discover a new river; a scientist, a natural law. For example, Newton discovered the law of gravity and Dr. William Harvey discovered the circulation of the blood. It is, however, incorrect to say, "Cellophane was *discovered* by scientists"; it was invented.

One who *invents* creates. An inventor conceives of or devises something that has not previously existed. Electricity, for example, was discovered; the light bulb, invented. *Discover* has the sense of "find"; *invent*, of "make."

DISCRIMINATE, DISTINGUISH

See DIFFERENTIATE, DISCRIMINATE, DISTINGUISH

DISINTERESTED, UNINTERESTED

Interest Rates High

Disinterested and *uninterested* should not be carelessly interchanged, even though some dictionaries, bowing to popular usage, assign to them the same meaning: "lacking interest." The English language is not enriched by words that lose precision.

Disinterested means "impartial." A disinterested person is one who has no self-interest or bias in the issue at hand. He seeks no benefit for himself. A judge, an arbitrator, a mediator— all are presumably disinterested participants. That is, they bear no prejudice toward the litigants and are not influenced by personal motives. Their stand on the issue at point is neutral. But a disinterested person need not be uninterested.

Uninterested means "bored," "having no interest in." A person who is not an investor will, in all likelihood, have no interest in watching a ticker tape. Anyone unfamiliar with Oriental art would be uninterested in visiting the Asiatic Museum. These people are truly uninterested, indifferent (a synonym that means "lacking in feeling"). And feeling is entirely lacking toward a matter in which one has no interest.

The word *interest* has several definitions. One who has a share in the ownership of property has an interest in it. Or a person may have an interest in a venture and yet, in another sense, have no interest in it; that is, he may have a proprietary interest but feel no concern or stimulation.

DIVERT

See AVERT, AVOID

DOUBLE NEGATIVES

See CAN, COULD; HARDLY; MISTAKE

DOUBT

Beyond Doubt

A person in *doubt*, according to its Latin relative *duo*, is thinking "twice," a sign of uncertainty. Indeed, the original sense of the parent of *doubt* (*dubitare*) was "to have to choose between two things." But there is no doubt that the word following an expression of doubt determines the kind of doubt it is. The words to choose from are *whether*, *if*, and *that*.

When a positive statement expressing genuine doubt is made, either *whether* or *if* may be used, as in "They *doubt whether* the problem will be solved within a week" and in "We *doubt if* he'll come." *Whether* is preferred in formal writing.

In negative statements, *doubt* is regularly followed by *that*. Here the idea conveyed is not of real doubt, but a denial of it: "Esther has *no doubt that* her husband loves her." "We do *not doubt that* he has ability." Questions also take *that*: "Does anybody *doubt that* he is honest?" "Do you really *doubt that* it was said?"

The careless use of one of these words for another can change the meaning of the sentence. Replacing *whether* with *that*, for instance, converts doubt into firm disbelief. Uncertainty in "They doubt *whether* he stole the money" becomes incredulity in "They doubt *that* he stole the money."

The adjective *doubtful* is governed by these same rules. Either *whether* or *if* follows *doubtful* in positive statements. As with *doubt*, *whether* is preferred, since *whether* normally introduces noun clauses: "We are *doubtful whether* we will see the sun again today." *That* follows *doubtful* in negative statements or in interrogatives: "Can anyone be *doubtful that* Morgan was guilty?"

One who is *doubtful* about the success of a venture is said to be *in doubt* about its chances for success. Both *doubtful* and *in doubt* connote a sense of uncertainty. In some instances, however, *doubtful* expresses stronger overtones of genuine doubt than *in doubt*. For example, "The funding of the project is *in doubt*" means that no one at the present time is certain about the final decision, but "The funding of the project is *doubtful*" implies a belief that the funding is unlikely.

DUE TO

How Do You Due?

Very few among us have not misused the term *due to* at one time or another. Its most frequent misusage is in these kinds of constructions: "*Due to* bad weather all airplanes have been grounded" and in "He lost the game *due to* a sore arm." In those examples *due* is treated as a preposition (which it is not), mistakenly suggesting a reason for what follows, thus ousting such legitimate expressions as "owing to," "on account of," "as a result of," and "because of": "*Owing to* bad weather all airplanes have been grounded." "He lost the game *because of* his sore arm."

Since *due* is an adjective, it needs a noun or pronoun to modify. To assure this functioning, the safest place for *due to* is after a form of the verb *to be* because there it always serves as an adjective: "The cancellation *was due to* bad weather" (*due* modifies the noun *cancellation*). "My failure to pay promptly was *due to* an oversight" (*due* modifies *failure*).

The most dangerous placement of *due to* is at the head of a sentence. In "*Due to* rain" or in "*Due to* the lateness of the hour" or in "*Due to* a cold I was unable to attend," *due to* is treated as an adverbial phrase. This is a misuse. English has not yet surrendered the adjectival character of *due*.

A test to determine whether *due to* is being used correctly is to replace it with *caused by* or *attributed to*, which is what *due to* means. If the replacements make sense, *due to* is correctly used, as it is in "The explosion was *due to* (*caused by* or *attributed to*) carelessness."

Criticizing adverbial *due to* may be futile, since its entrenched colloquial use has overwhelmed its grammatical origin—but this is not to say that its misusage need be condoned or encouraged.

$\mathcal{E}$

EACH

To Each His Very Own

Each sounds like a singular word. It is ("*Each* one *is* a good worker"). Yet in some constructions the nouns and verbs associated with it are plural.

The distributive pronoun *each* is always singular for it singles out an individual from the group—and it always takes a singular verb: "*Each has* to do what is right." It is singular even though an *of* phrase modifying *each* has a plural object: "*Each of the men has* to do what is right." "*Each of us knows* what is right." The same rule governs when *each* as an adjective modifies the subject: "*Each* officer (implying that there were many) *was* invited personally." As the subject of the sentence, *each* sets the number for related pronouns. For example, "*Each of them* has to fend for *himself*" (not *themselves*).

But when *each* is in apposition with a plural noun, it precedes the verb, and the following noun is plural. "The *employees each* expect to receive their *bonuses* soon," not "The *employees each* expect to receive their *bonus* soon." "The *salesmen each* have their own *techniques*," not "...their own *technique*." When *each* follows the verb, it expresses a singular sense and accordingly takes a singular pronoun and noun: "The employees *expect each* to receive *his bonus* soon." "These uses are clear, *each* in *its* own *way*."

EFFECT

See AFFECT, EFFECT

EITHER . . . OR

See CORRELATIVE CONJUNCTIONS

ELLIPSIS

No Sin of Omission

Words may be omitted from a sentence when their sense can be clearly and grammatically supplied by a parallel part. This is known as ellipsis. In "His argument was impressive: it was well researched, it was concise, and it was cleverly presented," for example, the "it was's" are unnecessary. In fact, without them, the statement becomes more forceful: "His argument was impressive—well-researched, concise, and cleverly presented." Too much has been deleted, however, in "The pie was large but the strawberries small," for the singular *was* cannot grammatically carry the plural *strawberries.*" The sentence needs rephrasing: "The pie was large, but the strawberries *were* small."

When a sentence consists of a single verb phrase, it must be set out completely. But when two verb phrases appear in sequence, one part may be omitted if it agrees in number and form with the corresponding part of the other. Thus in "The roast will *be ready* in an hour, and the potatoes will *be ready then*, too," *be ready then* may be omitted because it is clearly understood ("The roast *will be ready* in an hour, and the potatoes will [*be ready then*], too"). But in "The Committee always *has* and always *will offer* the best publications available," the verb phrases do not correspond, and a correction is needed: "The Committee always *has offered* and always *will offer....*"

Somewhat less obvious is the error in this sentence. "The book is well done and therefore useful." The *is* is there serving in two capacities—as an auxiliary to the past participle *done* (the book *is* well done) and as a linking verb to *book* and *useful* (the book *is* useful). Since a verb ought not be called upon to perform two jobs at the same time, the sentence should be rephrased: "The book *is* well done and *is* therefore useful."

Whether to repeat articles and prepositions is usually a writer's choice. Repetition drives home valuable words or thoughts. In "We enjoyed seeing the trees, the flowers, and the bushes," the last two *the*'s are unnecessary, but they emphasize the nouns by making them distinct. Unnecessary prepositions, however, should be omitted as a regular practice. In "He has tremendous admiration and affection for his partner," *for* was not used after *admiration* because the *for* after *affection* served both nouns. If it is ungrammatical or confusing to omit an article or preposition, of course it must stay. For instance, in "He has an understanding but no confidence in those policies," *of* is required after *understanding*. And in "We saw the secretary and treasurer," one person is referred to, but two persons are indicated in "We saw *the* secretary and *the* treasurer."

When a noun or pronoun serves as the object of two prepositional phrases (called suspended prepositional phrases), both prepositions should be given. For example, "His devotion and respect *for* his parents was applauded" needs "devotion *to* and respect *for*." "We have no interest or love *for* the project" should be rephrased "no interest *in* or love *for*."

Omitting the one preposition required in certain constructions is a widely perpetrated fault. For one thing, an *of* is needed between the noun *type* and a following noun when *type* means "sort." Just as one would not say "What kind man is he?" instead of "kind *of* man," so one should not say *type man* for *type of man*. In "We expect him in a couple days," the *of* also has been carelessly dropped. Replaced, the sentence would read: "We expect him in a couple *of* days."

Personal pronouns in the genitive case are possessive adjectives and should be repeated before each noun modified. For example, "I met *his* mother and *his* father" is correctly given, not "I met *his* mother and father." Or "We saw *her* house and *her* automobile," not "We saw *her* house and automobile."

Infinitives have their own rules. It is unnecessary to repeat *to* with infinitive phrases unless qualifying words intervene. For example, "To eat and drink seems to be the chief pastime of some people" needs no *to* before *drink*. But one is required in "To eat in the finest restaurants and *to* drink in the best bars is the chief pastime of some people."

ELSE

So What Else Is New?

There are two things to keep in mind about *else*. First, it should not be used in the same sentence with *except, but,* or similar words that serve the same distinguishing purpose. For example, in "No one *else* but you," *else* is superfluous, as it is in "There was no one *else* in the store *except* the janitor." In both instances *else* should be excised. Although the expression *nothing else but* ("We saw *nothing else but* swampland") is used for emphasis in everyday language, it is not acceptable in formal writing. Either *else* should be omitted ("We saw *nothing but* swampland") or *but* replaced by *than* ("We saw nothing *else than* swampland"). As another illustration, "Nothing *else but* a full rehearsal will do" should be rephrased: "Nothing *but* a..." or "Nothing *else than* a. ..." Second, expressions such as *everyone else* or *somebody else* are no longer converted to possessives by attaching *'s* to the pronoun—*everyone's else, somebody's else,* logical though they be. To avoid these clumsy phrases, the *'s* is now appended to *else: everyone else's; somebody else's.*

EMBLEM, SYMBOL

A Symbolic Gesture

The words *emblem* and *symbol* derive from the Greek; the former derives from *emblema*, meaning "insertion," and the latter from *symbolon*, meaning "a token." The terms are interchangeable in that they refer to visible signs that suggest something else. *Symbol* has a wider application, however, because it may be used of any outward sign.

In its most common use, a *symbol* is a sign that stands for something abstract, like peace. The symbol for peace is a white dove with an olive branch in its beak. The symbol of the American dollar is the letter *s* with two vertical lines through it ($).

An *emblem*, on the other hand, originally an inlaid ornament, is a design or pictorial representation specially created to signify an idea or object associated with it. For example, the emblem of justice is a blindfolded woman holding a scale. The spread eagle is the emblem of the United States; the hammer and sickle, of Russia. Usually an emblem is inscribed with a verse or motto. At one time emblems were used on family shields, but they now appear on flags, banners, school crests, coins, and so forth. Although the words are readily distinguishable in some cases (for example, one speaks of an emblem, not a symbol, on a blazer, or a miter as a symbol, not an emblem, of office), the cross may be termed either the emblem or the symbol of Christianity, just as the Star of David may be described as either the emblem or the symbol of Judaism.

The adjective forms *emblematic* and *symbolic* are preferred to *emblematical* and *symbolical. Symbolic* is usually followed by *of.*

EMIGRANT, IMMIGRANT

Coming or Going

When a person leaves his country to take up permanent residence in another country, he becomes an *emigrant* and an *immigrant.* He is an emigrant upon leaving his homeland and an immigrant upon arriving at his destination.

Careful writers distinguish between these words by using them with different prepositions. A movement *from* a place of departure is an emigration *from.* An entering *into* a new country is an immigration *to.* For example, "A Spaniard emigrates *from* Spain and immigrates *to* Mexico." *Emigrate* is spelled with one *m; immigrate* with two.

One who keeps moving about loses both labels and becomes a *migrant,* a person who periodically changes his residence. Birds also *migrate,* seasonally; and then there are *migratory* workers who travel from place to place seeking work. But these migrations are not necessarily from one country to another.

EMPTY, VACANT

Something's Missing

Something *empty* or *vacant* contains nothing; it is devoid of content. Though synonyms, those words are used in different senses.

Empty is the opposite of "full." An empty bottle, for instance, lacks its usual or customary contents. An empty house has no furniture and no inhabitants. Figuratively an empty life has no purpose; empty promises, no value; empty hours, no activity.

A primary distinction in usage between *empty* and *vacant* is that the latter refers to a temporary condition. A parking lot may be vacant, a position may be vacant, a hotel room may be vacant—but all will be filled, most likely, before very long.

Vacant, when used figuratively, is a synonym for *expressionless* ("a vacant stare") or *blank* ("a vacant mind").

ENDORSE

Back Support

On the highest levels of writing, *to endorse* has come to mean "to sanction" or "to have a favorable opinion of." Advertising promoters may now, with grammatical propriety, solicit prominent persons to endorse a product, that is, express approval and recommend it to others. Candidates for public office, too, may seek to be endorsed, to receive support from well-known persons. Formerly this usage of *endorse* was deplored by some authorities, but almost all have been won over by its popular acceptance. *Endorse,* which literally means "to write on the back," refers to a signature written on the back of a negotiable instrument by the payee. *Endorse* has a variant spelling, *indorse,* but the former one predominates.

The expression *endorse on the back,* meaning "to validate a check by putting one's signature on the back," is etymologically redundant because *endorse* derives from the Latin *dorsum,* "the back," through the French *en dos,* "put on the back." Accordingly, a signature to serve as an endorsement must appear on the reverse side of the check or other instrument. Nevertheless, *endorse on the back* is so widely used that except in formal writing, it deserves as little attention as the flick of a fin—a *dorsal,* that is. The expression may even be helpful if some papers are to be signed on the back and others on the front.

ENHANCE

Let's Make It Better

Since *enhance* and *increase* are not exact synonyms, they are seldom interchangeable. To *increase* means "to make something larger or greater." To *enhance* means "to increase value, worth, or appearance." It therefore presupposes that something already has some value or worth.

Enhance may be used of physical entities, but more often it refers to the abstract. It points to the augmenting of a quality, like a person's reputation, or to a condition, such as the usefulness of a building: "The parking lot has *enhanced* the usability of the office building." But it should be noted that it is not the person who gets enhanced. It is inaccurate, therefore, to say "The award *enhanced* her" or "She has been *enhanced* by it." The award may enhance her prestige in the community. A lavaliere may enhance the attractiveness of a gown. But neither an award nor a lavaliere can enhance a woman personally. The rule to remember is that *enhance* cannot have a person either as a direct object in the active voice or as a subject in the passive.

ENIGMA, PUZZLE, RIDDLE

Life Is a Puzzle

"I cannot forecast to you the action of Russia. It is a riddle wrapped in an enigma." This well-known statement of Winston Churchill, made in a radio broadcast during World War II, distinguishes the sense of *riddle* and *enigma*.

A *riddle* is a question or verbal problem, its parts seemingly paradoxical or contradictory. Often intentionally obscure, it is answerable only by guessing or by a flash of insight. Oedipus saved his life by solving the riddle propounded by the Sphinx: "What animal is it that in the morning goes on four feet, at noon on two, and in the evening upon three?" His reply was "Man, who in childhood creeps on hands and knees, in manhood walks erect, and in old age goes with the aid of a staff." The ancient Greeks took their riddles seriously. The penalty for failing to solve a riddle was servitude to whoever posed the riddle—a fate not much better than that imposed by the mythological Sphinx: death.

The evolution of the word *riddle* was unorthodox. It began with *raeden*, an Old English word for "to guess" or "to read." Later, what was to be read or interpreted was called a *raedels*. Still later, the final *s* was dropped, and from *raedel*, *riddle* emerged. Today *riddle*, when used as a verb, has the specialized meaning of "to pierce with numerous holes" (as in "The wall was *riddled* with bullet holes").

Puzzles are problems or contrivances that amuse while challenging the mind. Some concern themselves with words (like crossword puzzles), but most are toys and other devices (like jigsaw puzzles) that test one's ingenuity: "Larry's favorite *puzzle* is the Chinese ring trick." The verb *to puzzle* means "to baffle" or "to mystify": "Annette's behavior *puzzles* everyone on shipboard."

An *enigma* is something that is inexplicable or puzzling. Things or people may be enigmas: "The effect of the sun on many aspects of life is still an *enigma*." "Competent though he is, the treasurer is still an *enigma* to his colleagues." The adjective *enigmatic*, meaning "difficult to interpret," is more common than its noun form: "The *enigmatic* smile of the Mona Lisa is known the world over." "The monoliths of Easter Island are enormous and *enigmatic*."

ENOUGH, SUFFICIENT

More than You Need

Enough and *sufficient* are synonymous in that both words mean "adequate or equal to the required amount." But that fact does not always make them interchangeable. For one thing, *sufficient* is an adjective only, whereas *enough* is an adjective, an adverb, and a noun. This means that *sufficient* does not have the flexibility of *enough*. For example, a person may be said to have *enough* but not *sufficient*. For another, *enough* is preferred to *sufficient* adjectivally when the reference is to amount—"We have *enough* sugar" rather than "We have *sufficient* sugar."

In fact, in this regard *enough* is so well established that it is known as an adjective of amount. Nevertheless, in some areas the more refined-sounding *sufficient* should displace the more ordinary *enough*. For instance, one speaks of a *sufficient quantity*, not an *enough quantity*. Likewise, when quality or kind is considered, *sufficient* is the word to use: "The honors bestowed upon him were *sufficient* to satisfy any reasonable person." "*Sufficient* unto the day is the evil thereof." In those examples *enough* would not qualify.

Caution: One should be careful not to follow *sufficiently* by a *so that* construction, as in "The computer operators' training was *sufficiently* long *so that* they can manage without supervision." The adverb *sufficiently* calls for either a *to* infinitive or a *for* with a noun. Hence a proper rewording of the example would be "was sufficiently long *to enable them*" or "was sufficiently long *for them* to."

ENSURE

See ASSURE, ENSURE, INSURE

ENVELOP, EXPLICATE, IMPLICATE

Don't Fold the Envelopes

Both *explicate* and *implicate* mean "to fold"; the folding, however, occurs in opposite directions—outward versus inward.

From the meaning of *explicate*, "to fold out," has developed the sense "making clearly known." That which is thoroughly explained (in effect, unfolded) has been explicated. *Implicate* means "to enfold," implying a movement toward the inside. A person implicated in a crime is entwined or incriminatingly involved. That last word, *involved*, also refers to someone enmeshed, for it means "enveloped." But *implicate* goes a step further. Saying that someone is implicated suggests wrongdoing. The word *involved* contains no such suggestion. One involved in a scheme or venture, for example, is simply connected with it in some way.

Involve, from the Latin *involvere*, "to envelop," raises another point. *Envelop* means "to encase; to enclose with or as if with a cover; to surround." A term resembling it—*envelope*—is a wrapper that encloses, something that envelops. Not only the spellings but also the pronunciations of these words differ. The verb *envelop*, with no final *e,* is pronounced ehn-*vell*-uhp; the noun *envelope*, ending in an *e,* is pronounced *ehn*-vuh-lohp or *ahn*-vuh-lohp. The latter pronunciation, however, sounds affected. This same *ahn* is sometimes heard with *enclave* and *envoy*. But here again it sounds like an effort to add a bit of class. Those words should be pronounced with a normal *en*: ehn-claive, ehn-voy.

ENVY, JEALOUSY

The Envy of All

The words *envy* and *jealousy* indicate a person's ill will toward another because of the latter's possessions or accomplishments, but the words are not synonymous.

Envy, which is derived from the Latin *invidere* ("to look maliciously at"), stresses covetousness—a discontented longing for what another person has. The dictionary interprets *envy* as "a resentful awareness of an advantage enjoyed by another, and a desire to possess the same advantage." A person's style of living or his successful career may be the cause of envy among his neighbors.

Jealousy has two senses—one admirable, the other not. Its more common use suggests the suspicion of a husband whose attractive wife is always the center of male attention. Inherent in *jealousy* is the fear of rivalry that manifests itself not only in matters of the heart but also in political or business relationships. The admirable sense is the protecting of one's name and reputation, as a professional person may be watchful in guarding his standing in the community or as anyone may be who is solicitous of his rights. *Jealousy* is the noun form of *jealous*, from the Latin *zelus*, meaning "zeal."

EPITOME

See **SUMMARY AND RELATED WORDS**

EQUIVOCAL

See **AMBIGUOUS, EQUIVOCAL**

EQUIVOCATOR, LIAR, PREVARICATOR

Don't Play the Lyre

To tell the truth, a liar, strictly speaking, is neither an *equivocator* nor a *prevaricator*. A *liar* tells lies.

An *equivocator* speaks in ambiguities, refusing to commit himself to what he says; he is intentionally confusing. (Equivocation applies to actions as well; an equivocator, therefore, may also engage in confusing, even suspicious, acts: "His *equivocal* behavior made everyone at the summit meeting nervous.")

A *prevaricator* likewise evades the truth. The word derives from a Latin verb meaning "to walk crookedly" or "bent." One who prevaricates straddles the truth; he quibbles. It is said that Pliny used *prevaricate* in reference to one who ploughed in crooked lines and that later the term came to refer to anyone who gave crooked answers.

In everyday usage, *prevaricator* is often used as a euphemism for *liar*. Some people find it hard to mouth the word *liar*; they reach the same result, but with a less abrasive tone, by using *prevaricator*.

ESSENTIAL, INDISPENSABLE, VITAL

Vital Signs

What is *vital* is always important, but what is important is not always *vital*. This distinction is too important to be ignored.

Vital, from the Latin *vitalis*, "of life," means "necessary for existence" or "indispensable." It is often wrongly used for *desirable, useful, important,* or *helpful*—words that do not contain the element of indispensability. It is inaccurate to say "Ruthie's service as a hostess is vital" unless the affair absolutely could not proceed without her. It may be said that one should not be so careless with matters "of life."

Essential denotes either that which is of the essence of a thing (such as the essential serenity of a Chinese brush painting) or that which is basic or indispensable (as water is essential to life). Without an essential, the very nature of a thing or even the thing itself is impaired or destroyed. *Essential* and *vital* are equivalents.

Essential, like *vital*, is an absolute term and therefore is not expressed in degrees; that is, what is essential or vital cannot be properly termed more essential or more vital than something else. It is wrong, for example, to say that "The Bibliography is *more* (or *less*) *essential* than the Appendix" or that "The carburetor is the *most essential* part of the engine."

Indispensable, also a synonym of *essential*, has a somewhat different association. It pertains to what is required, often as an integral component. The indispensable cannot be relinquished, waived, or omitted without impairing the fundamental purpose or usefulness of a thing. Thus a motor is indispensable to an automobile, a director to a department, freedom of speech to a democratic society. In simple terms, *essential* concerns the nature of a thing; *indispensable* concerns its purpose.

The need implied by *necessary* is sometimes not so pressing as that suggested by *essential* or *indispensable*. Something necessary to complete a project may be unavailable, but a suitable substitute may be found; there are no substitutes for what is essential or indispensable.

-EVER

See WHATEVER, WHENEVER, WHOEVER

EVERY

Every Word for Itself

The word *every* in "We assemble *every* once in a while" makes the statement colloquial. In formal writing one should say, "We assemble *once in a while*"; likewise, the phrases *every so often* and *every now and then* should be replaced by *occasionally, at irregular intervals,* or *at intervals of,* say, "two hours."

In "Barbara has *every* confidence in her sister," *every* should be excised. *Confidence* is an abstract idea; *every* modifies countable things. But in "*Every* confidence was respected," in which *every* qualifies something countable, it is used correctly. Saying "I have *every reason* to expect him to be successful" is also correctly expressed because it implies that individual reasons had been considered.

Every is grammatically singular: "*Every* man of military age *is* likely to be drafted." The number of the verb remains constant, even though the subject contains two *every*'s and the conjunction *and*: "*Every* boy *and every* girl *has* been told what to do." The pronouns referring to *every* are likewise singular: "*Every* boy and *every* man *was* told to remove *his* overshoes."

Every can be distinguished from *each,* for, although both words refer to individuals, the sense of *every* is inclusiveness, individuals that make up the whole. *Each* emphasizes the individuals considered separately. "*Every* student must register. Later *each* one will receive a matriculation card."

Everybody is written as a single word. *Everyone* is also a single word unless the *one* is stressed: "*Everyone* is here," but "*Every one* of the soldiers in Unit E reported ill." *Every place* should always be written as two words, never *everyplace*: "*Every place* was searched, but unsuccessfully."

(Use of singular or plural verbs with *everyone* is discussed under INDEFINITE PRONOUNS.)

EXCEPT

We Must Take Exception

The words *except* and *excepting* are prepositions when introducing an exclusion. Both, in fact, mean "excluding." When *but* means "except," it, too, is a preposition but is less emphatic than *except* ("You may have all the books *but* that one").

In the sentence "Everyone was present *except you and I*," *except,* since it is a preposition, should take the objective case: *except you and me.* It is correctly used in "No one was paid *except him.*" The object of *but,* likewise, is in the objective case: "Everyone left *but me.*"

Usually *except* is preferred to *excepting,* except in "not excepting"—a phrase that means "including" (as in "The athletes all did well, not *excepting* those from our school"). When *excepting* is preceded by *always,* instead of *not,* its meaning is completely turned around: it then means "excluding" ("All students, *always excepting* commuters, must attend chapel services").

"And this is no *exception*" is wordy phraseology. "Most of the cartons delivered last week arrived broken, and *this* (or *this one*) is no *exception*" is more economically expressed: "Like most of the cartons delivered last week, *this one* arrived broken."

EXPLETIVES

There Is and There Isn't

Writing instructors have for generations railed against the use of expletives—not meaning profanity or an exclamatory statement, but a sentence construction that begins with *it is, here is, here are, there is,* or *there are.* Saying "*There were* five more failures noted" reads better if worded simply "Five more failures were noted." Even more clumsy are those sentences in which the auxiliary *has* or *have* has been added. "*There have been* three budgets proposed" is more direct and smoother without *there have been*: "Three budgets have been proposed."

This is not to say, however, that all *there are* and *there were* constructions should be condemned out of hand. In some instances there are good reasons to use them. For one thing, rhythm is an important ingredient in an effective sentence, and sometimes *there are* or *there were* supplies a pleasing stress. At other times, a shift in emphasis from the true subject to a more suitable word conveys a more forceful message. This is so in the Biblical quotation: "There were giants in the earth those days," in which the submerging of the subject *giants* into the middle of the sentence strengthens it and makes for a pleasing rhythm.

The *it, here,* or *there* in an expletive is not a real subject. It is merely an *anticipatory subject,* which serves no grammatical function. For example, in *"There are always more hands here than we need,"* the real subject is *hands*, as is clearly seen if the sentence is placed in regular order: "More *hands* are always here than we need."

Ordinarily the noun following *there is* is singular (*"There is* one napkin for each person") and the one following *there are* is plural (*"There are* two blankets for each child"). Restructuring the sentence will make clear whether *there is* or *there are* is called for: "One napkin *is there* for each person." "Two blankets *are there* for each child." Multiple nouns following an expletive, however, may cause a problem, for the number of the verb depends upon the construction of the rest of the sentence. In "There are two spoons, one fork, and one knife in each place setting," the items are, of course, introduced by the plural *there are*. But if the wording is reversed, with "two spoons" placed last, one may then choose between "There *are* a fork, a knife, and two spoons in each place setting" and "There *is* a fork. . . ." This latter phrasing is more common because the number of the verb is influenced by the proximity of the singular noun *fork*—"There *is* a fork. . . ." But this style is not sanctioned for formal writing; a plural verb is preferable.

The expletive *it* is always followed by a singular verb: "It *is* the *woman* who pays." "It *is* the *women* who pay."

EXPLICATE

See ENVELOPE, EXPLICATE, IMPLICATE

EXPLOIT

See USAGE, USE, UTILIZE

7

FACE

On the Face of It

Everyone has a face, that part of the front of the head that extends from the forehead to the chin and from ear to ear. *Face* has no exact synonym. Those that are listed in dictionaries have decidedly different connotations.

Countenance refers to the expression of the face—its appearance—smiling, dour, quizzical: "His *countenance* expressed good humor." The verb *to countenance* denotes tacit approval. A parent who countenances his son's behavior condones it.

Physiognomy originally referred to the art of judging a person's character from facial features. Although the art has few supporters, the word, although obsolescent in this sense, still implies that character and temperament are revealed by facial appearance. Today's more acceptable usage is of an inanimate or abstract entity, in the sense of "external aspect," a particular or peculiar shape or contour, especially revealing outwardly an inner quality or character (as in the physiognomy of a union or a political party or of Mt. Fuji).

Although a person's *visage* is his face, the implication is that the face is expressing a mental state: a wolfish visage; a stern visage; a tearful visage. The difference between *countenance* and *visage* is that the latter emphasizes what the observer sees in the other's face.

Face has spawned many colloquial expressions, such as *to face the music* (which implies the confronting of an unpleasant situation) or *to make an about face* (which indicates a reversal of a point of view or opinion). The idiom *face up*, as in "We must *face up* to it," is accepted by many respected writers. The *up* is what gives the phrase the idea of a courageous stand, a disregard of consequences. One who faces a bad situation may beat a sudden retreat. But one who faces up to a bad situation is determined, at all cost, to see it through. And if he perseveres, he will *save face*.

FACTITIOUS

See ARTIFICIAL

FACTOR

Just the Facts, Ma'am

A fact is something made or done, anything that has objective reality. The word *fact* derives from the Latin *facere*, "to make or do," the root of many English words. One of these, *factor*, means "agent or deputy." It also is "a cause contributing to a result." In this latter sense it has become a vogue word, applied with indifference to almost every contingency. Fowler's Second Edition describes *factor* as "one of those words which are so popular as thought-saving, reach-me-downs that all meaning is being rubbed off them by constant use." It has, unfortunately, come to oust more concrete terms. For example, in "One of the *factors* that made the play successful was the unusual costuming," *features* would be better. And *circumstances* is called for in "The horrible *factors* leading to this accident should be investigated." Perhaps *factor* should be reserved for use in biology and mathematics, where it has precise meaning. In general contexts suitable substitutes are *force, element, phase, aspect, component, ingredient, constituent,* or those suggested in the preceding examples—*feature* and *circumstance*.

The use of *factor* in other constructions should be scrutinized, too. Sometimes it is superfluous, as in "The personal *safety factor* must be taken into account," which needs only "Personal safety must be...." At other times it is unnecessarily modified, as in *a contributing factor* (all factors contribute). Even by itself *factor* may be verbiage. "Muscle and grit *were the factors that* were responsible for Harold's success" may be stated simply, "Muscle and grit were responsible for Harold's success."

FARTHER, FURTHER

Nothing Could Be Further from the Truth

The chief point of contention between dictionaries and traditional grammarians over the words *farther* and *further* is whether both words may be employed figuratively and literally or whether their uses should be distinguished. Those who recommend that *farther* be used only in reference to physical distance predominate. As a comparative form of *far*, it literally means "a greater distance or space." This is so in "We walked *farther* than we had planned," in which *farther* serves as an adverb, and in "Mars is *farther* away than scientists had originally thought," in which it is an adjective.

Further is also a comparative form of *far*. But it lends itself best to abstract meanings, referring to degree, quantity, or time, as in "Let us consider the matter *further*" or in "We have to move the plan *further* along." The distinction in use between these words—*farther* for physical distances that can be measured and *further* when physical measurement is not possible—although blurred because of their frequent interchange, should be maintained in formal writing.

Only *further* may serve when the meaning is "additional" ("There is no *further* reason to spend more money") or "moreover" ("*Further*, we think we should go"). As a verb, *further* means "to help the progress of." It is so used in "Leonard did what he could to *further* the cause of the Big Brothers."

FATAL, FATEFUL

Quirks of Fate

Fateful events affect one's destiny or future. A person considers the beginning of something of extreme importance a fateful moment. Although that which is fateful may bring death or disaster, neither result need follow. On the contrary, it may bring joy or even a happy event of momentous consequence: "What a *fateful* day it was—being named a Nobel Prize winner."

Fate derives from the Latin *fatum*, meaning "an utterance; a prophetic declaration." According to ancient religions, after the gods had spoken, usually through the mouth of a soothsayer, destiny was set. In Greek mythology, the Fates were the three goddesses whose actions determined the course of human life. *Clotho* held the spindle, *Lachesis* drew the thread of life, and *Atropos* snipped it off.

A word derived from the same root is *fatal*. Its usual meaning is "causing death, destruction, or ruin" (as in "The *fatal* shot was fired in Dallas"), but a less frequently used meaning is "influencing fate." Its figurative sense implies doom: "Shutting off the lines of supply proved *fatal* to the army's advance."

FAZE, PHASE

Unfazed

Phase, as in the phases of the moon, implies a temporary appearance. It may therefore signify a limited or fleeting aspect but not a general appearance. It also may refer to a stage in development. The misuse of *phase* for *faze* is not uncommon. *Faze* means "to disconcert or daunt." Although not accepted on the highest literary levels, it has well established itself informally and is frequently seen in print, usually in a negative sense: "Stumpf was *not fazed* by the approach of the two policemen."

FEW

How Many Are Few?

Although grammatically it makes no difference whether one says "Very few are here," "A very few are here," or "Comparatively few are here," it is incorrect to say "A comparatively few are here." The reason for this lies in the parts of speech involved.

In all four examples *few* is a pronoun, which in the first two examples is properly modified by *very*, an adjective. (Some people may disagree with that statement, thinking that *very* is only an adverb because it usually functions as one. But that argument is refutable by such a sentence as "That was the *very thing* you mentioned," in which *very* clearly serves as an adjective qualifying a noun.)

In the third example ("Comparatively few are here"), *comparatively* serves as a sentence adverb, modifying the entire sentence. Other everyday examples of this adverbial use are

"*Generally* I read the newspapers on Sunday afternoon" and "*Usually* we leave at five o'clock."

In example four, the adverb *comparatively* is employed to modify a pronoun, a function beyond its capability, since adverbs do not modify pronouns. It should be replaced by the adjective *comparative,* which may be preceded by *a,* since *comparative* is used idiomatically after *a: "A comparative* few are here."

FIGURES, NUMBERS

Numbers Figure, Too

Whether the words *number* and *figure* may be interchanged depends on the context. Both the Arabic 2 and the Roman numeral II are numbers as well as figures. Figures are symbols representing the spelled-out versions. The word *two,* on the other hand, is not a symbol and is therefore not a figure. It may be said that all figures are numbers but that not all numbers are figures.

People count by numbers. Ordinarily they use figures (1, 2, 3, 4...). These are cardinal numbers. Ordinal numbers designate the place of an item in a sequence: *first, second, third,* and so on. When ordinal and cardinal numbers are used next to each other, the ordinal precedes: "The *first 15* men will go to Room B; the *second 15* to Room C." The word *last* is treated like an ordinal number in this kind of sentence: "The *last three* days are most imporant," not "The *three last* days," despite Coleridge's "the fifty or sixty last years of her life."

FIGURES OF SPEECH

Watch Your Figure

Everyone uses figures of speech, some purposely, some unwittingly. They are important rhetorical devices because they add color and illustrative meaning to a thought that might otherwise be dull, unclear, and possibly misunderstood.

The most common figure of speech is the *hyperbole,* a word that derives from the Greek *hyper,* "over," and *ballein,* "to throw." Like an overthrown ball, a *hyperbole* has gone too far. It is an extravagant statement or fanciful exaggeration: "I am starving" for *hungry* or "My grandson weighs a ton" for *is heavy.*

The intent, however, is to emphasize, not to deceive. One who says "The books on the desk are piled a mile high" does not mislead anyone.

Metaphors and *similes* compare objects essentially unlike each other. A *metaphor* speaks of one thing in terms of another. It is an implied comparison, one that does not use *like* or *as*: "He is a lion." "His words were arrows piercing her heart." A *simile*, which always begins with *like* or *as*, is an explicit comparison: "He roars *like* a lion." "Her smile was *as* warm *as* a summer's day." Both these common figures of speech are particularly useful because they instantly conjure up identifiable pictures. Although original metaphors and similes are especially effective, trite ones—clinging vine, sharp as a tack, budding genius—are no longer evocative and therefore are best avoided. Mixing metaphors, a failure to stay with one image, is a serious stylistic fault, for the picture it draws is ludicrous: "Bad luck follows one who changes horses after setting sail." It's like not letting your left hand know that you should step off with the right foot.

FIRST

First Things First

First of all needs no *of all*. And *first* should not precede *before*, since *before* encompasses the sense of *first*. In "*Before* beginning our journey, let's *first* review our itinerary," *first* is unnecessary.

The expression *first-rate* is an adjective, not an adverb. One may properly say, "She is a *first-rate* singer" (hyphening *first-rate* is good style), but not "She sings *first-rate*." There, one should use either *well* or *excellently*.

The sister phrase *first grade*, as in "Mr. Foster is a *first-grade* accountant," means he is "top-ranking," not that he is in the first grade of his studies. The expression is sanctioned in formal usage.

Another *first* is often found in a combination of words like *the first two*: "The *first two* who come to my office will be hired." The rule is that when *first* and a cardinal number are written next to each other, *first* precedes. Saying the *two first* would be incongruous because there cannot be two *firsts*. The adjective *last* is treated likewise: "The *last two* chapters will keep you in suspense." Referring to the *two last chapters* may be confusing because a person might imagine that there were two last chapters.

FIX

Fixations

Talk about being in a fix. The noun *fix*, as in "Howard is in a terrible *fix*," is labeled slang by some dictionaries and simply informal by others. Informal terms, sometimes called standard colloquial English, are a cut above slang and are employed by educated people everywhere except in literary usage. Apparently, then, *fix* is no longer in the fix it used to be in; it is finally achieving respectability. Nevertheless, in formal writing, a more explicit expression is recommended; for example, *predicament, plight,* or *quandary:* "Edgar kept finding himself in the same *predicament*" rather than *in the same sorry fix. (Fix,* unfortunately, has acquired a new and ugly connotation. "A fix" is what a drug addict calls *a shot.)*

The verb *to fix* has even wider informal acceptance. Its ancestor was the Latin *fixus,* past participle of *figere,* to "fasten or pierce," but its present meaning is "to make fast, firm, stable, or permanent." This three-letter word has sprouted about two dozen unrelated meanings from fixing a chair (repairing) to fixing a meal (preparing—with all the fixings). But since its many uses are not confusing, it continues, especially because of its crisp sound, to gain supporters. Nonetheless, when exactness in language is demanded, *to fix* is best replaced by something more precise. For example, instead of "fix the scale," *repair* or *adjust* is more suitable; instead of "fix him," *punish;* instead of "fix the potatoes," *cook;* instead of "fix a fight"— better not.

FLAT ADVERBS

Double-Duty Words

Some people fail to realize that many modifiers, without changing form, may serve either as adjectives or as adverbs. These adjective-adverbs, commonly called flat adverbs, have no -*ly* ending. Representative flat adverbs are *far, hard, fast, little, much, first, straight,* and *well.* A fast driver drives *fast,* not *fastly,* for example, and the first child in line goes *first,* not *firstly.*

Some words have two adverbial forms, the flat form and the -*ly* ending. Examples are *right, near, close,* and *loud:* "Do it right," "He *rightly* decided to speak to them." "The dog slept *close* to the fire," but "We looked *closely* at the dog."

If both forms have the same meaning, either may be used. Some writers prefer the -*ly* form before the modified word and the flat form after: "He *loudly* protested their claims," but "He spoke *loud.*" "The figures are *wrongly* added," but "The figures are added *wrong.*" Other writers regard the -*ly* form as being more elegant in either position, and formal style is on their side. They would write, "Come *quickly*" rather than "Come *quick.*" In some cases, however, idiom overrules preference; a clock, for example, runs *slow,* not *slowly,* and a controlled ship holds *steady,* not *steadily.*

If the -*ly* ending changes the meaning of an adverb, the form that expresses the desired sense must of course be used: "We camped *high* in the mountains," but "She is a *highly* skilled technician." "He rises *late,*" but "*Lately* she has been worried about her parents." "He stopped *short,*" but "He is expected *shortly.*"

FLOTSAM AND JETSAM

The Jet Set

The useless trifles, the odds and ends, that are a part of almost every attic may be labeled *flotsam* and *jetsam.* Perhaps a more apt name would be junk. The phrase "flotsam and jetsam" is used metaphorically to describe many kinds of debris, human or other, ranging from vagrants and drifters to the excrement on barn floors. It makes for good description but suffers from overuse.

At one time *flotsam* and *jetsam* had distinct meanings; they were not, as they are now, a single coinage. *Flotsam* referred to that part of the wreckage of a ship still afloat; *jetsam,* from the Latin verb "to throw," was that part of a cargo tossed overboard to make the ship more seaworthy. From that action arose the word *jettison.*

Once upon a time, the story goes, the king of the realm owned all the flotsam, all the wreckage still afloat. However, the debris that washed ashore, the jetsam, belonged to the lord of the manor on whose property it landed. Other terms that pertained to this wreckage were *lagan, findals,* and *derelict.* But no one ever saw fit to make metaphors out of them.

FLOUNDER, FOUNDER

Lost and Founder

In the sense of struggling awkwardly, *flounder* is believed to be a variant of *founder.* Both words indicate that trouble is brewing—that there is distress—but only *founder* implies the need for an SOS.

To *founder* is "to stumble" or "to break down." In the case of ships, it means "to fill with water and sink." And since the sense of *sinking* is inherent in "foundering," saying "The ship *foundered* and sank" is redundant. Possibly *founder* is derived from the Latin "fundus," which means "bottom." Certainly a ship that founders goes to the bottom.

A fish out of water is likely to flounder, that is, struggle or thrash about. (The category of flatfishes, like the halibut or the plaice, known as flounders, has no connection with the verb "to flounder." In fact, *flounder* is supposedly a blend word from *blunder* and *founder.*) Animals also flounder, that is, struggle clumsily if mired in mud. Indeed, any living thing in a strange environment, if confused or trapped, may flounder.

FOLLOW, SUCCEED

Nothing Succeeds Like . . .

Although both *succeed* and *follow* mean "come after something else in a natural sequence," the words are not interchangeable. *Follow* is an everyday word. It means "to move along the course of" or "to move behind in the same direction," as in "The cows *follow* one another along the old footpath" and in "The players will *follow* the captain onto the field." It also denotes what comes after in time ("The fullback's kick *followed* the referee's whistle by less than a second") or as a result or consequence ("It *follows* that a frugal person is less likely to go bankrupt than a spendthrift").

The sense of *succeed* is "to follow or come next in time or order." Ordinarily a person succeeding another in an office, position, or role replaces him: "Upon the death of the president the vice president will *succeed* him." *Succession* may come about in many ways—through inheritance, as with a monarchy; through election, as with United States Presidents; or through appointment, as with federal agency chairmen.

Saying that a person succeeds or follows himself is absurd; he may only succeed or follow a predecessor.

FOOT

A Great Feat

Idiom that involves measurement, like many another idiom, conforms to no grammatical analysis. (The phrase *many another* in the preceding sentence is a case in point—*many* has a plural sense; *another*, a singular.) Compounds involving the word *foot* or *feet*, in particular, are laws unto themselves.

A *foot* is a part of a body or a unit of length. It is, of course, a singular noun. Yet a person with his two feet jumps over a *two* (plural) *foot* (singular) wall. The wall is two *feet* high, however, not *two* (plural) *foot* (singular) high. Likewise, a man may be a six-footer (that is, a six-*foot* man), but he is six *feet* tall. Which shows what the English language can do to a catchy tune: "Five foot two, eyes of blue."

Compound adjectives ordinarily are formed with *foot*, not *feet*, and spelled as one word: *flatfoot, footnote, barefoot, footpad.* Another group uses *footed*, but never *feeted: slow-footed, sure-footed, heavy-footed.*

FORBID, PROHIBIT

4 Bid 2 Is Right

Idiom dictates that a preposition following *forbid* should be *to*, not *from*. A teacher, therefore, may grammatically forbid a student *to* leave, but not *from* leaving. This requirement applies as well to the past tense ("The doctor *forbade* him *to* swim," not

"The doctor *forbade* him *from* swimming") and the past participle ("The inmates were *forbidden to* vote," not "The inmates were *forbidden from* voting"). Although the gerund construction (an -*ing* form of a verb used as a noun) may replace the infinitive, it weakens the message. "The teacher *forbade his smoking* in the halls," for example, is less commanding than "The teacher *forbade him to smoke* in the halls."

The principal parts of *forbid* are *forbid, forbade* (pronounced "forbad"), and *forbidden.* The archaism "We have *forbid* them to do it" should be rephrased "have forbidden."

A sister word, *prohibit,* is treated differently. It is followed by a *from* phrase—"prohibit from doing," not "prohibit to do." The following are examples of correct usage in both the active and passive voices: "The rules *prohibit* employees *from* congregating on the premises after hours." "Unescorted children are *prohibited from* entering the museum." But a sign saying "All children are *prohibited from* this area" is expressed incorrectly. Although children may be prohibited *from entering* an area, they cannot be *prohibited from* a place.

FOREIGN

See ALIEN, FOREIGN

FOREIGN WORDS

Speaking in Tongues

Foreign words or expressions sometimes supply, as the French say, *le mot juste,* "the right word." In some instances no English substitute seems to convey so correct a flavor or to be so precise. For example, referring to someone as a bosom friend or one's second self is clear, but *alter ego,* which literally means "another I," says it better: "Damon was Pythias' *alter ego.*" Using *alter ego* to mean another aspect of one's own personality is inaccurate.

The literal meaning of *sub rosa* is "under the rose." During the Renaissance, and even later, a common architectural motif in banquet halls was the rose. Whatever was said under the rose, it was generally agreed, must be kept confidential. This belief—that the rose is a symbol of silence—was founded in

Greek mythology by Cupid, who, upon presenting a rose to Harpocrates, obtained his pledge not to tell anyone that he had seen Venus in an amorous embrace. Today what is whispered in secrecy is said to be spoken *sub rosa.*

The term *lorelei* was derived from a legendary German siren on the Rhine who led sailors to their destruction. The words charmer, seductress, temptress, vamp, and sexpot are synonymous, but they describe women who lead men to their pleasure, not necessarily to their doom.

Ad infinitum literally means "to infinity." It has replaced "forever" and serves for "endlessly": "It is believed that the moon will shine and the sun will burn *ad infinitum.*"

The literal meaning of the French *vis-à-vis* is "face to face." Its connotation "confronting each other" makes it a useful phrase, worthy of being retained in its native form. Many dictionaries, however, give it far-fetched Americanized definitions, equating it with *concerning* and *regarding,* and even with *toward, in relation to,* and *in comparison with.* In the following sentences, *vis-à-vis* should be replaced: "This meeting should be postponed *vis-à-vis* the president's return." "*Vis-à-vis* the pharmacist's warning, I think it has merit." In the first example, *until* would do; in the second, *as to.* The term is used correctly in "After living many years on separate continents, they suddenly found themselves *vis-à-vis* in a train station." The word is pronounced *vee-zah-vee.*

Another common French expression is *tête-à-tête,* supposedly coined by the French dramatist Molière in the seventeenth century. It means "head to head" and suggests a private meeting or a confidential conversation, usually between two persons: "That couple by the door are engrossed in a *tête-à-tête.*" It is pronounced *taet-uh-taet,* and the accent marks are dropped in informal usage.

Neither *vis-à-vis* nor *tête-à-tête* should be italicized, or underlined if in typescript, since they are now common English phrases.

A third useful Gallic expression is *sang-froid,* which conveys the idea of coolness under stress and marked self-possession. Although its literal meaning is "cold blood," the French phrase has no connotation of insensitivity or lack of compunction. Rather, it suggests the "cold blood" required to cool down "hot heads." It is an essential ingredient in the life of successful foreign diplomats and arbitrators.

Many Italian terms that pertain to music have been all but absorbed into the English language. American musicians use *allegro* to mean "brisk" or "happy" and *a mezza voce* (pronounced *mehd*-zah *vo*-chi) for "softly." An *arpeggio* (ahr-*pae*-joh) is a chord whose notes are played up the scale in rapid succession; and an *obbligato* (spelled with two *b*'s) is an indispensable instrumental accompaniment. These words are still italicized. But not *aria* (pronounced *ah*-ree-ah), a song for a single voice in an opera ("We enjoyed best the aria from the first act"), nor is the adjective *coloratura,* as in "a coloratura soprano." Italicizing or underlining *maestro,* the conductor of the orchestra or an eminent musician, is passé. Words borrowed into the English language need no longer be emphasized.

FORMER, LATTER

> *See* LAST, LATEST

FORTHWITH, PRESENTLY

Presently There's a Problem

The problem with *presently* is that no one is quite sure what it means. For centuries it meant "at once," as in "I need it *presently* ("now"), not sometime tomorrow." It eventually came to mean "before long": "He'll do it *presently* ("soon"), but he's busy now." The old sense is experiencing a revival but is objected to on the grounds that giving a word two meanings, each making sense in the same context, is bound to be confusing. The objection, of course, is valid. It would be helpful if the obsolete meaning of *presently* were ignored and only the current meaning ("soon") survived, thus letting bygones be bygones.

Forthwith, another double-edged word, means both "immediately" and "in a reasonable time." The first meaning is the correct one in textual writing. Certainly someone in pain who has been told he will be relieved forthwith hopes that *forthwith* means immediately, and not "in a reasonable time"— whenever that may be. When *forthwith* means "thereupon," its sense is clear: "Students who are suspended must *forthwith* leave."

FORTUITOUS, FORTUNATE

Good Luck—You Can't Beat It

Etymologically *fortuitous* and *fortunate* stem from the same Latin root, *fors,* meaning "chance or luck." But from that common ancestor their meanings have diverged. The words are therefore not interchangeable, even though some dictionaries regard them as synonyms. They may, in fact, be used in tandem without being redundant. "A series of *fortuitous, fortunate* circumstances made her prominent" indicates that the circumstances were undesigned but turned out to her advantage.

Fortunate means "favored by fortune," or "marked by good luck." What is fortunate may result from chance or plain luck, the strong implication being of unexpected good fortune. "Your careful driving was *fortunate*; a police car was behind you." "It was *fortunate* for Easton that he found the money he had lost."

The term *fortuitous* has within it no sense of good fortune—or bad, either. It merely suggests that what happened was unplanned, something unexpected or accidental as in a fortuitous encounter. That which is fortuitous, therefore, can be unlucky or lucky. In law, a *fortuitous event* is defined by *Black's* as an "event...occurring unexpectedly, without known cause." And a *fortuitous collision* is the "accidental running afoul of (maritime) vessels." The noun form that designates such a happening is *fortuity.*

FRACTIONS

A Fraction of the Amount

Fractions in text are expressed in words: "There were three quarters of an inch left, since only an inch and a half were used." Ordinarily hyphens are used between a numerator and a denominator (four-fifths, nine-tenths) and within a fraction used as an adjective before the word it modifies: a one-third part; a two-thirds majority. But a hyphen is not used, in the opinion of many authorities, when a fraction serves as a noun, in which case the numerator is an adjective: *one third* of the book; *two thirds* of the pie. A guide to this problem of hyphening is to remember not to hyphen a fraction that is followed by an *of* phrase: "A two-thirds vote wins, but *two thirds of the votes* for any one person is not to be expected."

An objection to the phrase *a fraction* (as in *"A fraction* of the students rose when the president entered the room"') is that the intended sense is a small part, whereas *a fraction* may be a large part of the whole. No objection is ever raised when *only* precedes the phrase—*only a fraction* is always a small part.

(See also HALF, QUARTER.)

FREQUENTLY, OFTEN, USUAL

What Frequency Are You On?

One makes no great mistake by interchanging *often* and *frequently*. *Often* is defined as "frequently" or "repeatedly"; *frequently,* as "occurring or appearing often." Perhaps the simpler word *often* is more forceful.

However, *often,* more so than *frequently,* suggests regularity of recurrence, something that happens repeatedly ("We *often* go to the corner grocery store." "Herman visits his sick mother *often*"). *Frequently* indicates repetition at close intervals ("Athletes *frequently* dislocate their shoulders when learning to shot-put." "In the spring, blue warblers are *frequently* seen flying south").

Frequently has an adjective form, *frequent* ("My brother's *frequent* visits please me"); *often* has no such form. *Often,* pronounced *aw*-fin—the *t* is silent—is an impermissible substitute for *in many instances.* For example, "Maple furniture is *often* selected for damp climates" should be reworded: "In many instances maple furniture is...." *Oftentime, oftentimes,* and *ofttimes,* all of which mean "often," are obsolescent. *Oftentimes* retains some vitality and is occasionally found in literary writings, but its use is not recommended.

That which is commonly or frequently encountered is termed *usual:* the usual time; the usual place. Its adverb form, *usually,* should come immediately before or after the verb: "Matilda's aunt is eating more than she *usually does*" or "Matilda's aunt is eating more than she *does usually.*" When modifying an adjective, *usually* should precede it, as in "She is *usually* loud" or "She was more than *usually* loud," not "She was more loud than *usually.*" In positions other than these, *usual* is called for, not *usually:* "The barber took more time than *usual.*" "This season the orchestra played more sonatas than *usual.*"

FULSOME

See -SOME

FURTHER

See FARTHER, FURTHER

G

GAMUT, GANTLET, GAUNTLET

G-Words That String Along

Almost everyone at one time has used the expression "to run the gantlet" or "to run the gauntlet." The latter phrasing, "to run the gauntlet," despite its approval by some dictionaries, is not technically correct.

A *gauntlet* was the name of a protective glove; a *gantlet,* on the other hand, was a military form of punishment in which a person ran between two rows of men who beat him with clubs or other weapons. Although this practice no longer exists, the expression has survived, figuratively, in the sense of a severe trial or ordeal: run a gantlet of disapproving looks; run a gantlet of critical remarks.

Another G-word steeped in "runs" is *gamut.* In the eleventh century, Guido D'Arezzo, a monk, devised a musical scale (known as Guido's scale) that has since been the basis of musical notation. To the earlier six-note scale, Guido added a low G, which he called *gamma* after the Greek letter. It became known as the *gamma-ut. Gamma* later was named "G" as in G-clef; *ut* was renamed *do,* as in *do-re-mi;* and *gamut* entered the English language as a generalized word designating the complete range or extent of anything—notes, prices, choices. "To run the gamut" is to run through an entire series of musical notes, a full display of figures, or a whole range of colors. It is the alphabetical A-to-Z, of any subject: "Defense counsel *ran the gamut* of emotions in pleading for clemency—he laughed, he begged, he harangued, he cried." *Gamut* is pronounced *gam*-uht.

Spectrum (denoting "a continuous range or sequence") has, to a large extent, replaced *gamut* in everyday usage. In physics, it refers to bands of light or radio waves that provide various kinds of information. Oddly, lay people rarely use it unmodified: one surveys *a broad spectrum, a wide spectrum,* or *the whole spectrum,* but not just a *spectrum*, unless he lives in Philadelphia, where *Spectrum* is spelled with a capital *S*.

GAY

Query: Can Sex Be Colloquial?

Many plain, simple words with no emotional overtones have developed sexual connotations. How and why this happens is not always clear.

A common example is the word *queer*. It refers to what is odd or eccentric, "differing from the normal or expected," as in "His ideas on how to conduct a class are queer." "A clown purposely tries to look queer." But *queer* has become a contemptuous term for "homosexual." The vernacular expression is not only misleading but unfair, in that it connotes censure and derision. Other disparaging synonyms are *fruit, fag, dyke,* and *fairy*.

Today the word preferred by homosexuals is *gay*. No one seems to know where this label came from nor what justified it. *Gay* literally means "merry or lively," implying high spirits and freedom from care. These attributes suit homosexuals no more than they do artists or bankers or Bavarians. The label will probably remain, however, and with it the self-consciousness of those people who would like to use the word in its original sense but no longer feel free to do so.

GENERAL

See COMMON, GENERAL, UNIVERSAL

GENUINE

See AUTHENTIC, AUTHORITATIVE, GENUINE

GET

Got it? Got it. Good!

The original meaning of *get* was "seize" or "take hold of." But with the passage of time *get* has acquired so many definitions that today few verbs can match it in number of meanings. First, there are all its standard senses—for example, to obtain ("get a dictionary"); to fetch ("get the ball"); to persuade ("get him to go"); to receive ("get an award"); to become ill ("get sick")—followed by its various idioms. Then there are its informal uses, which in some dictionaries take up an entire column. And finally its slang expressions.

Some writers avoid using the word entirely because they consider it inelegant; others think that such a maneuver is merely an affectation. In any event, one will often see *obtain, receive,* or *earn* where the simple word *get* would serve as well and sound more natural.

In colloquial language, one "gets out of bed" and "gets up from a chair." A doctor may say, "The secretary didn't *get the point*" for "understand" and "We *got* to the church on time" rather than "reached." But those expressions, although clear, are inappropriate in serious writing.

The past participle of *get* is *got* or *gotten.* When the sense is of progression ("His condition has *gotten* worse"), *gotten* is the preferred choice. The past tense of *get* is *got.* Except in casual conversation, this form is a poor substitute for *must, should,* or *ought to:* "I *must (should* or *ought to)* study now," not "I *got* to study now." Adding *have* to *got to* ("I *have got to study* now") changes no ratings on the literary scale. There is no argument, however, that when emphasis is needed, it is more effective to say "He's *got* to go" than "He *has* to go." Got it?

GIBE, JIBE

Gibberish

Are the verbs *gibe* and *jibe* in the sense of "sneer at," "scoff at," or "scorn" interchangeable? Can *jibe,* for example, replace *gibe* in "I cannot forget that my best friend *gibed* at me"? Not in formal writing. Although dictionaries equate the words by offering *jibe* as a variant spelling, in educated language *gibe* alone should be used when taunting or scoffing is meant. *Jibe* is best restricted to its nautical meaning ("to cause a sail to swing from one side of a sailing vessel to another") and to its colloquial sense ("match or agree," as in "The accounts of the two witnesses did not *jibe*").

No one knows for sure, but the word *gibbet* may have some connection with *gibe*. A *gibbet* was an upright post with a projecting arm from which the bodies of executed criminals were hanged. There they were exposed to public scorn so that the citizenry could gibe at them.

The verb *gibe,* when used intransitively, takes the preposition *at. Jibe* and *gibe* rhyme with *bribe.*

GIVE, PRESENT

Highly Gifted

Although *to gift* is recognized by some dictionaries as a verb, meaning "to bestow gifts upon," it does not belong in serious writing. To a beneficiary it may be of no concern whether largess is said to be given, donated, presented, or gifted. But to a sensitive ear, "He *gifted* her with a cockatoo" sounds awkward.

The everyday word for "to make a present of" is *give.* A fitting verb for formal occasions is *present:* "The Lodge *presented* a plaque to the Secretary." Another "giving" verb, but one that sounds heavy in ordinary situations, is *donate.* It is best reserved for the giving of goods, money, or services without charge, as to a charity: "The doctor *donated* two hours of service daily to the clinic." The simpler word *give* still remains the most suitable choice in most instances.

GLANCE, GLIMPSE

Short-Sighted

The words *glance* and *glimpse* connote a momentary, incomplete view. A *glimpse* is what one sees at a *glance.*

To *glance* is to look indirectly, rapidly; to cast a brief look at: "He *glanced* at the playbill just as the lights dimmed." "He would not be so rude as to stare at the Queen, but he did *glance* at her." Expressions such as *brief glance* or *a glance for only a second* are redundant.

A *glimpse* is a quick but imperfect sight of something: "One could get only a passing *glimpse* of the Prime Minister as he sped by."

Practically speaking, the difference in meaning between these words is so slight (*glance* pertains to an act of looking; *glimpse,* to what is seen) that they are interchangeable if used with their correct prepositions (respectively *at* and *of*). It may be said that since a person has *a glimpse of,* and gets *to glance at,* someone or something, *glance* is what he does, and a *glimpse* is what he gets.

GLUTTON, GOURMAND, GOURMET

Food for Thought

A person may resent being called a *gourmand* but be pleased to be known as a *gourmet.* Both terms apply to someone who knows and enjoys good food. A *gourmand,* a person with a voracious appetite, eats often and enthusiastically, devouring large quantities of food. Euphemistically he is called a "hearty eater." A *gourmet,* an esthete, is more fastidious; he chooses his food carefully, regarding it as a source of keen and subtle pleasure.

Both *gourmands* and *gluttons* eat to excess, but at that point the meanings of the words diverge. A *gourmand,* despite his large consumption of food, knows something about cuisine and can discriminate between the good and the bad. A *glutton* is an unrestrained eater who is indifferent to the quality of his food. As long as it is available, he will eat, allowing nothing—not even table manners—to interfere with his pleasure. Henry VIII supposedly was such a person.

A *gourmet* is quite the opposite. He is a gastronomic connoisseur and often, too, a judge of vintage wine. He is respected for his refined taste in food and his equally refined manners. He regards eating and drinking as acts that should do more than satisfy hunger and thirst—they should delight the senses. A synonym of *gourmet* is *epicure.*

GOT, GOTTEN

See GET

GRADUATE

Making the Grade

One who has successfully completed a course of study at a school is *graduated,* that is (from the Latin *gradus*) has moved a "step," "degree," or "grade." This achievement may properly be expressed in two ways: *graduated from* or *was graduated from.* The active voice is preferable: "He *graduated from* college last week." The passive, *was graduated from,* sounds old-fashioned. The key to correct usage lies in the preposition *from,* which must be used in either case. Omitting it, as in "He *graduated* college last week," destroys the formal status of the sentence.

A graduate may become a member of the Alumni Society, but membership is not open to a dropout, even though he or she is as much an *alumnus* (male) or an *alumna* (female) as a *summa cum laude* graduate. An *alumnus* or *alumna* (in Latin, literally a foster son or daughter) is a person who attended a school, whether or not a diploma was received.

GRAFFITI

The Writing on the Wall

The proliferation of writings on walls and public vehicles has made *graffiti* a common word, especially in some Eastern cities. Its respectable ancestor, the Italian *graffiare* ("to scratch"), was an archaeological term referring to a primitive method of writing or drawing by scratching on walls or other surfaces.

Graffiti is plural; its singular is *graffito.* Thus a local newspaper headline, "Philadelphia graffiti reflects the illiteracy of its writers," needs either "Philadelphia *graffito reflects*" or "Philadelphia *graffiti reflect.*" The sentence, especially on such literate matters, must be consistently singular or plural. *Graffiti,* it should be noted, is spelled with a double *f* and a single *t.*

GREATLY

See **CHIEFLY, LARGELY, GREATLY, MATERIALLY**

GREEK ROOTS

It's Greek to Me

It is not true that Greek roots are used only in scientific terms or in other academic disciplines. Many ordinary English words also depend on Greek for their origin. For example, *auto-* in *automobile* and *autobiography* is Greek for "self." The *cycl-* in *bicycle, motorcycle, cyclone,* or any other *cycle* is Greek for "circle." *Graph-,* as in *telegraph, photograph, graphite,* means "write"; *dyna-* in *dynamite, dynamic,* and *heterodyne,* "power"; *chronos-* in *chronometer, synchronize,* and *chronic,* "time" (a *chronic* disease is one of long duration); *bio-,* in *biography, biology,* and *antibiotic,* "life"; and *micro-* in *microscope, microbe,* and *microfilm,* "small."

The Greek *poly-* means "much" or "many." The language abounds in words stemming from that root—*polysyllabic,* "having many syllables," *polytheism,* "belief in many gods," *polychromatic,* "having many colors," *polyglot,* "speaking or writing many languages." The same prefix appears in less commonly used words, such as *polyandry* "having more than one husband," or *polygyny,* "having more than one wife." This latter word at one time also referred to the practice of having more than one mistress or concubine at a time. *Polygamy* refers to having two or more marriage partners simultaneously. The accent in *polyandry* is on the first syllable (*pawl*-ih-ahn-drih) and in *polygyny* and *polygamy* on the second (poh-*lij*-ih-nih, puh-*lihg*-uh-mee).

GUARANTEE

Promises, Promises

One who offers security may be called a *guarantee* or a *guarantor.* The latter term is generally preferred, especially since the word *guarantee* has other uses. As a verb meaning "to secure, as by taking collateral" ("The Society will *guarantee* the mortgage"), and as a noun signifying a warrant or pledge ("We hold the *guarantee* of the Society"), it refers to an assurance that a promise will be kept or that something will perform satisfactorily.

The word *guaranty* also may serve as a verb or noun. Its everyday business use, however, is as a noun, meaning "a pledge, accepting responsibility for another's liabilities" or "an offer of security," virtually eliminating its function as a verb. The contract which guarantees that an obligation will be duly honored or that a product will perform as specified is, in the world of commerce, the *guaranty*. But *guarantee* in all these uses is never wrong. In fact, it is always a safe word to use. It may be said that one who guarantees is a *guarantee* or *guarantor*, for he has given a *guarantee* or *guaranty*.

H

HABIT

See CUSTOM, HABIT, PRACTICE

HACKNEYED EXPRESSIONS

See TRITE EXPRESSIONS

HAD BETTER, OUGHT

Place Your Betters!

When the doing of something is highly advisable, *had better* is an appropriate idiom to express it: "If Elmer wants to keep his job, he *had better* arrive on time." "We *had better* clean the place before Mom comes home." In informal language *had* is normally omitted and *better* used alone: "Larry *better* plan carefully, or else he'll be in trouble." "We *better* leave now." In formal writing, where this omission is impermissible, *had better* or *ought to* or *should* are equally satisfactory choices: "He *had better* (or *ought to* or *should*) consult with his doctor before taking such a long journey." *Ought* and *should* convey a sense of obligation; *had better,* a feeling of expediency. If *had better* is reversed, it becomes ungrammatical. "Christine *better had* see the doctor before her condition worsens" should be "Christine *had better* ...." The same rule applies to *had best.*

The formal idiom for expressing preference is *had rather.* Even more formal is *would rather:* "He *would rather* lecture than write." In speech, the contraction *he'd* could stand either for *he would* or for *he had.*

Particular care should be taken to avoid illiteracies such as *had have, had of, had ought,* or *hadn't ought.* "Had I known it, I would have been quicker" is correct as stated, but not "*Had* I *have* known it..." or "*Had* I *of* known it...." "If *he'd (he had) have* known it, he would not have come" is wrong, too. The *have* is unnecessary. Similarly, "That sentence *hadn't ought* to be written that way" should be rephrased, "That sentence *ought not* be written that way." Using any part of the verb *have* with *ought* is ungrammatical.

(See also **OUGHT, SHOULD**.)

HAIL, HALE

Hail, Hail, the Gang All Went

A felon carted to the hoosegow hardly cares whether he is being *hailed* or *haled* to prison. But others might want to know that he was *haled*. *Haled*, meaning "hauled," is a synonym of *carted*. It is frequently used in the sense "to compel a person to go"; hence the familiar "hale into court."

A person may *hail* a taxicab (that is, signal it), or he may get the *hail* out of a rowboat (remove the ice pellets). As most commonly used, however, *hail* means "to salute or greet." For example, "The people along the parade route *hailed* the new mayor."

Hale as an adjective means "free from disease." A robust person is "*hale* and hearty," but is not a "*hale* fellow well met." The idiom is "*hail*-fellow-well-met" and refers to geniality and pleasantness upon being greeted, not to health. It is always hyphened.

HALF, QUARTER

Two Quarters for a Half

People who are quartered are provided with shelter ("The troops were *quartered* in the barracks at the edge of town") or they are dismembered, their bodies divided into four parts ("The traitor was hanged and *quartered*").

In expressions of time it is correct to say either "It is now *quarter* to four" or "I will meet my teacher at *quarter* past four." The omission of *a* before *quarter* is well established, although technically incorrect. In all other cases *quarter* needs a preceding *a* or number: "She gave me *a quarter* of a pound." "*One quarter* of the pie was eaten."

Except when time is expressed, *quarter* and *half* are treated differently. *Half,* unlike quarter, needs no preceding article or number: "*Half* the students were absent" makes sense, but "*Quarter* the students were absent" does not. Or again, "It is *half* finished," but "It is *a quarter* finished."

As nouns, *half* and *quarter* may be followed by *of* and actually or impliedly by another noun or pronoun: "Sixteen students entered that year. *Half* of them failed; one *quarter* (of them) went on to college." The number of the verb is determined by the number of the accompanying noun or pronoun, even if it is not expressed, as in "Half (of the *store*) *was* destroyed." "One quarter (of the *men*) *are* gone."

(See also FRACTIONS.)

The Halves and Half Nots

Something divided may have two halves. In formal English the expression "Divide it *in halves*" is preferred to "Divide it *in half.*" But no consensus has established that choice. Those writers who prefer *in half* contend that it sounds more natural; and it does, even though it is grammatically illogical. Nevertheless, expressions such as "break in half" and "cut in half" are entrenched in the language. Certainly no one has ever seen a magician saw a woman in halves. It is always *in half.*

Half may be treated as a singular or a plural word. When the noun or pronoun to which it refers is singular, it is followed by a verb in the singular ("*Half* the pie *has* been eaten"), but it takes a plural verb when the noun or pronoun is plural ("*Half* the books *are* obsolete").

As a prefix to an adjective or a noun, *half* is hyphened: half-brother, half-afraid, half-jokingly, half-moon, half-full. But there are exceptions: half dollar, half hour, halfhearted, halftime. *Two halves* is not hyphened in "The *two halves* were rapidly eaten, one after the other" because it is not a fraction.

It is preferable to say "We waited *a half hour*" to "We waited *half an hour*"; likewise, "*a half cup* of coffee" rather than "*half a cup* of coffee." Although the latter expression ("half a cup of coffee") is acceptable because of its common usage, extending it further with a redundant *a* ("*a half a cup of coffee*") is not.

HAMSTRING

In technical language the verb *to hamstring* refers to the cutting of a tendon, the hamstring, in the back of the knee. It is more commonly used, however, in a general sense, meaning "to disable" or "to render powerless" or "to hinder the efficiency of": "Every time Betty decides to have a party, her younger sister manages to *hamstring* the plans." Although the present tense of *hamstring* raises no problems, opinions differ on the proper form of the past tense and the past participle— *hamstringed* or *hamstrung*, or both. *Hamstringed* is logical because the verb means "to cut the hamstring," and it is unrelated to the verb *string*. Yet the preference, based upon prevailing usage, is *hamstrung;* this is doubtlessly influenced by the principal parts of the verb *to string—string, strung, strung*: "The revenue bill has been *hamstrung* by a conservative faction in the Senate."

HANDLE, MANAGE

Get a Handle on It

Handle and *manage* share the same meaning, "to control or influence." In "Jack can *handle* (or *manage*) the most demanding customers" or in "Mildred can *handle* (or *manage*) any family problem," either verb may serve. However, *handle* literally means "to take with the hands," whereas *manage* (from the Latin manus, "hand"—the root of many words in which hands play a part) simply means "the use of hands." *Amanuensis, manipulate, manuscript,* and *manufacture* have this same stem. Although both *handle* and *manage* still retain their original senses ("Please *handle* the crystal vase carefully." "It is surprising how well he *managed* that unruly horse"), they have now assumed figurative meanings that have little to do with touching, as in "The chairman *managed* the committee meeting with ease."

Manage also signifies the directing and carrying on of business affairs, sometimes by a *manager*, the person in charge of these activities. The word *handle* is more commonly used when hands are actually employed: "Annie Oakley *handled* a gun as if she'd been born with it."

HARDLY

Sooner Than You Think

It is idiomatically incorrect to say "*Hardly* had we begun to put the material together *than* we were told to stop." Also unidiomatic is "The schoolboard had *barely* announced the new schedule *than* a group of protestors condemned it." In both these examples *than* has wrongly displaced *when*. Perhaps this kind of error is induced by the analogy of the adverbs *hardly* and *barely* to the *sooner* in *no sooner ... than*, which is established idiom. For instance, if *hardly* were used in the following sentence, "The students had *no sooner* sat down *than* the teacher entered," a recasting would be needed: "The students had *hardly* sat down *when* the teacher entered."

To distinguish the expressions *hardly when* and *barely when* from *no sooner than*, one should remember that a comparison made between a thing or situation greater or smaller than another requires an adjective or adverb in the comparative degree (of which *sooner* is one) followed by *than* to introduce the second element: "Their needs are greater *than* ours." "His salary is smaller *than* his wife's."

This also means, quite clearly, that *when* should not be misused for *than*. For example, in "*No sooner* did we tee off *when* it began to rain," *than* should replace *when*.

There's Scarcely Anything Between Us

The differences in sense between *hardly, scarcely,* and *barely* are hardly, scarcely, or barely noticeable. They all suggest a happening by the narrowest of margins. In popular usage, the words are interchanged with no loss in clarity: "After that vicious tackle, the quarterback was *hardly (scarcely or barely)* able to raise his arm." Strictly speaking, however, *hardly* suggests a degree of difficulty ("He can *hardly* walk") and *scarcely* a quantity that is unbelievably small ("There is *scarcely* any ice cream left"). *Barely* implies narrowness and thinness ("He *barely* missed that tree").

These three adverbs, since they imply a negative, should not be used with other negative words. This restriction, a guard against the illogical "double negative," poses no problem in ordinary constructions. One would be unlikely to say, "The storekeeper said she could *not hardly* read the order" or "After that purchase, I *scarcely* had *no* money left." But some pitfalls are less obvious. For example, in "Our neighbors do not have a single relative or *hardly* any friends," the negative sense of *hardly* requires that it have its own affirmative verb to negate. Otherwise, the preceding *not* carries through and in effect combines *not* and *hardly*. The sentence should be rephrased, "Our neighbors do not have a single relative and *have hardly* any friends" or "Our neighbors *have no* relatives and *hardly* any friends." In "*Without hardly* any money, he managed to buy a wardrobe," two words with negative force are used where only one belongs. Either *with* should replace *without* ("*With* hardly any money") or *without* should remain and *hardly* be removed ("*Without* any money").

HAVOC

See **RAVAGE, RAVISH**

HESITATE, VACILLATE, WAVER

Slow Down

Hesitate, vacillate, and *waver* are synonyms in that they all denote a lack of determination. Their uses should be distinguished, however, for their meanings have shades of differences.

A person who *hesitates* is undecided and is therefore slow to act. If he *vacillates,* his mind swings back and forth, like a pendulum. First he believes he should follow one course of action, then another, and so on; he keeps changing his mind and cannot reach a final, firm decision. One who *wavers* is irresolute. Having made a decision, he then is reluctant to see it through; he falters and wonders if he should retract.

Another term that suggests irresoluteness is *fluctuate.* It derives from the Latin *fluctuare,* "to float about." Whatever rises and falls, as waves do, is said to *fluctuate.* Figuratively *fluctuate* implies irregular movement and is commonly used of moods, feelings, and prices. A synonym for *fluctuation,* its noun form, is *unsteadiness.*

HIRE, LEASE, RENT

The Rent Goes Hire and Hire

Hire means "to engage the services of," as in "Fred hired a bodyguard last night." When applied to inanimate objects, *hire* is interchangeable with *rent.* In this sense both words suggest the procurement of something for temporary use by paying money. One may hire or rent a bus, for example. *Hire* is the more general word, for almost anything can be hired. Ordinarily, however, *hire* is applied to labor, halls, and automobiles. With apartments or buildings, the terms used are *rent* and *lease.* They are also used of equipment. One hires a typist, for example, but rents or leases a typewriter. Yet, strictly speaking, a piece of equipment or an automobile made available for rental to the public is *leased* by the owner to someone who wants to *hire* it. Nonetheless, *hire* is no longer a common term except for a horse and buggy: "We have Old Bess and a two-wheeler for hire."

Lease, as a noun, refers to an instrument that conveys a property, usually for a definite period, for an agreed compensation called *rent.* As verbs, *rent* and *lease* are synonymous. However, they may be a source of confusion, for they do not point to a specific doer. A person who says that he has just leased or rented a suite of rooms may be the lessee or the lessor.

HISTORY OF THE ENGLISH LANGUAGE

Polyglottos

The English vocabulary has developed from many languages; it is a babel of strange tongues. Primarily it is Germanic, descended from the language of the Angles, Saxons, and Jutes— Teutonic invaders of the British Isles in the fifth and sixth centuries. The dialects of the Anglians (who gave their name to "England") and the Saxons came to be known as Anglo-Saxon or Old English.

Viking invasions of England during the following centuries and the conquest in 1066 by the Norman-French, led by William the Conqueror, further influenced the language. After the Battle of Hastings, French became the country's official language, and although the common people continued to speak English, those who wished to advance socially or politically considered it wise to learn French. French became the language of government, diplomacy, and aristocracy. Many of the country's leaders, however, were bilingual. The law finally established English as the official language of the realm in 1362 by the Statute of Pleadings, which required that all court proceedings be conducted in English.

In the sixteenth century, when knowledge of Latin became a mark of culture, a stream of Latin words poured into the English language. But its development did not stop there. English continued borrowing words from sources around the world; for example, from Japanese (*kimono*), Chinese (*tea, typhoon*), Hebrew (*cherub, kosher*), Spanish (*canyon, stevedore, vanilla*), Arabic (*assassin, giraffe, checkers, alcohol*), Hindu (*jungle, cashmere, bungalow, khaki, pajamas*), Italian (*grotto, novel, opera, concert, piano*), Persian (*bazaar, shawl, orange, lemon, candy*), Dutch (*furlough, buoy, yacht, cruise, deck, cole slaw*), Turkish (*coffee, caviar, sherbet*), and Hungarian (*paprika, goulash*).

The additions were not acquired from foreign sources alone, however. Some were home grown, especially in the English colonies. The Indians, the native Americans, supplied *succotash, caucus, pecan, mugwump, toboggan,* and *moccasin,* among others. In addition, the Pilgrims and immigrants to the "New World" created new words to convey new meanings—words such as *backwoods, bowie knife* (named for its inventor, Colonel James Bowie), and *gerrymander* (after Massachusetts Governor Elbridge Gerry). Meanwhile England itself was fashioning words. *Boycott* got its name from Charles C. Boycott, a British estates agent in Ireland whose tenants successfully ostracized him when he refused to reduce rents; and *macadam,* from John L. McAdam, the British engineer who invented the macadam road surface.

American coinages have also kept pace with changing times, encompassing everything from the long to the short: *long-johns, bulls and bears, G.I.'s, H-bombs,* and *short-wave radios.* American-English terms are now completely integrated into daily speech, and many are used even in formal writing. As H. L. Mencken said, "Today it is no longer necessary for an American writer to apologize for writing American."

HOME

A Home Is for Pleasure, Too

Discriminating writers distinguish between the words *house* and *home*. This is as it should be. Dictionaries, however, regard them as synonyms, and real estate dealers purposely confuse them, believing that a *home* is more salable than a house.

A *house* is a building designed to be a residence. A *home* is the center of private or family life. Therefore, a home may be in a house, an apartment, a condominium, or even a cave. It is any shelter in which a person or family lives. But a home is more than a structure; it connotes warmth, love, and security, and evokes recollections of domestic comfort and the pleasant sentiments that attach to family living. Hence a house, in itself, cannot be regarded as a home. Certainly a house of gambling or prostitution would not be so considered. The commercial practice, therefore, of offering one's home for sale is ludicrous. Only a house or a dwelling can be bought or sold; a home, which is a concept, can never be put on the marketplace.

Whether *home* may be employed adverbially for *at home* is a matter of context and tone. Formal style calls for *at home:* "Mrs. Kirk is *at home.*" In general usage, however, the preposition is often omitted: "She was *home* all day." And rightly it does not belong after verbs that imply motion, such as *coming* and *going:* "The soldiers are *coming home.*" "The students will be *going home* for Thanksgiving." But in "We're going to *stay at home* on Sunday," *stay* does not suggest motion; hence the *at.*

HOMICIDE

Deadly Relations

Ever since Cain slew Abel, man has been killing man. The relationship of the victim to the killer has as many variations as human relationships, and words have been invented to distinguish the kinship involved in a particular killing.

A general word meaning "the killing of one person by another" is *homicide.* That term, from the Latin *homo,* "man," and -*cide* from *cidium,* "killer and killing," does not imply criminality. Some homicides are justifiable, as in self-defense or in the performance of a legal duty. Specific felonious killings have distinctive names, such as *matricide* or *patricide,* the killing of a mother or a father by a son or daughter. A broader term, encompassing the killing of either a parent or a person whose relationship resembles that of a parent, such as a ruler or a pope, is *parricide. Fratricide* is the killing of one's brother and *sororicide,* the killing of one's sister. *Regicide* is the killing of a king; *suicide,* the killing of oneself.

Then there are general words meaning "to kill unlawfully," particularly *murder* which is any malicious killing of a human being by another, and *manslaughter* which, unlike murder, is a killing with no malice aforethought. An *assassination* is a murder for political reasons. The name is derived from the Arabic *hashshashin,* a Muslim sect, which, supposedly while under the influence of the drug hashish, but probably motivated by religious fervor, attacked Christians during the Crusades.

HOMONYMS, HOMOGRAPHS, HOMOPHONES

Homogenized

Many common spelling errors are caused by mistaking one word for another. Particularly confusing are words with similar sounds or spellings. Consider *peek, peak,* and *pique,* or *idle, idol,* and *idyll,* or *rode, rowed,* and *road.*

Words that resemble each other in spelling or pronunciation, or in both, are called variously *homonyms, homographs,* or *homophones.* What these words have in common is the Greek prefix *homo,* meaning "of the same kind."

Homonyms are the same words, literally "same name" or "namesake." They are spelled and pronounced alike, but have different meanings: *pool* (collection of water, a game, a betting group); *bear* (an animal, to carry, to endure); *redress* (to dress again, to requite a loss); *cashier* (one who handles cash, to discharge); *pale* (colorless, an enclosure); *toll* (a tax or duty, to sound a bell).

Homographs, meaning "the same writing," are words that are spelled alike but differ in pronunciation and meaning: *row* (a straight line) and *row* (a noisy dispute); *lead* (to conduct) and *lead* (a metal); *wind* (gust of air) and *wind* (to twist); *bow* (a fancy knot) and *bow* (to bend at the waist).

Homophones are words having the same sound, but different meanings and spellings: *toe* and *tow; alter* and *altar; fete* and *fate; marshal* and *martial; feet* and *feat; canvas* and *canvass; brake* and *break; sole* and *soul; palate, palette,* and *pallet.*

Dictionaries do not agree on the definitions of these labels. Some equate homonym and homophone. Others list all three words as synonyms. Some chronicle as homonyms *hour* and *our, aid* and *aide,* and *cite* and *sight,* for example, even though, precisely speaking, these words are homophones. *Tear* (to make a rent in) and *tear* (a weeping drop from an eye) and *bass* (a fish) and *bass* (the lowest pitch of the voice) are also regarded as homonyms, but to be accurate, they should be regarded as homographs.

Some words can have several labels. For example, *air* is a homonym in that it may refer to a melody or to the atmosphere, but it also is a homophone of *heir.*

HOPEFULLY

A Hopeless Case

Hopefully is a good old English word meaning either "with hope" or "in a hopeful mood or manner." It is used correctly in "The crew is searching *hopefully* for a break in the clouds" and in "My husband looked *hopefully* at the doctor's report," for both the crew and the husband were full of hope. Today, however, it is most often used to mean "let us hope" or "it is to be hoped that," as in "*Hopefully,* the program will end soon" or in "*Hopefully,* the ship will anchor near the shore." These examples say that the program and the ship are full of hope— a meaning, of course, not intended.

The newer sense is, in spite of widespread popularity, deplored by those concerned with the purity of the language. Among careful writers the prevailing opinion is to reject this usage as a solecism.

Unfortunately, English, unlike some other languages, lacks a word meaning "let's hope" or "it is hoped." *Hopefully* is being made to serve. But it then becomes a hanging adverb, ungrammatical and illogical. The desired sense can be expressed properly only by expending a few extra words. Perhaps one day the argument that an inanimate object cannot harbor hope will be overlooked, but that day has not yet arrived.

The verb "to hope" is also often misused, but in a different way. The caution with this verb is that it should not be employed in the passive except as an impersonal verb, with *it* as its subject. In "The Federal Reserve is creating what *is hoped* will be a healthier economic climate," *it* has erroneously been omitted: "what *it* is hoped will be."

The expression *no hope* is singular, of course. And it should remain that way. "The patient has *no hope* of surviving" is correctly put. It is wrong to say *has no hopes of.*

HOWEVER

However You Look at It

The conjunctive adverbs *furthermore, accordingly, consequently,* and *moreover,* like all such adverbs, join independent clauses, but these words are so heavy that they are best confined to formal texts.

A lighter adverb, and one that is therefore appropriate to both formal and informal writing, is *however.* Rather than as a conjunctive adverb, however, it more often is used transitionally to emphasize a statement or word by contrasting it with a preceding one, as in this sentence or in "Michael has not had time to repair the machine. We are certain, *however,* that he will begin work soon."

When *however* introduces a sentence, the contrast it should effect is with the preceding sentence—something it usually fails to do. In fact, in an introductory position, *however* will in all likelihood be serving either as a conjunction meaning "but" ("*However [But]* we will leave soon") or as a pure adverb meaning "in whatever manner" ("*However* long we wait, we will keep smiling").

The punctuation marks that *however* takes depend on how it is used. As a conjunctive adverb, it is preceded by a semicolon and followed by a comma ("We will reconvene at one; *however,* we do not know when we will adjourn"). When used transitionally, it is set off by commas ("He wants to be sure, *however,* that everything arrives promptly"), which, if misplaced, could change the meaning in some sentences ("We will leave, *however* regretfully, to return to our distant village" is less forlorn than "We will leave, *however*, regretfully to return to our distant village"). The pure adverb *however* is never troublesome. It may be positioned almost anywhere and with no punctuation: "*However* hard he struggled, he could not succeed." "He could not succeed *however* hard he struggled."

HUNG, HANGED

See MISUSED WORDS

HYPERBOLE

See FIGURES OF SPEECH

-IC, -ICS

The Numbers Game

The basic grammatical principle that a verb must agree with its subject in number is easily understood but not always easily followed, for certain nouns are plural in form but singular in meaning. They, of course, take singular verbs: *molasses, measles, news* ("The news *is* all bad"). Other nouns may take either a singular or a plural verb, depending on the exact meaning of the noun. (*See* SINGULAR NOUNS THAT APPEAR PLURAL.)

This duality in number applies to many *icky* words. For example, *politics* is a singular noun when it refers to a science or a profession: "*Politics is* everyone's concern." When *politics* means opinions or principles, its sense is plural, and the governing verb must accordingly be plural: "The President's *politics raise* debatable issues." As a system of training, *athletics* is singular: "*Athletics is* recommended for the young." But when used of sports in general, it is a plural noun: "*Athletics are* activities for the young." Other examples are "*Physics is* a required subject," but "The *physics* of this engineering project *need* review." "*Acoustics is* what tells us that the *acoustics* here *are* intolerable."

Words of cultural bearing that end in *ic,* rather than *ics,* such as *rhetoric, logic,* or *music,* entered the English language before the sixteenth century. Words absorbed later added *ics.* The additional *s* has had no effect on meaning. The *ic* words, however, are always singular: "*Rhetoric is* . . . ," "*We are pleased by her logic,* which is . . . ," "The *music goes* round and round."

IDEA

What an Idea

A wit might exclaim, "Before using the word *idea,* one should get a better idea." Actually, *idea* is a good word. In fact, it is so good that it is used too often—and therein lies its fault. Overuse makes for monotony and vagueness.

Although dictionaries offer many meanings for *idea,* it chiefly means "conception." *Idea* is best applied to reflect a serious or elaborate thought, but not one that is detailed and intricate (as is a *concept*) or one that is fleeting and imperfectly formed (as is a *notion*). The term is accurately employed in "General Arnold weighed the *idea* of an immediate withdrawal" and in "The *idea* of enlarging our operation is appealing."

Almost any emanation of the mind may be called an *idea.* But some thoughts are more precisely conveyed by more appropriate synonyms. For example: "Dorothy's idea *(intention)* is to take two courses." "The idea *(proposal)* to merge was well received." "What an idea *(whim)*—to go swimming at night." "The idea *(theory)* of the defense was that the plaintiff had no knowledge of the occurrence." "The idea *(thesis)* of the lecture was easily comprehended." "Myer's idea *(belief, opinion)* is that everyone should write a letter to his congressman." "The doctor got the idea *(impression)* that the patient didn't like him." And then there are *views, convictions,* and *hypotheses*—all more specific descriptives than *idea.* Perhaps that wit back in the first paragraph was right.

IDLE, INDOLENT, LAZY, SLOTHFUL

Lazybones

"He must be lazy, since he's idle every afternoon" is a fallacious statement. An idle person may be far from lazy. He may, in fact, be energetic.

Lazy implies unwillingness to work. It is a disparaging term, in that it labels a person as one who dislikes to exert himself. It is not derogatory, however, when used to refer to things other than people: "a *lazy* afternoon"; "the *lazy* drifting of a canoe." No one is certain of the derivation of *lazy* (perhaps everyone was too lazy to find out), but it may have come from the Latin *laxus,* "loose," or from the French *a l'aise,* "at ease." Dr. Samuel Johnson believed it derived from the latter. Its verb form, *laze,* is a back formation from *lazy.*

The derivative meaning of the word *idle* is "useless," a definition no longer current except in the sense of groundless (as in idle rumors). *Idle* refers either to things that at the moment are not in use or to persons who are unemployed or not involved in business. But idleness may not necessarily be self-imposed. A person may be made idle by an illness or a lockout at his place of employment—causes beyond his control and for which no reproach is justified: "The typist was made *idle* by the breakdown of her typewriter." "Our computers are *idle* during our vacation periods." *Idleness* implies temporary inactivity. *Laziness* is a permanent trait.

Indolent—the word in Latin literally means "free from pain" (*non-dolorous*)—implies a disinclination to engage in any activity that interferes with one's comfort. An indolent person seeks not to exert himself but to relax as much as possible: "My *indolent* friend whittled twigs all summer." Dictionaries enter *slothful* as a synonym for *indolent*, but *slothful* is a stronger, more pejorative word. A slothful person is totally unwilling to do what he should. Another synonym is *otiose*, derived from a Latin word meaning "at leisure." It suggests a lack of purpose, a lazy nature—true indolence.

IF AND WHEN, UNLESS AND UNTIL

Make Up Your Mind

A man who says he will pay you if and when the package is received expresses doubt that he will receive it. But only seldom is the cliché *if and when* used with this purpose in mind. Ordinarily the words follow each other automatically, with no conscious thought on the speaker's part. Yet the person has said too much. If cut in half, *if and when* loses nothing in meaning or emphasis. Although *if* expresses possible consequences ("*If* the train is late, we'll miss the first half of the concert") and *when*, time ("*When* the train runs late, we always miss the first half"), the sense of both words together can be expressed by either one alone. This is made clear in "*If and when* the Braves win the pennant, the town will go wild." The result will be the same whether it is *if* or *when.*

The analysis made in the preceding paragraph may, in good part, be applied to *unless and until.* It, too, is often merely a reflex action, for one word or the other ordinarily may be dropped with no loss in sense. A difference between the two phrases is that *unless and until* is usually used in negative statements: "We will not pay the bill *unless and until* we receive the package."

Until raises another matter: Is it preferred to *till*? It is not. *Till* is just as good a word. Both mean "before," "up to," or "when," and either may properly begin a sentence. Although *until* predominates over *till* in that position, rhythm should determine the choice. Abbreviations of *till* are not recommended in serious writing: *'til* is informal and *'till* substandard.

IF CLAUSES

Subjoined

Some people have a mistaken belief that a clause beginning with *if* must always be in the subjunctive mood, reflecting a doubtful fulfillment of the condition or a condition contrary to fact. This is not so. A clause introduced by *if* may express a simple condition relating to the past and take the indicative form of the verb. For example, in "If Allan *was* there, he was drunk," the *if* clause introduces a supposition, hence a verb in the indicative mood. And so with the sentences "If Curran *was* absent, he was probably out of town" and "If I *was* long-winded, I'm sorry." None of the examples imply doubt or suggest a circumstance contrary to fact, as in "If I *were* President, I wouldn't pardon him."

(*See also* SUBJUNCTIVE MOOD.)

ILLUSION

See ALLUSION, ILLUSION, DELUSION

IMITATION

See ARTIFICIAL

IMMIGRANT

See EMIGRANT, IMMIGRANT

IMPEACH

See MISUSED WORDS

IMPLICATE

See ENVELOP, EXPLICATE, IMPLICATE

IMPLY, INFER

He Had It Infer Me

Perhaps the two words in the English language that are most often confused are *infer* and *imply*. They are interchanged so frequently as to lead many people to regard them as synonyms. But they are not. In fact, their meanings are far apart.

The problem usually lies with *infer,* as in this sentence: "Do you mean to *infer* I don't know what I'm doing?" *Imply,* of course, not *infer,* is the word required.

To *imply* is to suggest without explicitly stating, to express indirectly: "The doctor *implied* that he knows more than he is saying." *Infer* means "to surmise; to deduce; to draw a conclusion from": "We must *infer* from his remarks that he did not tell us everything." Speakers who hint *imply;* hearers who recognize the hint *infer.* To put it another way, the implier initiates; the inferrer receives.

One way to remember the distinction between these words is to think of their alphabetical sequence—*im* comes before *in;* therefore one must *imply* before another can *infer.* In "The book *implied* that Napoleon's moods affected his decisions; hence we must *infer* that some of his military strategy was not carefully considered," the author implied; the reader inferred.

IMPROPRIETIES

See TYPES OF ERRORS

IN

In Trouble

Perhaps more than any other preposition in the English language, *in* leads to wastefulness and awkwardness. It introduces many phrases that not only are wordy but also ring of pretension—*in close proximity* for "near," *in lieu of* for "instead of," *in possession of* for "with" or "having." Writing gains in grace and brevity if *in* phrases are replaced by simpler, shorter locutions.

It would be difficult to defend sensibly the use of *in the neighborhood of* or *vicinity of* for "about" or "around," or *in the near future* for "soon" or "shortly." The phrase *in the amount of* is prolix for *for;* and *in the course of,* for "during" or "when."

"*In spite of* all this" is more succinctly put as "*despite* all this." However, some *in* phrases are useful and are not easily replaced. One such is *in the light of,* which implies that what follows is information that has just been or is about to be disclosed. What must be guarded against there is the inadvertent omission of *the,* not *in light of* but *in the light of:* "*In the light of* the latest chart, we can no longer object." A sister phrase, *in view of,* means "with regard to." It has no internal *the:* "*In view of* the city's programs, we commend the mayor."

IN-, UN-

A Not-ty Problem

Not all *not*'s are the same. The meanings of words prefixed by *in-* and *un-,* both of which usually convert a positive word into a negative, differ from each other. For example, that which does not conform to the canons of art is *inartistic* ("a pretty but *inartistic* picture"), whereas a person lacking artistic ability is *unartistic.* Similarly, *inapt* means "inappropriate," "unqualified," but *unapt,* "not likely."

Some words, whether prefixed by *in-* or *un-,* retain the same sense. A sedentary person may be described as *inactive* or *unactive,* with no change in meaning. This is also true of the following words, although the second of each pair is the more common: *unsupportable* and *insupportable; unsubstantial* and *insubstantial; unfrequent* and *infrequent; insanitary* and *unsanitary.* The Declaration of Independence speaks of "unalienable rights," but today those rights are almost always rendered *inalienable.* In most cases the *in-* form is preferred.

In some words, *in-* does not serve as a negative at all. For instance, *invaluable* does not mean "of no value" or "valueless." In fact, its meaning is just the opposite—"of value so great that no estimate can be conceived."

A negative form preceding a word with a negative prefix can sometimes be confusing. In "Not an unintelligent student among them," what was meant was "all were intelligent." And in "No unwanted books are on display," all the books are wanted.

INAUGURATE

See BEGIN

INCLUDE

See COMPOSE, COMPRISE, INCLUDE

INCOMPARABLE, UNCOMPARABLE

When in Doubt, Don't Compare

In some contexts, *incomparable* and *uncomparable* are synonymous, since both mean "incapable of being compared." But even when this is so, one or the other is usually more appropriate. *Incomparable* also means "peerless," "unequaled," "unsurpassed," or "unmatched." It implies excellence more than dissimilarity. It may be said that reaching the moon is an incomparable achievement or that the Bible is an incomparable tome. *Uncomparable* would have been less suitable.

Uncomparable means only "that which cannot be compared." A baseball bat and a tennis racquet are uncomparable objects as are a golf bag and a hockey stick. As a grammatical term, however, it describes words that are "matchless," that is, absolute in meaning. Such words admit of no comparisons and therefore have no comparative or superlative degrees. For example, *eternal* is "forever," and therefore nothing can be *more* or *most* eternal. And since *unique* identifies "the only one of its kind," something cannot be *more* or *most* unique or *rather* or *very* unique. One looking to qualify such words may do so with a word that does not imply degree (such as "almost") or say that something is "more nearly so" (as in "more nearly round," "more nearly equal," or "more nearly unique").

INCREDIBLE, INCREDULOUS

Believe It or Not

Something *incredible* is something that is not credible—in other words, unworthy of belief. *Incredible* and *unbelievable* are synonymous. *Incredible,* however, has come to mean not only difficulty in believing, but a refusal to believe. A person who says it is incredible that his sister ignored her sore throat and walked in the pouring rain is not suggesting that it did not happen. He is implying that his sister was extremely, or "incredibly," foolish. Similarly, a person who says kidnapping is incredible does not doubt that it occurs, but rather that he thinks it incomprehensible that anyone would commit such a heinous act.

Unbelievable, too, is occasionally used in this sense. People who are surprised by something out of the ordinary might call it unbelievable. What they mean is that it is difficult to believe; still they do believe it.

Another word akin to "disbelief" is *incredulous.* But it pertains to someone who is doubting or distrustful, a skeptic rather than a confirmed disbeliever. Such a person remains unbelieving until validity has been established: "The story he told the police officers left them *incredulous.*" The police were unbelieving or, as is said in the vernacular, not sold on it. A situation is *incredible* or *unbelievable;* a person informed of it, *incredulous.*

The antonyms of *incredible* and *incredulous* are *credible* and *credulous. Credible* means "believable" or "trustworthy." A witness's testimony, a document, or an account—all may be credible; that is, worthy of belief.

Credulous refers to an overtrustful person, one prone to believe on slight evidence. A synonym is *gullible.* It may be said that although a fable sounds credible to a child, adults are bound to be less credulous.

INDEFINITE NOUNS AND PRONOUNS

Tennis Anyone?

Indefinite nouns and pronouns are so called because their antecedents are persons or things not specifically named. These words convey merely general impressions, yet their sense is easily grasped. For example, in "Everything is in order," *every-thing* points to nothing specific, but nobody is befuddled by it. And who is *nobody?* That unspecific word misleads no one. In fact, *no one,* like *nobody,* is itself an indefinite pronoun, which *everyone* understands.

Although *everyone* and *every one* have the same meanings, they are not always interchangeable. The two-word form is used when the meaning is every one of a number. The *one* is stressed—every *one*—emphasizing the separateness of the people or things. Ordinarily an *of* phrase follows: "*Every one of the senators* rose at the same time." "*Every one of them* had the same hopes." "Those boxes? *Every one of them* is broken." The pronoun *everyone,* meaning "everybody," is written as one word. It refers to people who are not singled out: "*Everyone* must appear promptly." Both *everyone* and *every one* take singular verbs.

Some indefinite pronouns—*another, each, either, nobody, no one,* for example—are always singular and take singular verbs. Others, like *both, many,* and *several,* are always plural and take plural verbs. But some may take either a singular or a plural verb. And therein lies a source of confusion.

The indefinite pronouns that may be either singular or plural are *all, any, most, none,* and *some.* They are singular when referring to a quantity but plural when referring to a number. The following examples are illustrative (the first part of each pertains to quantity and the second to number): "*All* the sand we bought *has* not been shipped, but *all* the books *have* arrived." "*None* of the rubbish *has* been collected, and *none* of the bottles *have* as yet been picked up." "*Some* of the cement *is* dry; *some* of their molds *have* broken." "*Most* of the trouble *is* over, but *most* of his fears *remain.*"

Not everyone agrees that *none* may be used as a plural. Purists insist that since it is the etymological equivalent of "not one," it should be treated only as a singular. According to accepted practice, however, *none* becomes plural when it means "not any." Therefore, although "*None* (No one) *has* done his duty" is correct as stated, so is "We had ten apple pies, but *none* (not any) *are* left." Today the use of the plural with *none* is acceptable on all levels of writing. The timid, of course, may continue to employ only the singular form—sometimes awkward but always safe.

Whether a noun or pronoun referent following *everyone* must always be singular or whether it may be plural, when called for by common sense, is also a matter of controversy. Strictly speaking, a singular pronoun should follow: "Everyone removed *his or her* coat (rather than *their* coats) before entering the room." But the plural *they* or *them* is more widely used in a sentence such as "If everyone is ready for dinner, let *them* come in" or in "Everyone was singing, but *they* sounded off key." To avoid the awkwardness of a singular pronoun and the ungrammatical structure of a plural pronoun, the sentence may be recast without *everyone:* "If the *guests* are ready for dinner, let *them* come in."

INDIRECT OBJECTS, OBJECTIVE COMPLEMENTS

The Pattern Maker

English sentences follow various patterns. The two simplest are those with a subject and a verb ("Lance Bernheimer died") and a subject, verb, and object ("Barry Preston bought a house"). More complex patterns are those that contain either an objective complement or an indirect object.

Objective complements are nouns or adjectives that complete the meaning of a noun or pronoun object, renaming or describing it. Examples are "The association elected Millie Roberts *president*" and "Thomas Mehan made the librarian *angry*." The construction is used with special verbs—*appoint, call, elect, judge, make, name,* and the like.

An indirect object also is used with special verbs—*ask, bring, buy, give, hand, lead, lend, offer, pay, receive, say, send, take, teach, tell, throw,* and so forth. Always preceding the direct object, the indirect object names the receiver of the action, designating the person for whom or to whom the action of the verb is being done: "Please read *him* the letter." "The jeweler made *her* a handsome gold bracelet." An object is determined to be indirect if a prepositional phrase could replace it and express the same meaning, as in the following examples: "Send *him* the book" and "Send the book *to him.*" "The office gave *her* a farewell party" and "The office gave a farewell party *for her.*"

INDISPENSABLE

See ESSENTIAL, INDISPENSABLE, VITAL

INDIVIDUAL

See PEOPLE, PERSONS

INDOLENT

See IDLE, INDOLENT, LAZY, SLOTHFUL

INFECTIOUS

See CONTAGIOUS, INFECTIOUS

INFER

See IMPLY, INFER

INFINITIVES

Infinitives Without End

The word *infinitive* derives from the Latin *in,* meaning "not," and *finitus,* meaning "limited." According to its original definition, an infinitive is a form of a verb that is not restricted, not limited by person or number.

Most people recognize an infinitive as a verbal preceded by *to,* the sign of the infinitive. Examples of its common use are "I like *to read*" and "The judge decided *to clear* the courtroom."

Infinitives have two tense forms, present and perfect: *to strike, to have struck.* The present tense is used of time contemporaneous with that of the main verb ("I want to go now") or at a time future to it ("I am being asked to seek funds"). The perfect tense, consisting of a form of the auxiliary verb *to have* and a past participle, points to action that has taken place before the action of its principal verb: "I am delighted *to have assisted* your uncle."

Infinitives in the perfect tense normally do not accompany principal verbs that are also in the perfect tense—the so-called . . . *have.* . . *have* construction. A present infinitive is used instead. For example, it is correct to say "Marc Alston would have liked to study"—implying that he had a desire to study at the time indicated by the verb; it is wrong, however, to change the present tense to a perfect: "Marc Alston would *have* liked to *have* studied." Other examples of proper and improper usage are "The chairman had expected *to see* (not *to have seen*) the treasurer" and "Reynold would have liked *to attend*" (not *to have attended*).

The sentence "Ira hoped to have visited the Museum" presents a similar case. Its prime fault is that the auxiliary misplaces the time sequence. It should read "Ira *had* hoped to visit the Museum," putting the principal verb in the perfect tense and the infinitive in the present so that it is clear that the *hoping* preceded the *disappointment.* But if Ira were expressing a present feeling, he might say "I *would like* (now) *to have visited* (then) the Museum."

The commonly heard "I wish to be among the first to have congratulated you" confuses warmth with grammar. It should be reworded, "I wish to be among the first *to congratulate you.*"

INFLAMMABLE

All Burned Up

The conventional word meaning "capable of being set on fire" or "combustible" is *inflammable.* The problem is that it may be construed to mean the very opposite ("not flammable" or "not ignitable"), for one meaning of the prefix *in-* is "not" (as in *incoherent, indefinite,* and *injudicious*).

Fire underwriters, concerned with potential claims by those who might be injured because of their mistaken belief that the word *inflammable* meant "nonburnable," worked to adopt an unambiguous word—*flammable.* Today *flammable* is the more commonly used warning on petroleum trucks and perhaps the more commonly used form generally. It has even been accepted into formal English, interchangeable with *inflammable.*

Only *inflammable,* however, is appropriate in the figurative sense of excitable or easily aroused to strong emotion, as in "The boss is known for his *inflammable* temper." *Flammable* would not serve. Its sister word *inflammatory* (which means "tending to excite the senses, kindling passion or anger") is also employed only figuratively: "*Inflammatory* speeches are heard every day in Hyde Park." The antonym of both *flammable* and *inflammable* is *nonflammable.*

INFLICT

See **AFFLICT, INFLICT**

INGENIOUS, INGENUOUS

The "In" Thing

The words *ingenious* and *ingenuous* are easily confused look-alikes. Both bear within them the same Greek root, *gen*, which means "to beget," suggesting that one possessing these qualities is born with them.

Ingenious means "skillfull in contriving, resourceful, inventive." An ingenious person is said to be clever, talented, imaginative—an ingenious mechanic, an ingenious executive, an ingenious accountant.

Ingenuous describes a person who acts with artless frankness, innocence, or extreme naiveté: "The class adviser considers Essie the most *ingenuous* freshman at Vassar." A person unsophisticated in worldly affairs or free from guile and deceit is ingenuous: an ingenuous clergyman, an ingenuous young lady. Not only a person but a statement or manner may be ingenuous.

The second syllable of *ingenious* is pronounced *jeen;* of *ingenuous, jehn.* The noun forms of these words are *ingenuity* and *ingenuousness,* respectively.

An *ingénue,* a word developed by the French (pronounced ahn-zhae-*nyoo*) is an "ingenuous girl or woman," more often an actress who portrays a naive girl. The acute accent mark over the first *e,* though permissible, is unnecessary, since it does not alter the normal anglicized sound of the middle syllable.

INHERENT, INNATE, INTRINSIC

Born with It

Inherent denotes the "existence of something as an essential constituent or characteristic." It refers to what is firmly fixed by nature, a permanent and inseparable element, such as an inherent attribute. It may be used of both persons and things: "The human mind has certain *inherent* qualities." "A gutteral sound is *inherent* in the German language."

Innate means "possessed at birth." That which is innate is integral to a person's makeup. It may be as physical as a harelip—although *congenital* more aptly describes physical defects existing at birth—or it may be an abstract quality that pertains to a part of a person's essential character, like modesty. *Innate* also points to what arises from the mind: innate ideas. Its closest synonym is *inborn,* which refers, of course, to qualities only of living beings.

Intrinsic, a synonym of *inherent,* also means "pertaining to the essential nature of a thing." It refers to properties of the thing itself, unaffected by outside considerations or circumstances. It may be applied to both persons and things (intrinsic worth, for example, is inherent worth, a measurement of actual utility or desirability): "The intrinsic value of this misprinted stamp is fifteen cents, but its extrinsic worth, that is, what it would sell for on the open market, is considerably more."

The antonym of *intrinsic* is *extrinsic.* It means "being outside of a thing" or "operating or coming from without." Something extrinsic is unessential or foreign, having no vital part of, or bearing on, the matter in question: "Sympathy is extrinsic to an impartial judgment." *Extraneous,* a similar word, also pertains to what is external; it refers to what has been introduced from the outside. One difference between *extrinsic* and *extraneous* is that although extrinsic matter remains "on the outside," extraneous matter can be found within—such as an uncalled-for comment or a fly in the soup.

INITIATE

See BEGIN

INNATE

See INHERENT, INNATE, INTRINSIC

INQUIRE

See ASCERTAIN, INQUIRE

INSURE

See ASSURE, ENSURE, INSURE

INTELLECTUAL, INTELLIGENT

More than Intelligence

An intelligent person has a high mental capacity. He has a good understanding, is quick to comprehend, and can meet and solve problems, especially those that are practical: "Mr. Brown is so *intelligent* that he arrived quickly at a workable solution." *Intelligence* is a native faculty, independent of education. Even an animal can be intelligent, but not intellectual.

That which is *intellectual* engages the intellect, "the faculty of mind which enables it to function by way of thought and reason and to some extent of intuition." *Intellectual* implies a high degree of knowledge and understanding, manifested by a person's utterances, acts, and qualities. Although an intellectual person is likely to be intelligent (otherwise he would shun mental exercises), the converse need not follow. An intelligent person is not necessarily intellectual, for, although his mental capabilities are great and his understanding quick, he may have no interest in academic matters or matters of the mind.

Those involved in academic pursuits—the intellectuals—may be called members of the *intelligentsia*. Imported from Russia, the term refers to the professional and highly educated classes. But since it stems from the Russian Revolution, it has acquired unfavorable connotations. Intelligentsia is a collective noun: "The *intelligentsia was* here in force." But its signification is singular, and therefore it may not be immediately preceded by a numeral. "Four *members* of the *intelligentsia* sat on the platform" is properly expressed, not "Four *intelligentsia* sat. . . ."

INTRACTABLE, INTRANSIGENT

Who's Keeping Tract?

One who is *intractable* may be *intransigent*, but those words are not synonymous. *Intransigent* means "refusing to moderate an extreme position." Derived from the Spanish *los intransigentes,* "the uncompromising," it retains this sense in English. An *intransigent* (the form is used for both noun and adjective) is one who chronically disagrees: "Mr. Browne has shown himself to be an *intransigent* union leader at the negotiating table." "*Intransigent* youths often become more tractable with maturity."

An *intractable* person is also stubborn, but "stubborn" in the sense of "difficult to manage or govern." One who is intractable does not want to learn or to acquire a sense of discipline. With animals, *intractable* means "unruly." The word is also used of metal that is not easily wrought and of ailments that are not responsive to medicine.

A more familiar word to describe a person who objects to restraint is *recalcitrant.* Derived from the Latin *recalcitro* ("kick backwards"), it was used by the Romans to describe stubbornly resistant horses. It now refers to a rebellious or obstinate person.

INTRINSIC

See INHERENT, INNATE, INTRINSIC

INTRODUCTORY EXPRESSIONS

Can Out-of-Place Be Normal?

Traditionally, an adverb out of normal word order—like *traditionally* in this sentence—was followed by a comma. This is not invariably so today. The trend is to use a comma after an introductory adverb only if it improves rhythm, promotes emphasis, or aids clarity.

Introductory transitional expressions—those that relate a preceding idea to one that follows—offer no choice. They always take commas. Typical "transitionals" are *above all, as a result, conversely, finally, first, for example, further, however, in addition, in conclusion, on the contrary, to sum up,* and *what is more: "Above all,* one must be sure he's right." "*In conclusion,* we believe the budget should be adopted by voice vote."

A writer's independent opinion or attitude toward a succeeding thought, when expressed within a sentence, should have commas placed before and after it. Some of the most common such expressions are *for instance, fortunately, in essence, most of all, obviously,* and *strictly speaking: "Geoffrey is, obviously,* not to be believed."

If, however, the rhythm of the sentence in the writer's judgment is more pleasing without commas, they need not be used: "Geoffrey is *obviously* not to be believed."

INVENT

See DISCOVER, INVENT

ITALICS

Italics Are Not Greeks

Italics, a form of Renaissance script that slants to the right, came by its name logically, since it was invented by Italians. The style first appeared in a Virgil printed by Aldus Manutius in Venice in 1501. Italics is now a common typeface used primarily for the setting off of distinctive names, such as the names of ships, trains, or airplanes, and titles of books, plays, motion pictures, periodicals, or newspapers. It is also used to indicate that the word itself, rather than its meaning, is being considered, as in "Both *and* and *or* are common coordinate conjunctions." Although stylebooks differ on whether italics should set off letters, figures, and symbols—most recommend its use—they all agree that a pluralizing *s* should not be italicized. For example, "The *5*'s look like *s*'s; the *n*'s like *m*'s." Foreign words not yet accepted into the English language—*caveat emptor, nouveau riche*—are italicized.

Whether to indicate key words or phrases by italics is a matter of judgment, but it is not a preferred way of conveying emphasis. If used more than sparingly for this purpose, it will lose whatever force it has.

A pertinent question is whether to italicize *the* when it is part of the title of a periodical or newspaper. Preferably a *the* that begins a title should not be italicized when the syntax requires a *the:* "He reads the *New York Times*" rather than "He reads *The New York Times*." It certainly would be aimless to say, "He reads the *The New York Times*." In some constructions the *the* or the *a* is omitted entirely to avoid awkwardness.

This is so when a title beginning with *The* or *A* precedes a possessive form, as in "This is his (The) *New York Times*" or in "Here is Dicken's (A) *Tale of Two Cities*." If the preference is to include the initial article in the title, the title may be treated as an appositive, as in "Here is a copy of Dickens's book *A Tale of Two Cities.*

In manuscript or typescript, italics are indicated by underlining.

J

JEALOUSY

See ENVY, JEALOUSY

JIBE

See GIBE, JIBE

JUNCTION, JUNCTURE

Tuxedo Junction

The words *junction* and *juncture* are so much alike that their meanings in most dictionaries follow each other, converging to denote "the act of joining or the condition of being joined," as in "The *junction* (or *juncture*) of these two armies will enable them to defeat the enemy."

Past this "junction," however, their meanings digress. Although they both identify a place of joining, *junction* is preferred in the sense of "crossroads": "Pittsburgh lies at the *junction* of the Allegheny and the Monongahela rivers." When *juncture* is used as a place of joining, it is synonymous with *joint* or *connection,* the line or point where two things are joined—the juncture of the head and neck. More often *juncture* applies to a point in time. It is used of events that, if not simultaneous, occur at least during the same general time, often significantly or even critically: "The *juncture* of blizzards, derailments, and a power shortage may force us to close the station early today." "At this *juncture,* as imports soar and exports crash, we must decide whether to redistribute our holdings."

166

The phrases *at this juncture* and *at this moment* are sometimes confused. If the circumstances are not of great significance, or if the reference is not to a concurrence of events but only to a *moment,* the word juncture is inappropriate: "At this *moment* (not At this *juncture* in time) before greeting the president, you must be confident of your position on those issues."

JUST, QUITE

Is Just Enough Quite Enough?

"The manuscript is quite ready" can mean different things to different people—and each one's interpretation may be correct. The reason: *quite* means "completely" in its primary sense, but "somewhat" in informal English.

Dictionaries define *quite* as "wholly, entirely, altogether, positively"—or "completely" (as in "Our professor has not been *quite* the same since he fell") and "actually, really, and truly" (as in "My aunt is *quite* content with her new accommodations"). In formal writing any one of these senses is acceptable. In less formal writing, *quite* may mean "to a considerable extent," "rather," "very," or "somewhat," as in "It is *quite* late" or in "It is *quite* warm today." But to conform to the demands of standard English, the last two examples need recasting.

The use of *quite* in some popular expressions is well established but controversial. Among the most common are "quite a few" and "quite a number" meaning "many"; "quite a little" meaning "more than a little" or "much"; and "quite a bit" meaning "a considerable amount."

Just is another word that glories in informal meanings: "precisely" (just perfect); "narrowly" (just missed being struck); "recently" (just left); and "only" (just a morsel). The combination *just about* makes no sense; the words are contradictory—*just* points to what is precise, and *about,* to an approximation. Like *quite, just* is colloquial when used in the intensive sense of "very," as in "The dinner was *just* fine." It is repetitious in *just exactly*—*just* means "exactly." One may say "It is *just* two o'clock" or "*exactly* two o'clock." Either word will suffice. The phrase *just as* takes no intervening *the same:* "He was selected *just as* the others were" not "*just the same* as the others were."

K

KILT, KIN

Who Kilt My Kin?

The sentence "A kin can wear a kilt" raises a question of number; namely, whether *kin* and *kilt* are singular or plural nouns. *Kin* ordinarily refers to one's relations collectively but considered separately, and therefore takes a plural verb: "My kin *are* to gather here tomorrow." In the idiomatic expression "He is no *kin* to me," *kin* is regarded as a singular term; in no other case may one refer to only one person as *kin.* It is incorrect to say "Esmeralda is *a kin* of mine." *Kin* should not be confused with its steady companion *kith,* which means "acquaintances." The phrase *kith and kin,* denoting "friends and relatives," is archaic.

Kilt versus *kilts* presents a different problem. Again authorities are divided on correct usage. But most agree that this form of dress refers to a single garment, which should be treated accordingly: "Mac is wearing *a* handsome kilt." In the United States, following the lead of words like *pants* ("Mario's pants *are* too long"), the plural *kilts* predominates: "Scott's *kilts are* short." Its analogy to *pants,* however, is false because *pants,* though a single garment, is a plural word. Only when preceded by a singular term does its sense become singular: "*A pair of* blue serge pants *is* on the hanger."

KIND

Sort Out the Right Kind

One advantage in knowing the correct usage of *kind* is that many of the same rules apply to *sort, variety, species, breed, size, type, class, brand,* and *quality.* For example, *kind* as a singular form is qualified by *this* or *that,* not *these* or *those.* And so are the other listed words—*this* (not *these*) sort; *this* (not *these*) type; *that* (not *those*) variety.

168

The plural noun *kinds* is used with plural pronouns: these kinds; those kinds. "*These kinds* of sweaters are the warmest" is the way to say it, in spite of King Lear's "*These kind of* knaves I know." Although some authorities support Shakespeare's phrasing as good literary English and accepted idiom as well, preferably the plural form *kinds* should be used when more than one kind is meant so that it will agree in number with its referent: "Some *kinds of plants* survive best in direct sunlight."

Saying "I was *kind of* chagrined by what I heard" or "It's *kind of* cold today" is colloquial and awkward. *Rather* or *somewhat* would do better. The informal phrase *kind of a* is the least excusable of all, for the intrusion of *a* makes the expression illogical. *Kind* indicates an approximation of a class of objects; *a* points to a single thing. Instead of "What *kind of a* career appeals to you?" one should ask "What kind of career...." That kind may help one's career.

KNOT

See **NAUTICAL TERMS**

L

LACK, NEED, WANT

Less than Essential

Lack, want, and *need,* as either verbs or nouns, suggest the absence of something desirable. They imply that what is missing is more than a mere deficiency, although perhaps not an essential.

Lack is defined as "a deficiency of something requisite, desirable, or customary," thus indicating an insufficient supply, a shortage: "*Lack* of exercise often causes loss of muscle tone." *Want* suggests a lack of necessary things and an awareness of that lack: "We saw plants dying for *want* of rain" (*want,* meaning "lack," is the object of the preposition *for*). The word *need,* though not denoting great urgency, implies necessity: "Inherent in all of us is a *need* for recognition" (*need* connotes strong emotional appeal).

In their verbal usage the words are not interchangeable, for each has a distinctive meaning. "The student *needs* good grades" (for admission to college). "The student *wants* good grades" (he would like to have them). "The student *lacks* good grades" (he never earned them).

LARGELY

See CHIEFLY, LARGELY, GREATLY, MATERIALLY

LAST, LATEST

The Last Word

The words *last* and *latest* can be confusing because they both mean "most recent." The last or the latest news bulletin refers to the most recent one.

Generally *last,* a shortened form of *latest,* means "final," designating what follows the others in time or place. One refers to the last day of the month or to the last row in the theater. *Latest* refers to what follows all others in time only; that is, the most recent. More is expected. The latest report, the latest fashion, and the latest edition are usually not the last. They may turn out to be the last, but only if no more are forthcoming. *Latest* does not imply the finality that *last* does. It is more tactful, therefore, to request of an author a copy of his latest book rather than his last. Asking for his last may frighten him.

Former and *latter*, which also denotes placement, refer to only two persons, things, or parts. They are wrongly used of three or more, and, strictly speaking, they should refer only to nouns, not to pronouns. The words to use when more than two items are mentioned are *the first* or *the first-named* and *the last* or *the last-named.* Although *former* and *latter* most frequently simply replace names, they may annoy a reader by making him reread to find out who is who. Samuel Johnson expressed his intense distaste for those signposts. He said, "As long as you have the use of your pen, never be reduced to that shift."

LAWFUL, LEGAL

Law Abiding

Legal and *lawful* are synonyms to the extent that they both pertain to the law. The legal heir, for example, is also the lawful heir. The distinction between these terms is that *lawful* refers to the principles that underlie the law, whereas *legal* refers to the literal interpretation of the law.

What is *legal* is in conformity with the law, is according to law, is required by law, or is not expressly forbidden. *Lawful* is similar, in that it implies that something is authorized by law or not contrary to it. It denotes the substance of the law. *Legal* marks its form. Hence, in sum, what is lawful is permitted; what is legal is done in compliance with the law.

LAY, LIE

Play It as It Lays

One can always use the verbs *lie* and *lay* correctly if the difference between transitive and intransitive verbs is kept in mind. A transitive verb requires a direct object to complete its meaning, as in "You can *lay it* on the chair" or "The gardener *laid* the new *sod* today." But an intransitive verb, as is *lie,* cannot take a direct object: "Our dog *lies* in the sun every afternoon." "Please let it *lie* there."

To *lay* (*laid, laid*) means "to put or place"; to *lie* (*lay, lain*), "to recline in a prone position," "to repose." The confusion created by these words lies in part in the identicalness of the present tense of *to lay,* which is *lay,* and the past tense of *to lie,* which also is *lay.* The simplest way to distinguish the uses of *lay* is to note whether a noun following it is essential to the meaning of the sentence. If so, a form of *to lay* is required ("He will *lay* the *bricks* tomorrow"); otherwise, a form of *to lie* ("He *lay* down early in the evening").

Confusing the present participle and the past tense forms of these verbs is also not uncommon. For example, in "Not only was he *laying* on the floor, but he *laid* there feigning sleep," two forms of *to lay* are mistakenly used for the corresponding number of *to lie.* Properly rephrased, the sentence would read: "Not only was he *lying* on the floor, but he *lay* there feigning sleep."

LAZY

See **IDLE, INDOLENT, LAZY, SLOTHFUL**

LEASE

See **HIRE, LEASE, RENT**

LEGAL

See **LAWFUL, LEGAL**

LEGAL TERMS

Giving It Up

A *bequest* is a gift by will. Strictly speaking, it pertains only to personal property, in law called personalty. A gift of land or realty by will is a *devise.* Hence the antiquated terminology *devise and bequeath,* a phrase designed to cover the disposition of all property by will. Many testators now use only the word *leave—*

which is less cumbrous and more easily understood than the legal phraseology.

A *legacy* is a bequest. In a figurative sense, a *legacy* refers to anything received from an ancestor or coming from the past. It may be a code of moral principles, intellectual liveliness, or a sterling silver tea set.

The expression *last will and testament* is another legal relic. It was formerly believed that both terms had to be be used to validate a testamentary gift of realty and personalty. One who left realty was termed a devisor; one who left personal property, a testator. Today people write *wills*; the term *testament* is obsolete. A will can effectively dispose of all property; but the person making the will is still called a *testator*.

An *heir* is a person who inherits property by will or operation of law. Since an heir does not come into being until someone's death, it is improper to speak of the heirs of the living.

LEND, LOAN

See BALANCE, REMAINDER

LESSER

See LITTLE, SMALL

LEST

More or Lest

It would be inaccurate to say, "Be with us yet, less we forget." *Less* in its primary use is the comparative form of *little.* The word needed is *lest,* meaning "in order that . . . not." Kipling said it correctly: "Lord God of Hosts, be with us yet, Lest we forget—lest we forget!"

Lest expresses a sense of fear or doubt, as in "The soldiers decided against leaving the compound *lest* they be spotted," which says in effect that the soldiers were fearful of being seen. As so used, *lest* acts as a subordinate conjunction introducing a clause that shows the reason for the apprehension or concern.

The verb form following *lest* is usually in the subjunctive, as in the examples given. However, a *should* or *would* construction is more natural. "Joe did not tell his neighbors about his good luck *lest* he be surrounded by 'friends' seeking a hand out" becomes "Joe did not tell his neighbors about his good luck for fear *that he would be.* . . ."

LIAR

See **EQUIVOCATOR, LIAR, PREVARICATOR**

LIBEL, SLANDER

You Don't Say

Did he say it or write it? The distinction between *libel* and *slander* lies not in their content but in the manner of their delivery. A *slander* is a false and malicious statement spoken to harm someone. A *libel* is a written and published statement that damages a person's reputation.

The sense of both *libel* and *slander* is defamation—that which is injurious to the character and reputation of another. *Slander* may consist of defamatory talk or malicious gossip; *libel* is defamation of character expressed by print, writing, pictures, or signs.

Defamatory recordings and broadcasts are libelous. Slander is restricted to other spoken utterances or gestures: "The broadcasts of Tokyo Rose were *libelous,* but what your neighbor said at dinner about the mayor was *slanderous.*"

LIE, LAY

See **LAY, LIE**

LIKE

See **AS, LIKE**

LINKING VERBS

See **BAD, BADLY**

LITTLE, SMALL

Chicken Little

Idiomatically a *little* can go a long way. Someone having "a little difficulty," for example, may be encountering more difficulty than was expected: "How are you doing?" "Well, I'm having a *little* trouble." "Not a little" indicates an even greater problem—"I must admit that our troubles are *not a little.*"

In any of its uses *little* refers to what is small in size, quantity, or degree. Its comparative and superlative forms, indicating what are smaller and smallest, are *littler* and *littlest* or, alternatively, *less* (or *lesser*) and *least.* Formal style and idiom have established different uses for these various terms. *Little* itself is distinguished from *small* by having the narrower meaning: "a sharp reduction from the average." *Littler* and *littlest,* perhaps because they connote marked diminutiveness, often sound childish and so are replaced by the more widely applicable *smaller* and *smallest* to denote relative size.

Less and *least* are the preferred forms for matters other than size—duration, quantity, or degree, for example. *Lesser,* an exact synonym of *less,* was once reserved for use as an adjective before a noun, as in "the lesser portion" or "the lesser price." This usage, now considered too formal for most contexts, is disappearing. Occasionally *lesser* is employed in contrast to "greater," referring to value ("the lesser of two sums") or to importance ("the lesser evil") or to extent ("to a lesser extent"). The obsolescence of *lesser* is not a great loss to the language, for the words *lower, fewer,* and *smaller* often serve more precisely where *lesser* was once standard: lower rent; fewer marbles; smaller shares or earnings.

Less and *least* mean "a *smaller* (or *the smallest*) amount" as in "less time, less bulk, less heat" and in "the least expense, the least noise, the least waste." When items are compared, *less* should be used of two ("Which of these two lamps is the *less* expensive?") and *least,* the superlative, of three or more ("We would like to climb the *least* steep hill in San Francisco.").

The expressions *much less* and *still less* are good descriptive phrases but are sometimes mistakenly used in reverse. For example, "It is difficult enough to listen to him, much less to agree with him" should be reworded *much more.* Spelled out, the phrase would read: "It is difficult to listen to him; it is *much more* difficult to agree with him." As a general rule, affirmative statements take *much more;* negative ones, *much less:* "Leona did not even examine the books, *much less* buy them." *Least,* too, is sometimes mistakenly used for its opposite number, *most.* In "Urbanites dislike subzero weather, *least* of all blizzards," what was meant was "Urbanites dislike blizzards *most* of all."

LIVID, LURID

What Will Hue Do

The sense of the statement "The senator turned *livid* when he saw those *lurid* campaign posters" is clear to most people. *Livid* means "red" and *lurid* means "sensational." But these popularly accepted definitions of the words bear no resemblance to their precise meanings—those demanded by formal English.

Livid does not mean "red"; it means "the black and blue coloring of flesh that has received a contusion" or "the color of lead." In Latin, *lividus,* the root of the word *livid,* means "bluish" or "leaden-colored." If the face of a man in a rage turns livid, it becomes ashen rather than reddish, for *livid* has come to mean "pallid or gray." It is the grayish hue of death. All colors compounded with livid (livid brown, livid pink, livid purple, livid violet) have a grayish tone.

Lurid is pale yellow. A face described as lurid is wan. Its hue is ghastly. *Lurid,* like *livid,* is a color reminiscent of death. Today, because one with a ghastly pallor suggests aspects of death, *lurid* has come to be equated with *ghastly* in the sense of "gruesome." In informal language shocking occurrences are called *lurid,* especially by those intrigued by the phrase "lurid details." Through further extension, *lurid* has come to mean freakish activities or weirdly glaring, like the flashing multicolored lights found in some discotheques. What is meant is "so sensational as to be mind-boggling."

LORELEI

See FOREIGN WORDS

LOTS

See A LOT OF

LURID

See LIVID, LURID

LUXURIANT, LUXURIOUS

Super Deluxe

Although both *luxuriant* and *luxurious* stem from the Latin word *luxus*, "abundance," their meanings differ greatly. The first means "lush, thick, or growing abundantly"—something prolific or flourishing, as a luxuriant beard or a luxuriant symphonic style. The second implies luxury—a style of life identified with sumptuousness, costly comfort, and elegance. A dwelling, an automobile, a gown, or even a meal may be a luxurious thing. Jungle foliage is luxuriant, not luxurious; a Park Avenue apartment is luxurious, not luxuriant.

Words related to *luxurious,* found mostly in informal usage, are *posh* and *ritzy.* They originally described the ultrafashionable elegance reserved for the famous, the wealthy, and their hangers-on. Currently, however, the words are used of elegant affairs or accommodations.

It is said that *posh* is an acronym for "Port Out, Starboard Home." The coinage, so the story goes, developed when the British Empire was at its height and travel to and from India by steamer was common. To enjoy the most comfortable quarters available, away from the tropical sun, preferred guests were assigned cabins on the port side outwardbound and on the starboard side homebound. Now that's *posh!*

Ritzy is less flattering than *posh.* What is *ritzy* is considered ostentatiously fashionable, as in "putting on the ritz." Another meaning is "snobbish, haughty": "For a barmaid she's acting awfully *ritzy.*" The word derives from Cesar Ritz, the Swiss entrepreneur and founder of many fine hotels, including the Ritz-Carlton in New York City.

M

MAD

Mad Dogs and Englishmen

The word *mad* means "insane" or "frenzied." It suggests mental abnormality, a disorder of the mind. A mad man is insane; mad activities are frenzied; a mad scheme is senseless. As applied to dogs, *mad* means afflicted with rabies.

The expressions *mad about* and *mad over* are informal. One who says "I'm *mad about* chopped liver," meaning it is a favorite dish, or "I'm *mad over* Agatha Christie," meaning that her mystery stories never cease to fascinate him, uses colloquial language. "He ran *like mad,*" "He talks *like mad,*" and all the other *like mad* similes are slang.

Many words may replace *mad* in its everyday conversational sense of annoyance. For example, a person may be *irritated, exacerbated, chagrined,* or *vexed* by his accountant's miscalculations. Or he may be *disappointed* in or *dismayed* by his son's report card. He may be *angered* or *piqued* by a failure to receive an increase in salary. In any event, he is mad only if deranged.

MAJORITY

A Majority of Two

The several senses of the word *majority* should be clearly distinguished. Strictly speaking, it indicates the numerically larger part of two numbers considered as parts of a whole, as in "The *majority* of the cups on the tray have broken ears." *Majority* is properly used there, for it refers to a numerically divisible number that exceeds half the total. But it is wrongly used in "The *majority* of his research was aimlessly conducted," for *research* is an abstract, uncountable term. ("The majority" could be acceptably replaced by "The major part.")

178

In elections, *majority* means at least one more than half the total votes cast. Assuming that one candidate received twelve votes and the other ten, one may say "The winner had a slim *majority*" or "He had a *majority* of two."

Although colloquially *majority* is used as a synonym for *most* (as in "A *majority* of the land is arid" or in "The assistant did the *majority* of the work"), on a formal level it is applied to groups of at least three countable things or to the greater part of a number of things. For example, it may refer to the majority of the stockholders or to the majority of automobiles in a parking lot. It should not be employed when counting is impossible or when *most* would serve more logically or economically. Rough estimates are best given as *most, many,* or *the greater part:* "*Most* (not *The majority*) of the apples were ruined by the severe storm," but "A *majority* of the members voted to strike." "*The greater part* (not *The majority*) of the valley was inundated."

Majority is followed by a singular verb when the reference, whether stated or implied, is to a specific number: "The majority *is* five votes." "His majority *was* surprisingly small." Like other collective nouns, *majority* is normally plural when it refers to the individual members of a group: "The majority *are* taking different paths." It is singular when oneness is meant: "The majority *has* decided to terminate the session." When *majority* is followed by an *of* phrase, denoting most of the described group, it is plural: "The majority of the officers *are* planning to leave early."

Although the expression *great majority* is an accepted idiom, the *greater majority* and the *greatest majority* are not. They are incorrect forms of intensification.

Majority should not be confused with *plurality*. In a field of three or more candidates, if no one receives a majority of the vote, the one with the highest vote-count wins by a plurality. If, of 900 votes cast, the tally shows 400 for Ralph, 300 for Herb, and 200 for Mac, Ralph has garnered the winning vote with a plurality of 100—the difference between the number of his votes and that of the second highest vote-getter.

MALAPROPOS

See **APROPOS, MALAPROPOS**

MANAGE

See HANDLE, MANAGE

MARGINAL

Oleomarginal

There are so many synonyms for *small, narrow,* and *slight* that creating another one, *marginal,* is unnecessary. *Marginal* is a term in economics pertaining to a sale of goods that, at existing prices, barely covers costs. In general usage its meaning is "near the lower limits." That which is on the threshold of making do may be said to be *marginal.* From *margin* comes *marginalia,* used to refer to notes written in a margin or on a border of a sheet of paper. By extension, what falls on either side of a borderline may be called *marginal* (such as a marginal profit, which scarcely puts a company in the black).

The equating of *marginal* with "small" has been fostered by those writers who exploit vogue words, but it is better to be accurate than fashionable. For example, *small* is preferable in "The cost of repairing the garage was *marginal.*" *Slight* is better in "The doctor remarked on the *marginal* improvement in the patient's health." And *minimal* is clearer in "The theft of supplies at army depots is *marginal.*"

The adverbial form of *marginal* has been infected, too. For example, if one says "I passed the course *marginally,*" *barely* is meant. In "The system will improve only *marginally* if we change methods now," *slightly* is preferable.

The noun *margin,* meaning an outer part or edge, is synonymous with border: the margin or border of a page; the margin or border of a sheet of stamps. *Margin* also refers to geographical description: living at the margin of the forest, of a lake, of a glacier. Figuratively it denotes "something over and above what is strictly necessary," such as a margin for safety or for error; that is, a provision for emergencies. On the other hand, a margin may be a minimum standard of desirability: living on the margin of good taste, of respectability, of ethical conduct.

Some sportscasters habitually confuse the words *margin* and *score.* For example, *score* is called for in "The Mapleleafs defeated the Rangers by a three-to-one *margin.*" The word *margin* is correctly expressed only in a single number: "The Mapleleafs won by a two-goal *margin.*"

MARVEL, MIRACLE

Mirabile Dictu

A spectator who exclaims "That catch was a miracle" makes the catch seem supernatural, although probably no religious association was intended. Some people, however, see a divine spirit in every happening, particularly if it is fortunate: "My son's escape from the inferno was a miracle."

A more suitable word to signify something astonishing (that which evokes wonder or even admiration) is *marvel,* used either as a noun ("Yehudi Menuhin at age seven was a *marvel*") or as a verb ("People *marveled* at Menuhin's ability when he was only seven years old"). When used in its adjective form, *marvelous,* meaning "pleasant or splendid," it is a colloquialism, for it does not describe an event of wonder.

What constitutes a *miracle* is a matter of dispute. An event that cannot be explained by available information, especially in terms of the laws of nature, may be called a miracle—or simply a wonderment. Whether qualities that surpass human powers and knowledge should be ascribed to it depends on a person's attitude.

Marvel in other forms is spelled *marveled, marveling,* and *marvelous.* The final *l* is doubled only in Britain. The adjective form of *miracle* is *miraculous.*

MATERIALIZE

Mind over Material

The sense of *materialize* in "Nothing worth reporting *materialized* at the meeting" extends beyond good usage. The word is best employed to suggest that something will assume material form ("an investing of something nonmaterial with material attributes") or become physically perceptible ("At the seance, the medium expected the dear departed to *materialize*").

Figuratively something materializes when it evolves from the insubstantial to the substantial, as would be a tangible result from hopes, dreams, or plans. Using *materialize* as a substitute for "happen, occur, appear, or come about," however, is poor style. The following sentences are therefore not well expressed: "Despite the grumbling, walkouts never *materialized*" (took place). "Fortunately, the rain did not *materialize*" (happen).

Materialize is used correctly in "Herman's long-range plans finally *materialized* yesterday" and in "His dreams of becoming a commissioner *materialized* when the governor appointed him." Certainly a man is ill-advised who says, "I waited for two hours, but my wife failed to *materialize*"—unless she's a ghost.

MATERIALLY

See CHIEFLY, LARGELY, GREATLY, MATERIALLY

MAY

See CAN, MAY

MEAN

See AVERAGE, MEAN, MEDIAN

MEANWHILE

Meanwhile Back at the Ranch

Meanwhile, which means "during the interval," is an adverb in "*Meanwhile* he studied hard." It is a noun in "In the *meanwhile* he studied hard," but the phrase of which it is a part sounds clumsy and is not recommended. *Meantime* would be preferable. In "In the *meantime* he studied hard," *meantime* is the anchor word in an adverbial phrase. Whether it may be used solely as an adverb (as in "*Meantime* he studied hard") is a matter of controversy. Most authorities would say no. A good rule to follow is to regard *meanwhile* as an adverb only and *meantime* only as a noun.

The Latin phrase *ad interim* means "meanwhile" or "in the meantime." It applies to appointments that enable a department or agency to continue its work after someone's death or resignation pending confirmation or election of a successor. *In the interim*, when referring to an intervening period, is proper English. The word *interim* has been completely absorbed into the language and should not be italicized.

MEDIA, MEMENTO

Finding a Happy Medium

The meanings of *media* and *memento* mislead no one, but how to use the one and how to spell the other are often sources of confusion.

Media is the Latin plural form for *medium*. Its anglicized plural is *mediums*, which may replace *media* in any of its uses. But since the word *mediums* also refers to people who are clairvoyant, it is generally restricted to that use. The common error with *media* (referring to radio, television, and the press) is associating it with a singular verb, as in "The media *was* impressed by the candidate's oratory." Formal English maintains the distinction in number between *medium* and *media*. Perhaps one day *media* will be considered a group acting as an individual unit— a collective noun—and will then take a singular verb. But that day has not yet arrived.

Saying "A *momento* in the form of a plaque was presented to the media because it has ferreted out corruption on high levels of government" incorrectly spells *memento* and, in deference to the preceding paragraph, also errs in using *it has* for *they have* (media *have*). A mnemonic device that might aid in the correct spelling of *memento* is to think of *memory*, which is what *mementos* refresh. Both *memento* and *memory* begin with the same letters.

MEDIAN

See AVERAGE, MEAN, MEDIAN

MEMENTO

See MEDIA, MEMENTO

MERETRICIOUS

There's No Merit in Meretricious

Meretricious sounds like a glamorous word, but it is not. And it is unrelated to *meritorious*, which means "deserving of praise." The original forebear of *meretricious* was *meretrix*, "harlot." Although the word is no longer associated with courtesans, it suggests the traits of prostitutes or, more figuratively, of something deceitfully attractive or ornamental. Defined as "luring to a bad end (a bed end?) by false attractions," *meretricious* implies more than mere tawdriness—there is a concealment of something base or evil. The word is used, especially in law, to describe the relationship of a man and woman who live together but are not married to each other. In today's parlance this relationship, instead of *meretricious*, is called "meaningful."

METAPHORS

See FIGURES OF SPEECH

MIGHT

See CAN, MAY

MILITATE, MITIGATE

A Fence Mit a Gate

Many people would not find this statement curious: "I have been told that my absences will not mitigate against my appointment." Or this one either: "The fact that he is a Southerner mitigated unfairly against him." The word needed instead of *mitigate* was, of course, *militate*, "to affect or operate against": "The change in weather militated *against* a large attendance." "The obstinacy of some of the ministers militated *against* a prompt settlement."

Militate has a negative connotation; that is, something does not function or perform so well because of what militates against it. A minor school of thought sanctions its use in affirmative statements: "These facts militate *in favor* of his chances for election." But the word is seldom so employed.

The word *mitigate*, unlike *militate*, is never followed by *against*. It comes from the Latin *mitigare*, "to make soft, kind, or gentle," and means "to lessen or alleviate" in the sense of "to reduce the effect of, to make less severe": "Her gentle ways *mitigated* the anger rising within him." Often it is associated with a punishment, indicating a reduction of or a leniency. A judge, while imposing a milder sentence than the offense calls for, may say, "In the light of the defendant's cooperation, I will *mitigate* the sentence." A synonym is *to moderate*.

MILLION

What's a Million More or Less

Considering the rate of inflation, people will soon become accustomed to replacing *thousand* with *million*. Governments routinely use *billion*, which was only a theoretical figure in the nineteenth century.

A *million* is a thousand thousand or, more suitably expressed, 1,000 thousand. Sums of money that would be unwieldy if spelled out or given in figures may be expressed as in the following examples: "The costs now exceed 169 million dollars." "Increasing the budget by 2 million dollars can improve living conditions for 20 million people." Less formal is the figure accompanied by a dollar sign, which replaces the word *dollars*: "The museum paid $2.5 million for its latest acquisition."

Whether *million* is used in a singular or plural form depends on idiom. When a specific number is mentioned, especially in reference to money, the singular is required: "The school board budgeted four *million* dollars." In this case an accompanying verb is also singular: "Four million dollars *was* budgeted by the school board." In the absence of a preceding number, the plural form *millions* is used, followed by *of* and, if need be, a plural verb: "*Millions of* birds *are* in the forest." "There *were millions of* counterfeit bills to burn." When fractions are used with millions, the preferred style is *a million and a quarter* rather than *one and a quarter million; three million and a half* rather than *three and a half million*. When preceded by *few*, *million* is usually an adjective (*a few million votes*), but it is always a noun when preceded by *many* (*many millions of people*).

The word *billion* takes the same constructions that *million* does. A billion is one thousand million, a number followed by nine zeros: 1,000,000,000. (In Britain, a billion is a million million, and a thousand million is called a *milliard*.)

MIRACLE

See **MARVEL, MIRACLE**

MISHAP

See **ACCIDENT, MISHAP**

MISTAKE

Double Talk

The sentence "The teacher addressed the class in *no unmistakable* language" contains a not uncommon error. The phrase *no unmistakable* is a double negative meaning "mistakable." Certainly the intended meaning was not that the teacher spoke in mistakable language. Even a correct assemblage of these words—"no mistakable language"—is not entirely clear. It is best to say "The teacher addressed the class in language that was not mistakable" (but not to spell it *mistakeable*).

To *mistake* is to err or to commit a fault. The past participle of *mistake* is *mistaken*. One who is in error about, say, the direction to take or the day of the week is mistaken. But one who is not understood is, in the opinion of many grammarians, *misunderstood*, not *mistaken*. A person who misinterprets an announcement is mistaken; the announcement has been misunderstood.

MISUSED WORDS

An Alibi Is No Excuse

During the Watergate Affair *impeach* became a household word. Many people thought that *impeach* meant "remove" or "convict" and that Nixon, if impeached, would lose his pension rights. That was not so. *Impeach* means "to charge." One who has been impeached—charged with a crime—has not been proven guilty by virtue of the charge, and therefore forfeits no rights unless subsequently tried and convicted. Andrew Johnson, the seventeenth President of the United States, was impeached in 1868 by the House of Representatives. He was tried in the Senate and acquitted by a margin of one vote.

Another word often used carelessly is *alibi.* In colloquial speech it frequently replaces the noun "excuse" ("What is your *alibi* for coming late?") or the verb "to justify" ("You cannot *alibi* such conduct"). In formal writing *alibi* (in Latin *alius,* "another," and *ibi,* "in that place") must denote its literal meaning, "a plea or fact of having been elsewhere when an offense was committed," as in "The defendant's *alibi* is that at the time of the kidnapping, he was in Cincinnati."

Using *hung* for *hanged,* referring to capital punishment, is a misusage. A person is hanged, not hung, by the neck; Christmas stockings and paintings are hung.

The use of *collide* has been subject to some dispute. Strictly speaking, a collision is a coming together of two moving objects. An accident between a moving and a stationary vehicle, therefore, is not a collision, although in general usage a truck that rams the side of a barn is said to be in a collision. When an actual collision does occur—that is, two moving vehicles strike each other—it is redundant to say they collided *together.* Inherent in *collide* is a coming together.

MITIGATE

See **MILITATE, MITIGATE**

MODERATE, MODEST

Mod Is Neither Moderate Nor Modest

Whatever is *moderate* or *modest* is neither extreme nor excessive. On the contrary, it is something that is held within reasonable bounds, limited in scope or effect. It may be medium, mediocre, or temperate. One who lives modestly, for example, lives moderately. A person whose talent is not outstanding has moderate or modest talent.

Just as money can change people, so, too, it can change the meanings of these "mod" words. A moderate charge is a reasonable charge, but a modest charge is lower than is customary. A student might get along handily on a moderate allowance but struggle to make ends meet on a modest one.

Applied to persons, *modest* indicates a lack of egotism. A modest person is not boastful nor vain nor ostentatious nor extravagant: "Albert Einstein was a *modest* man; he accepted no awards or emoluments for his remarkable contributions to man's knowledge." A moderate person is fair-minded, temperate in speech and behavior: "Adlai Stevenson was known to be a person of *moderate* habits."

One who is modest is not necessarily *shy.* A shy person is timid and bashful, afraid to assert himself: "Jerry was so *shy* that he fled from the party to avoid making a dinner speech." A modest person has a humble opinion of his abilities; he is unassuming, unpretending. A shy person lacks confidence; he is diffident and oversensitive.

MOMENTARILY, MOMENTLY

Moment to Moment

Many dictionaries equate *momently* (a seldom heard word) with the commonly heard *momentarily.* But those words, strictly speaking, are not interchangeable; and the moribund state of *momently* is costing the English language a useful term.

Momentarily means "for a moment" or "for a short time." It is appropriately employed to convey a sense of short duration, as in "I was *momentarily* shocked." When the meaning shifts to "from moment to moment" or "at any moment," that thought is best expressed by *momently.* "We expect him *momently,*" for example, implies that he is expected soon, from one moment to another. *Momentarily,* however, has usurped this sense. Today it is usual to find *momentarily* meaning "at any moment," too. Unfortunately, while *momentarily* continues to thrive, the state of *momently* is so weak that its demise is expected momently.

The adjectives *momentary* and *momentous,* except for their first two syllables, bear no relationship to each other. The first means "lasting for a moment" ("We suffered only *momentary* inconvenience"); the second, "weighty or of great importance" ("The first walk on the moon was a *momentous* event").

MORE THAN, ONE OR MORE

One More, Please

Although the idiom *one or more* begins with the singular pronoun *one,* it takes a plural verb: "*One or more* of the waitresses *have* been sick every day this week." "*One or more* of the officers from Paulsboro *have* been hunting the fugitive." Yet the idiom *more than,* despite its plural sense, takes a singular verb if the following noun is singular: "*More than* one plan at a time *is* confusing." And although "More than one dollar *was* spent," "More dollars than one *were* spent."

MOST

See ALMOST, MOST

MS.

Madame X

As the courtesy title *Ms.* gains in popularity, the controversy surrounding its use becomes more heated. Designed to be as noncommital as *Mr.* is for men, *Ms.* is meant to be used for women regardless of their marital status. But many people object to it—some because of its harsh sound (pronounced *mizz*), some because it supplants two titles they prefer, *Mrs.* and *Miss,* and some because it is a fake abbreviation.

If a woman's preference for a courtesy title is unknown, how can one address her formally and tactfully? Should it be *Mrs., Miss,* or *Ms.*? The safe form of address has long been *Miss* on the theory that since all women once were *Misses,* it could not be offensive. The trend now, however, at least in America, is toward *Ms.* But *Ms.* still runs the risk of displeasing those who resent this newly created title. In Britain, there is a movement away from it. *The London Times* has officially banned *Ms.* in favor of *Mrs.* and *Miss,* saying that *Ms.* is "artificial, ugly, silly, means nothing and is rotten English."

One way around the controversy is to use *Madame,* borrowed from the French. Any woman in France may properly be so addressed, regardless of her marital status, even though *Madame* is specifically applicable to a married woman and *Mademoiselle* to a single woman. Several women together are addressed as *Mesdames* if married, or as *Mesdemoiselles* if unmarried. In English *Madame* (with the *e*) is the correct form for use without a surname, especially in addressing professional women, as in "Madame, may I introduce you to our new salesman." With a title of rank or office, *Madam* (without the *e*) is the proper style:

"Madam Vice President."

MUSICAL TERMS

See FOREIGN WORDS

MUST

See OUGHT, SHOULD

MYSTERIOUS

Mystery's Mystique

Many English words denote something not readily explained or comprehended, whether it is awesome, confusing, or frightening. The word with the widest application, and the one most commonly used, is *mysterious*. It means "full of mystery," *mystery* referring to what is unknown or puzzling.

Mysterious things or occurrences defy human reason and thus arouse curiosity or awe—primarily curiosity: "Many people are fascinated by the *mysterious* smile of the Mona Lisa." "My neighbor had a *mysterious* visitor last night." Although *mysterious* is used in different positions—as a predicate adjective ("The Sheik looks *mysterious*") or as an attributive adjective before a noun ("God moves in *mysterious* ways")—the word *mystery*, as an adjective, may serve only in the latter position and then only in such established phrases as mystery novel, mystery play, or mystery cult. Except as so used, adjectival *mystery* seldom serves well. The sentence "She is a *mystery* woman" is more appropriately worded, "She is a woman of mystery" or ". . . a mysterious woman."

Mystic and *mystical* both describe that which is spiritually significant without being apparent to the senses or easily grasped by the intellect. The word *mystic*, however, is a slightly more formal adjective and is also commonly used of occult practices: "A *mystic* communion among the dead and the living." "The *mystical* significance of religious symbols is inexplicable." Followers of a mystical way of life are known as *mystics*.

NAMES

Capitalize on Junior

Since there is nothing more personal than a person's own name, a name should be written in the manner preferred by the nameholder, even if it looks informal, as does Mike McQueen or B. Chas. Keats.

Ordinarily a name should not be abbreviated in formal writing. Richard Thompson may be called Dick or Rick by the writer, but the given name Richard is the only proper one to use where a dignified style is called for. And although Samuel Clemens frequently used Sam'l Clemens, a stranger certainly has no license to spell it that way.

Courtesy dictates that the abbreviation for "Junior" or "Senior" be capitalized when it is part of a fully spelled out personal name—that is, a given name or initials with the surname: "The chairmen for the event were Mr. Maxwell Haupt, Jr., and Mr. L. T. Shepherd, Sr." Whether to set off *Jr.* or *Sr.* with commas, as in the preceding example, is a question of style. In general, commas are preferred. When a name is written without a given name or initial, *Jr.* or *Sr.* is omitted: "We saw both Mr. Haupt and Mr. Shepherd later that evening."

The designations "Second" and "Third" following a name are written in Roman numerals (II, III, IV) or in ordinal numbers (2d [or 2nd], 3d [3rd], 4th), depending on personal preference. Roman numerals look better without commas; ordinal numbers need them: "We were addressed by Archibald R. Maxey II and his associate, R. B. Worthington, 2d."

NAUSEATED, NAUSEOUS

Ad Nauseam

People are frequently heard to say, upon becoming ill, that they feel nauseous. Perhaps a sick person should not have his

191

grammar questioned; he needs another kind of examination. But writers who write that way are not so kindly regarded.

A person with a queasy sensation is not *nauseous* but *nauseated,* which means "feeling sickness." *Nauseous* means "causing nausea." Anything that is repulsive—that turns one's stomach—is nauseous. It may be a bumpy ride in an airplane or fumes from a leaking gas line. One exposed to something *nauseous* becomes *nauseated.* If he were nauseous, he would make other people sick.

NAUTICAL TERMS

Knot So Fast

References to the sea should be expressed in pertinent terms. Clearly, one who says "The boat when under weigh steamed out of the harbor at 15 knots per hour" must be a landlubber.

Most vessels that travel the sea lanes are properly called *ships,* not *boats.* Small open vessels (those propelled by oars or sails) are boats. Some boats are motor driven; others are not so small—ferry boats, for instance. But seagoing craft that steam out of a harbor are ships.

A vessel that is moving is under way, not under weigh. In nautical language, *weigh* means "to lift." The ship's anchor must be weighed or hauled up before the ship can make any progress. Once the anchor is raised (weighed), the ship is under way. The words *weigh* and *way* are sometimes confused because they are pronounced alike and have associated functions.

The expression "15 knots per hour" is redundant. A *knot* is a measure of speed, which incorporates the sense of "per hour." One need say only 15 knots. This means that in one hour the ship will have traveled 15 nautical miles. For those concerned with measurements, it may be noted that a sea mile is slightly longer than a land mile, 6080 feet compared to 5280 feet. It is equally wrong to consider a knot a measure of distance. A ship will not travel 15 knots, say, in one hour. If it is moving at 15 knots, it will cover, as was previously shown, 15 nautical miles in an hour.

The word *knot,* referring to speed, originated from the kind of knot one makes with a string or rope. The speed of ships used to be calculated by reeling into the water a hogline divided by knots into 120 parts, each the same part of a nautical mile as a half minute is of an hour. In yesteryear measuring nautical speed was a knotty problem.

NÉE

Mistaken Identities

Née, which comes from *nâitre*, "to be born," is often used in wedding announcements to identify the bride by her maiden name: "Mrs. Mildred R. Gaines, *née* Blanck." Since *née* signifies a family name—the only name that a baby has at birth (the given name comes later)—it is illogical to say, "Mildred R. Gaines, *née* Mildred Blanck." Although *née* may be spelled without an acute accent on the first *e*, formal stylists prefer it. *Née* is pronounced *nay*, as is its rarely seen masculine form, *né*.

NEED

See LACK, NEED, WANT

NEEDLESS TO SAY

Take Nothing for Granted

Purists challenge the suitability of the expression *it goes without saying*, contending that what can go without saying is best left unsaid. *Needless to say* is also objected to on similar grounds. Why use it, the argument goes, when the information is immediately forthcoming? Perhaps *naturally* or *of course* would be better; at least they are shorter expressions. But the longer phrases do serve as a warning that a forthcoming statement—the one that "goes without saying" or is "needless to say"—must be understood as the groundwork for what follows. As a device to introduce this basic information—a clearing of the air, as it were—these phrases are useful. One should be cautious, however, not to employ them simply as "fillers," but that goes without saying.

NEITHER . . . NOR

See CORRELATIVE CONJUNCTIONS

NEOPHYTE

See AMATEUR

NEPOTISM, SALARY, SINECURE

My Nephew's Not Worth His Salt

Nepotism is favoritism shown to relatives, especially in political or business affairs. It is an appointment based on relationship rather than on merit.

The origin of nepotism may be found in the acts of early popes who conferred special favors on their natural children, referred to euphemistically as nephews. The word *nephew* (from the Latin *nepos*) had formerly meant "descendant," referring to a grandson. Today, of course, the term *nephew* denotes the son of one's sister or brother, and *nepotism* is favoritism shown to any family member or close friend. One who practices nepotism is a *nepotist*.

A nepotic appointment is likely to be a *sinecure,* a position requiring little or no work or responsibility. The word *sinecure* means "without a care" (Latin *sine,* "without," and *cura,* "care"). But *cura,* by itself, is a word of service. From it came terms such as *curate* (one entrusted with the care of souls) and *curator* (one entrusted with the care of museum collections). *Sinecure* is pronounced *sy-nih-kyoor.*

The *salary* paid in these and other cases is a word derived from the Latin *salarium.* Originally a *salarium* was an allowance given Roman soldiers to buy *sal* (Latin for salt), since salt was regarded as essential to their diet. From this practice evolved the expressions "not worth one's salt," meaning that a poor performance merited no salarium, and "to be below the salt," which designated an inferior social position. This latter phrase developed as a matter of seating arrangements. The precious salt was kept in saltcellars on the table from which the king and his dignitaries ate. The less important courtiers sat at a table lower than the king's. That they were in a less favored position was made clear, since they were seated "below the salt."

NEVERTHELESS, NONETHELESS, NOTWITHSTANDING

No More, No Less

Nevertheless is synonymous with *notwithstanding*, but the two words differ in connotation. *Nevertheless* implies weak concession: "The restaurant was noisy and poorly ventilated; *nevertheless*, the food was excellent." *Notwithstanding* presupposes stronger opposition, modification, or contrast. The sons of Plantagenet use it emphatically in Shakespeare's *Henry VI*, proclaiming that they "Should *notwithstanding* join our lights together / And over-shine the earth. . . ."

As adverbs, except for emphasis, they contribute little or nothing to the sense of the sentence; but they do serve usefully as other parts of speech. As a preposition or a conjunction, *notwithstanding* accentuates a contrasting thought. The preposition means "in spite of," as in "*Notwithstanding* expensive marketing, the new line is still not selling." The conjunction means "although": "The architect, *notwithstanding* he had forgotten his blueprints, delivered a fine lecture." The Latin equivalent of *notwithstanding* is *non obstante,* which in law usually accompanies *veredicto,* meaning a judgment that has been entered notwithstanding the verdict.

When defined as "not any the less," *nevertheless* comes into contrast with *nonetheless,* which means "not the less." Although not exact synonyms, the distinctions between them are so nebulous that, for all practical purposes, they are interchangeable. This is so in "We did not win; *nevertheless* (or *nonetheless*) we enjoyed ourselves." Sentences are made lighter, however, if these words are replaced by *but, still, yet,* or *however.*

The conjunction *albeit,* which derives from Middle English, "let it be entirely (that)," although obsolescent, is nevertheless useful when *notwithstanding, though,* or *although* does not supply the right feeling. It should be remembered, however, that *albeit* has a literary tone that is not always suitable.

NOISOME, NOXIOUS, OBNOXIOUS

Hold Your Breath

Because *noxious* and *obnoxious* derive from a common Latin root (*noxa,* meaning "harm"), the words are sometimes interchangeable. An ill-smelling gas, for example, may be described as either *noxious* or *obnoxious* (*obnoxious* originally meant—with its prefix *ob*, "in the way of"—"exposed to harm or evil").

Specifically, *noxious* denotes that which is injurious either to health (noxious fumes, noxious dust) or, in a figurative sense, to morals (noxious excesses, noxious lies). *Obnoxious* today means "offensive or odious," as in "If he were less *obnoxious*, he would be a better salesman." A sweet but deadly vapor, although not obnoxious, is noxious. On the other hand, an obnoxious vapor need not be noxious. Informally *noxious* suggests the "highly disagreeable": noxious neighbors, noxious situations. But only *obnoxious* refers to objectionable behavior or acts, such as drunkenness or brawling.

Another word that raises a feeling of repugnance is *noisome*. It pertains, not to noise, but to unpleasant and disagreeable odors. *Noxious* is sometimes mistakenly interchanged with it, but *noisome* implies that an odor is offensive (manure, garbage), not harmful. *Noisome* is more akin to *obnoxious* for either may suggest what is malodorous (as in "the *noisome* [or *obnoxious*] practice of dumping garbage into a stream").

NONE

See INDEFINITE PRONOUNS

NONETHELESS

See NEVERTHELESS, NONETHELESS, NOTWITHSTANDING

NONRESTRICTIVE CLAUSES

See THAT, WHICH

NOR

Nothing More Nor Less

Nor is seen most often as the second half of the correlative conjunction *neither . . . nor:* "He *neither* dances *nor* sings." It is the negative counterpart of *or* in *either . . . or.*

A question sometimes raised is whether *nor* or *or* should follow the words *no* and *not.* The answer depends on whether the sentence conveys one thought or embraces two or more ideas. A single negative idea expressed in two parts creates no problem. It takes *or:* "He enjoys *no* money *or* goodwill." "He has *not* a dime *or* even a pocket to put one in." The negative effect of *no* and *not* carries through with no change in sentence structure: "no money, no goodwill"; "not a dime, not even a pocket." Other examples are "They need *never* visit us, *or* write us, *or* even notice us" (*never* visit, *never* write, *never* notice) and "He added *nothing* useful *or* even sensible" (*nothing* useful, *nothing* sensible).

But if the negative force is so restricted that its effect is felt in only a part of the sentence, *nor* is required: "He thinks *nothing* of spending his money, *nor* is he concerned about spending other peoples' money." "We *no* longer visit each other, *nor* do we ever meet accidentally." In these examples each segment expresses a different idea. Hence the same negative cannot be applied throughout—*nothing is he concerned* and *no do we ever meet* make no sense.

NORMALCY

Normalcy—The Unknown State

President Warren G. Harding was wrongly chided for having invented the word *normalcy* when he used it in 1920 in a speech calling for a return to normal conditions. He said that America needed "not nostrums, but normalcy." Intellectuals ridiculed him for an unnecessary coinage, but they need not have scoffed at him, for the word had long been listed in many dictionaries. In fact, the history of *normalcy* antedates the Civil War.

Nevertheless, *normalcy* has never been fully accepted. Until this day, some dictionaries reject it, asserting that it was an irregularly formed word. Others deride it as a needless alternative for *normality,* since both words mean "the state of being normal." Between the two, the better choice is *normality.*

NOT ONLY ... BUT ALSO

Verbal Symmetry

Not only ... but also is a set of correlative conjunctions like *either ... or, neither ... nor,* and *whether ... or.* Such conjunctions connect phrases of equal grammatical value (*See* CORRELATIVE CONJUNCTIONS).

Not only . . . but also lends itself best to formal usage, in which careful planning is more likely. It makes emphasis explicit: "The prosecutor made the mistake of questioning the witness's credentials. As he then learned, she was *not only* a medical doctor *but also* a leading specialist in radiation therapy." The use of *also* is optional. If omitted, the word following *but* is made more emphatic: "Washington is *not only* the largest city I visited this year *but* the cleanest." "Fred is *not only* unemployed *but* bankrupt." Without *also,* the words *cleanest* and *bankrupt* receive greater stress.

When *and* can serve as well as the wordier, heavier *not only . . . but also,* it is preferable. For example, although "*Not only* the promotion *but also* the financing was his responsibility" is expressed correctly, *and* would be as clear and yet more economical: "The promotion *and* financing were his responsibility."

NOTWITHSTANDING

See NEVERTHELESS, NONETHELESS, NOTWITHSTANDING

NOUNS AS VERBS OR ADJECTIVES

Write It Strong

Many nouns are easily adapted to verbal use. This practice of conversion has long been established and is not objectionable. But what is best avoided is converting a noun into a verb merely for its startling effect. Saying "Foster *banqueted* his fraternity" is a case in point, as is "Seidel *chaired* the meeting." The first example should be recast entirely. In the second, *chaired* should be changed to "presided over." (*See also* BACK FORMATIONS.)

Nouns used as adjectives add a facility to the language. A sick person may wear a *bed jacket* while getting *bed rest.* Children given *television time* may learn of *storm warnings.* And in technical writing, noun combinations are indispensable. But unnecessary combinations of noun-adjectives should be guarded against, especially in literary writings. "We will report on the freshman-sophomore problems" is not only stilted but imprecise. For-mations such as "the sociological procedure study seminars," those in which a noun modifies two or more polysyllabic nouns, are particularly awkward and cumbersome. Much more readable is "the study for the seminars on sociological procedure."

If, when selecting a modifier, there is a choice between an adjective and a noun, the adjective form ordinarily is to be preferred (for example, *governmental action* rather than *government action*). It should be noted, however, that the meanings of some adjectives and nouns vary considerably; for instance, an ethics teacher is not necessarily an ethical teacher any more than a sanitation director is a sanitary director.

NOVICE

See AMATEUR

NOXIOUS

See NOISOME, NOXIOUS, OBNOXIOUS

NUMBERS

See FIGURES, NUMBERS and MILLION

(The word *number* as a noun is discussed under COLLECTIVE NOUNS.)

OBJECTIVE COMPLEMENTS

See INDIRECT OBJECTS, OBJECTIVE COMPLEMENTS

OBLIVIOUS

Forget Me Not

Seldom is *oblivious* used in its original narrow sense, "forgetful of something known in the past" or "lacking remembrance." In current usage it has acquired a broader sense—"unaware" or "unconscious." When employed according to its original tenor, *oblivious* takes *of:* "*Oblivious of* their past misfortunes, the explorers set out anew." In its popular connotation, it takes *of* or *to:* "*Oblivious of* their dilapidated surroundings, the children ate the food greedily." "After Henry was struck on the head, he was *oblivious to* the world." In a more formal style those sentences would be rephrased, "*Unaware* of their surroundings . . . ," in the first example, and ". . . he was *unconscious*," in the second.

Which brings up the difference between *aware* and *conscious*. One who is aware of something recognizes its existence, having become cognizant of it either through perception (*aware* of his torn coat) or through information (*aware* through a news broadcast of a storm brewing). Although *aware* and *conscious* are related terms, the distinction between them is that a person is *aware* of what goes on around him but is *conscious* of what is felt within. For example, although a man may be aware of his wife's anger, he is conscious of his own.

OBNOXIOUS

See NOISOME, NOXIOUS, OBNOXIOUS

OBTAIN, PREVAIL

Prevailing Wordage

Although the word *obtain* is synonymous with *prevail,* as in "The same opinion *obtains* with each specialist" or "*prevails* among specialists," a simpler phraseology is "Each specialist *has* the same opinion." In "It is a custom that still *obtains* among us," *prevails* would sound less stilted, but better yet would be "*is* still with us."

Prevail has many definitions and takes many prepositions. When it means "to triumph," it takes *over* or *against·* "The Liberals will *prevail over* the Conservatives." When it means "to succeed in persuading someone," it takes *on, upon,* or *with :* "One cannot always *prevail upon* his roommate to lend an extra dollar." "Foster could not *prevail with* Jill to dance with him."

ODD

See **WORDS OF APPROXIMATION** and **ODD, QUAINT, QUEER**

ODD, QUAINT, QUEER

The Odd Acquaintance

Queer and *odd* are synonyms that mean "differing from the ordinary." Something unusual may be called queer or odd, and so may a person whose actions are eccentric.

Although one or the other of these words may become a person's favorite to describe someone or something strange, generally unconventional behavior is called *queer;* freakish behavior, *odd:* "Timothy has a *queer* way of greeting people." "The chairman's taciturn manner at the board meeting struck everyone as *odd.*"

A related word is *quaint,* which also suggests the unusual. But *quaint,* unlike *queer* and *odd,* is seldom disparaging unless used sarcastically. In fact, *quaint* usually conveys a sense of pleasantness. Its meaning is "old fashioned, out of date but endearing," as in "The Victorian houses in Cape May, especially those with a widow's walk, are *quaint.*" "Williamsburg—what a *quaint* place to visit!"

OF

Of All Things

Of is possibly the most carelessly used preposition in the English language. Sometimes it is used needlessly; at other times it is not used when it should be.

In "We think the fugitive is *inside of* that house," *of* is unnecessary. In formal writing the double preposition *inside of,* and its cousin *outside of,* is not considered good style: "His body was found *inside* the garage" rather than "found *inside of* the garage." "This matter is entirely *outside* (instead of *outside of*) our control."

When *inside of* means "in less than," referring to time, it has some authoritative support for general usage: "The firemen arrived *inside of* five minutes." But *within* is preferred in more careful writing: "The project should be completed *within* (rather than *inside of*) a year."

Substituting the phrase *outside of* or *except for* for *besides* is a colloquialism rejected by formal stylists: "*Outside of* (better *Besides*) our family, no one will be there." "*Outside of* (better *Except for*) the 50-yard dashes, the relays are finished."

Rather than *of, by* should follow *frighten,* even though *afraid of* is good idiom: "Ellen is frightened *by* (not *of*) dogs." And equally desirable is *of* for *from* in "My uncle is ill *of* (not *from*) pneumonia." When the meaning is "to cease living," *die* takes *of:* "He died *of* (not *from*) yellow fever." A caution is that although a person cannot die *from* thirst (he dies *of* thirst), he dies *from* (not *of*) wounds.

The *of* is superfluous, and should therefore be deleted, in "He fell *off of* the platform" and in "We just had fluctuations in price *of between* four and five thousand dollars."

Saying "She should *of* known better" is an illiteracy for "should have known." The phrase *no use* needs a preceding *of,* since *use* is a noun ("All this is *of* no use"), even though Porgy and Bess sounded better without it: "No use complainin'." But the absence of a preposition makes formalists complain: "There is no use *in* (or *of*) complaining."

OFFICIAL, OFFICIOUS

Deteriorating Definitions

Although *official* and *officious* grew from the same source, their meanings are unalike. Simply stated, *official* means "authoritative," pertaining to an office or position: an official letter, an official representative. *Officious* means "excessively forward or meddlesome," as is one who offers unnecessary and unsolicited advice: an officious clerk, an officious barber.

Long ago, *officious* was not used pejoratively. In fact, it was a term of admiration. *Officious* then meant "ready to serve, ready to exercise one's appointed function." But like another good serviceable English word, *obsequious*, which once meant "dutiful and obedient" but now means "fawning and servile," the word *officious* has gradually assumed its present uncomplimentary sense of pressing one's service upon others obtrusively.

The terms *official* and *officer*, as applied to a government employee, may pertain to the same person. An official is one who holds a public position and is authorized to act in a specific capacity, as is an official of the postal department or a customs official. Since an officer is one invested with an official duty, an *official* of the Bureau of Internal Revenue, for example, may properly be called a revenue *officer*. Nevertheless, the term *officer* is usually restricted to those in uniformed services, especially if in authority. Nowadays policemen, park guards, and security patrolmen are called officers, although they hold no rank. The term is considered a polite form of address.

OFTEN

See FREQUENTLY, OFTEN, USUAL

ON, ONTO, ON TO

Hop on the Bandwagon

The distinctions between *on, onto,* and *on to* and those between *in, into,* and *in to* are similar. The first two words of each set are propositions; the third consists of an adverb and a preposition.

On indicates position. It refers to something in contact with a surface. It also means "time when" (*on* January 1) or "continued motion" (worked *on* through the night). An example of *on* indicating position is in "The banner guard is marching *on* the field."

Onto is sometimes interchanged with *on* when indicating movement toward a fixed position. In this regard, *onto* is more explicit, since it has only this one sense. As between "The irate customer jumped *on* the counter" and "The irate customer jumped *onto* the counter," the latter more clearly expresses movement toward the counter. The former might imply that the customer was using the counter for a trampoline.

The preposition *onto,* believed to have been first written by Keats, developed during the last century because of popular demand for a single word to correspond with *into*. *Into* expresses motion or direction, implying a penetration or entrance; *onto* was created to suggest movement toward: "He climbed *onto* the roof." "The football team marched *onto* the field."

When *on* is used as a separate adverb, the combination *on to* should be written as two words: "He passed the papers *on to* the students." "After visiting Cincinnati, she went *on to* Cleveland."

ONE

We're All One of a Kind

One mistake is one too many. And that is why caution is advised before using the word *one*. For example, it is a solecism to write, "One of the books that has the information you want is on the large desk." The pronoun *that,* since it refers to *books,* a plural noun, needs a plural verb: "One of the books that *have*." Likewise, "He is one of the few distinguished professors who has never served as a dean" needs correcting for the same reason: "One of the few distinguished professors who *have* . . . ." The phrase *one of those who* is always followed by a plural verb.

Another somewhat common misusage is in "*Fiddler on the Roof* was one of the best, if not the best, show of all times." If the sentence is parsed, it becomes clear that "one of the best" requires the plural *shows* ("One of the best shows"). A corrected version would read: "*Fiddler on the Roof* was one of the best *shows*, if not the best *show*, of all times."

Some *one* miscellany: The phrase "one of the reasons" as in "One of the reasons for leaving is the poor weather" is more economically expressed, "One reason. . . ." Except for *no one,* all words compounded with *one—everyone, someone, anyone*—are written solid. The reflexive pronoun *oneself* is also preferably written solid, although *one's self* is acceptable. The possessive form *one's* is unique among pronouns. It is the only one that takes an apostrophe. *Hers* and *theirs* are spelled as given, for example, with no apostrophe—not *her's,* not *their's.*

ONE . . . ONE

One Plus One

When the impersonal *one* begins a sentence, the word that should later refer to it, in strict formal contexts, is *one.* By and large, this style has been employed by the great writers of the past. But the enthusiasm of modern-day writers for this usage has waned. It is now generally believed that constructions using *one . . . one* instead of *one . . . he* are stodgy and pedantic. In fact, some grammarians contend that once *one* has been clearly established as an antecedent, repeating it is faulty. Shakespeare must have subscribed to this thinking, for in *As You Like It* he put the following words into the mouth of Corin, the shepherd: ". . . I know the more *one* sickens, the worse at ease *he* is."

The personal pronoun *you* is correctly used when addressing a person ("If *you* go, I will go with *you*"), but it is entirely out of place as an indefinite pronoun coupled with *one.* For example, the sentence "If *one* wants the job, it is wise for *you* to apply early" should be recast using *one . . . him or her* or *you . . . you.* In those constructions in which the indefinite pronoun *one* means "anyone," clearly pointing to an experience common to almost everyone, the employment of *you* is particularly inappropriate. "If *you* jump from a hot shower into a pool of cold water, *you* will immediately feel the difference in temperature" should be reworded: "If *one* jumps from a hot shower into a pool of cold water, *he or she* will. . . ."

ONE OR MORE

See **MORE THAN, ONE OR MORE**

ONLY

The Only Way

A modifier, for the sake of clarity, should stand close to the word modified, preferably immediately before it: "We play *only* tennis and squash." "Howell deals *only* in first editions." But general usage is more liberal. It recognizes other placements if they make sense and are unambiguous. The meaning in "It can *only* be thought of in terms of astronomical figures" is clear in most minds, even though "It can be thought of *only* in terms of astronomical figures" is more precise. The placing of *only* before the verb, however, is not sanctioned by English formalists, for fear that a sense different from the one intended might be conveyed. Certainly the meanings and the emphases change as *only* shifts its position in a sentence. The following examples underscore this point.

1. She said that she would sing *only* opera.
   [She would sing no other kind of music.]
2. She said that she would *only* sing opera.
   [She would sing opera, not teach it.]
3. She said that she *only* would sing opera.
   [She would sing opera, not dance.]
4. She said that *only* she would sing opera.
   [No one else would sing it.]
5. She said *only* that she would sing opera.
   [She said nothing else.]
6. She *only* said that she would sing opera.
   [She said so but did not do so.]
7. *Only* she said that she would sing opera.
   [She was the only one who said it.]

Some of the examples may, of course, be interpreted differently. The caution is that unless modifiers refer clearly and logically to the words they modify, the result may be confusion.

OR

Don't Stick Your Oar In

When two nouns or pronouns acting as the subjects of a verb are linked by the conjunction *or*, the following rules govern: First, two singular subjects joined by *or* take a singular verb, as in "This book *or* that one *has* the answer." Second, two plural subjects take a plural verb: "Either the Bottomleys *or* the Hubbels *have* the material." Third, if one subject is singular and one plural, the verb agrees with the nearer subject: "Signals *or* a sign *is* what we want". "A sign *or* signals *are* what we want." The latter sentence, with its plural noun next to the verb, sounds better. If it still seems awkward, the order may be inverted: "We want signals or a sign." "We want a sign or signals."

Or may introduce an appositive ("It is a teepee, *or* an Indian tent") or an alternative ("You may come on Monday or Tuesday"). An appositive *or* is preceded by a comma; an alternative *or* is not.

ORAL, VERBAL

Out of the Mouths . . .

It is a mistake to believe that what is verbal must be unwritten (that is, spoken) for the word *verbal,* from the Latin *verbum,* "word," means merely "pertaining to or consisting of words." It does not distinguish the written from the spoken.

The word *oral,* which also comes from the Latin (*os,* genitive *oris,* "mouth"), denotes "what pertains to the mouth" and therefore, in this connection, means "spoken rather than written." Hence what is oral is verbal (it is put "in words"—spoken words), but what is verbal may not necessarily be oral (it may be written). A contract made in conversation, therefore, is best called an *oral* agreement and one reduced to writing, a *written* agreement.

Even such sentences as "The Provost *verbally* took the Dean to task" or "The doctor gave him *verbal* instructions" are not so clear as they would be with *oral* or *written.*

The use of *verbal* should perhaps be restricted to comparisons of matters in words, signs, and symbols, but not of utterances.

ORIENT

Being in the West Is No Occident

The *Orient* refers to the Far East. (The term Far East is capitalized only when it refers to East Asia. Otherwise, it should be in lower case: "To a Chicagoan, Philadelphia seems to be in the far east.") The word was adopted from the Latin *oriens*, which means "rising," because it was assumed in ancient days that the sun actually rose from that distant place. *Occident*, its natural opposite, is from *occidens*, which means "setting."

Orient is the source of two verb forms—*orient* and *orientate*—both of which mean "to face toward the east." But their current sense is "to set right by adjusting to facts or principles." The preferred form is *orient*: "The moderator's remarks should *orient* the audience to the format of the debate." The longer *orientate* sounds pretentious and, except for an extra syllable, adds nothing to the shorter word. Their noun form is *orientation*: "All freshmen must attend *orientation* classes a week before school begins."

OSCILLATE, OSCULATE

Big Show Off!

When reading about an osculating fan, one might think that it refers to a stage-door Johnnie who insists on kissing his movie idol. If what was meant, however, was a fan that fluttered or vibrated to circulate air, the misspelling would then be obvious.

Osculate means "to kiss." *Oscillate* means "to move to and fro." An oscillating fan "swings back and forth with a steady uninterrupted rhythm." Its root can be found in the Latin *oscillum* ("swing"), originally a mask of Bacchus hanging from a tree in a vineyard to swing in the wind. The "mask" can be seen in the first syllable, *os*, which means not only "mouth" and "bone" but also "the face." *Oscillate* is also used to mean "a wavering between two or more thoughts." In this sense it is a synonym for *vacillate*.

The Latin *ostendere*, "to show," has given rise to many English words and the sense of "show" is a part of each one: *ostensible*, "professed," "seeming"; *ostensive*, "apparent," "showing"; *ostentatious*, "characterized by or given to ostentation," "showy."

Except for *ostensive*, a term used primarily in logic and mathematics, those are fairly common words. The adjective *ostentatious* (and its noun form *ostentation*) suggests a display that is in poor taste. *Ostensible* implies a belief that what seems to be is not so. It is something pretended to deceive others: "His *ostensible* motive was to aid the underprivileged. Actually, he wanted to control the charity for his own benefit."

OTHER, OTHERWISE

Why Be Otherwise?

A sentence such as "His difficulties, financial and otherwise, seem endless" would, as a matter of grammar, disturb few people because the misusing of *otherwise* for *other* has permeated every level of writing and is no longer a concern except, perhaps, to those linguistically sensitive to their proper usage. Strictly speaking, *other* is an adjective. It means "different." *Otherwise* is an adverb, and it means "in a different manner," "in different circumstances," or "in other respects."

Otherwise is correctly used in "The piece must be played slowly; *otherwise*, it will not sound right" and in "We all knew he could not handle it *otherwise*." It is incorrectly used in "Winston's problems, marital and *otherwise*, are beyond resolution" and in "The facts appear *otherwise* than as published." In the first example, *otherwise*, an adverb, is improperly paired with *marital*, an adjective. In the second, *appear* is a linking verb, which takes adjectives, not adverbs.

Some sentences require the plural form *others* for *otherwise* ("Maintenance employees—electricians or *otherwise* [should be *others*]—must attend today's meeting), whereas others need rephrasing ("Not all the team's supporters, players or *otherwise* [players or *other supporters*], think well of the coach").

The adjective *other*, although not so much a malefactor as *otherwise*, is occasionally misused. For instance, in "The teacher could not stare *other* than with chagrin at the condition of the classroom," *otherwise* is needed. Otherwise, it's all wrong.

OTHER THAN

Forsaking All Others

The word *other* should be used prudently to avoid illogical sentences and misunderstanding. For example, "No *other* dresses *except* those on the rack are reduced" and "We have no *other* books *but* these to show you" are not uncommon statements. However, in those sentences *except* and *but* should be replaced by *than*, since idiom calls for *other than* to suggest differences or opposition (no *other* dresses *than*; no *other* books *than*). Even the correct phraseology (*other than*) is not always the best choice, since it sometimes leads to wordiness. Suitable economical substitutes are *unless* and *except*: "All those matriculating, *unless* they have attended night school, must meet the dean at 10 o'clock" (preferred to *other than those who*). "The animals in the lower cages, *except* those that are pregnant, should be fed only at night" (instead of *other than those that are*).

Occasionally *other than* wrongly displaces more appropriate phrases such as *apart from* and *aside from*. "After stating his name, the defendant said nothing more, *other than* to nod his head when asked to plead" should be worded ". . . *apart* (or *aside*) *from* nodding his head."

The pronoun after *other than* is in the objective case: "Other than *him*, there is no one else," not "Other than *he* . . ."

Other is needed in comparisons between two persons or things belonging to the same class. The sentence "This drama is better than any I have ever seen" should be rephrased: "This drama is better than any *other*. . . ." But when the classes are different, *other* is unnecessary. "This drama is more enjoyable than any comedy I have ever seen." No *other*.

OUGHT, SHOULD

Let's Drive to the Ought-to Shop

Ought and *should* share a sense of obligation. They are therefore used more or less interchangeably. *Should* expresses a feeling of appropriateness or fitness; *ought*, which sounds more imperative, implies a general moral judgment. One may say, "A man *should* remove his wet overshoes before entering the house," but "She *ought to* reject his licentious advances."

Ought must be followed by an infinitive. "He *ought* but does not want to learn" should be reworded: "He *ought to learn* but does not want to." Since *ought* is currently used only as an auxiliary, it may not have an auxiliary of its own. For example, "She *had ought* (or *didn't ought*) to do that" should be rephrased:

"She *ought* (or *ought not*) to do that." "The teacher *ought to of* warned us about a test sooner" also needs correcting ("ought to *have* warned us"). The expression *can* and *ought* is in proper sequence for these words (not *ought* and *can*): "He *can and ought to go*." This arrangement also guards against the faulty omission of *to*, as in "He ought and can go." (*See also* **HAD BETTER, OUGHT**.)

The word to convey a sense of compulsion is *must*. If one *must* do something, he has no choice but to do it. Although *must* may also imply necessity or obligation, these weaker senses are ordinarily expressed by *ought to* and *should*. *Must*, formerly a past tense, is now only a present tense: "Students *must* pass these tests to merit promotion."

The colloquialism *must of* is poor English. In "He *must of* done it," *have* should replace *of* (*must have* done it). In "Attendance at the meetings is a *must*," *must* is a noun meaning "necessity." In "These are *must* arrangements," it is an adjective meaning "essential." In formal writing, these sentences must be recast.

OUGHT NOT

An Ought Is More than Nothing

Whether *to*, as part of an infinitive following *ought*, may be omitted in negative statements has been a matter of dispute among grammarians. The consensus supports the use of *to* in positive statements, whether the infinitive is expressed (as in "Cara *ought to* leave now") or implied (as in "Jill said she would go and we ought to" [go]). But with the negative expression *ought not to* ("He *ought not* spend so much money" and "Despite her infidelity, he *ought never* leave her"), the omission of *to*, though deplored by some authorities, is sanctioned by many others. Those in the latter group argue that *ought* (a past tense form of the obsolete verb *owe*) has no imperative and that omitting the *to* creates a resemblance of one. Certainly everyone might concede that *to* weakens a negative effect. "You *ought not* do that" is imperative; "You *ought not to* do that" sounds like a recommendation. Nevertheless, the *to* construction is more widely used. A suggestion is to employ *to* only in those negative statements made awkward by its omission, as is the case in "He ought not pay." Perhaps that recipe will satisfy everyone.

OVER

A Short Lay Over

"It costs *over* twenty dollars" is preferably written "The cost *exceeds* twenty dollars." *Over*, strictly speaking, refers to physical location: "A blue awning stretches *over* the window." But so many respected writers now use *over* to mean "more than" or "in excess of" a given number that this loose, figurative sense has become established. Such sentences as "He is *over* fifty years of age" or "She brought back *over* 100 green apples" are common. Nevertheless, *over* sounds colloquial, whereas *more than* has a tone of formality. This seems clear when comparing "*Over* ten scholars spoke" with "*More than* ten scholars spoke."

Accepting the meaning of *over* as "more than" is no sanction to use it to mean "less than." In "The average was down seventy-eight points *over* last year's" and in "Reductions *over* what had been planned have not been met," *from* should replace *over*.

The combination of *with* and *over* is redundant: "Let's get it *over*" (not *over with*). And although *over* is correctly used in "Is the concert *over*?" a better wording is "Has the concert ended?" In "We went *over* the Golden Gate Bridge," *across* is more precise.

Combining *over* and *lie* or *lay* to make a compound verb creates problems not unlike those attending the verbs *lie* and *lay* themselves. What is further confusing is that although *lie* is an intransitive verb and *lay* a transitive, the prefix *over* converts *lie* into a transitive verb, so that it, too, takes an object: "The North Sea *overlies* a rich oil deposit."

Overlay means "to lay or spread over" or "to superimpose," as to overlay wood with silver. The past tense and past participle of this transitive verb, *overlaid*, is usually used in the passive voice: "The walk was *overlaid* with petals." *Overlie* refers "to lying over or upon"—moss overlying the boulders. Its past tense is *overlay* and its past participle is *overlain*: "Ominous clouds *overlay* (have *overlain*) the valley." In some instances *overlie* is interchangeable with its opposite number, *underlie*: "His kindness, which *underlies* (or *overlies*) everything he does, is well known."

OVERALL, SITUATION

Vogue Today, Vague Tomorrow

Why use the word *overall*? What advantage does it have, for example, over *total, whole, general, complete,* or *comprehensive*? Or *aggregate, net, overriding,* or *supreme*? Are not *overall* views *comprehensive* views, *overall* costs *total* costs, *overall* designs *general* designs? And what is "his best *overall* record"? It is simply his best record. *Overall* contributes nothing useful in those phrases, nor is it helpful in *overall opinion* or *overall majority*. Perhaps all those *overalls* belong in a workmen's clothing store. Yet—and this is not meant to be contradictory—*overall* is a precise adjective. It means "between two extreme points" or "from one end to the other," as in "From the window to the corner, we measure 14 feet; however, the *overall frontage* (front corner to corner) is 32 feet."

Another vigorless word is *situation*. In common usage it can mean almost anything—or almost nothing. Thus one hears of "a serious economic *situation*" instead of "an economic problem," "a storm *situation* instead of "a storm warning," "an international *situation* rather than "an international incident." Derived from the Latin *situs* ("a site"), *situation* is best employed in its proper sense—that of a relative position—as in the following sentence: "Because of its *situation* high above the town, the castle, even though abandoned, was thought to influence the lives of the people below."

OVERLOOK, OVERSEE

Oh, What a Mission

An *omission* is something that has been left out deliberately, accidentally, or through apathy or negligence: "Because of the *omission* of the conductor's name, the program has to be reprinted." An *oversight* is a failure either to notice or to consider, or a careless error of omission, as in "The mortgage payment was not made on time because of an *oversight*." "Through an *oversight*, Vernon failed to invite his mother-in-law." Oversights are caused not by overseeing but by overlooking. Another meaning of *oversight*, used in governmental circles but not in general usage, is "supervision or careful watching and review."

The equating of *oversee* and *overlook* by some dictionaries, in the sense of "supervise" or "examine" ("The editor will *overlook* [or *oversee*] the new publication project") has been a source of confusion. One definition of *overlook* is "to ignore"— the very opposite of "to examine." Obviously precision would be best served if *overlook* were restricted to its meaning "to fail to look, see, or notice, either intentionally or inadvertently" (as in "The principal will not *overlook* Eddie's disobedience") or even to its extended sense, "to disregard" (as in "The vice president purposely *overlooked* the critical point"). *Oversee* alone would continue to mean "supervising," which fits perfectly with its noun form, *overseer* (one who supervises work).

In the light of the ambiguity that these words may occasion, a careful writer makes certain that the context will not leave the intended meaning in doubt.

$\mathcal{P}$

PAIR WORDS

Pairing Off

Which is correctly put: "Here *is* your pliers" or "Here *are* your pliers"? The general rule is that instruments spelled with a final *s* are treated as plural nouns: "The *tongs are* heavy." "The *clippers were* delivered."

When *pair*, which refers to two things that are inseparably used together, is employed as the subject of a sentence (a pair of tongs, that pair of shears), it usually governs a singular verb: "A *pair* of shears *is* needed right away by the sewing class teacher." Although less often employed as a plural, it can be: "That *pair were* named the winners." Following a numeral other than one, the plural form *pairs* is recommended: "Six *pairs* of scissors are on the work bench" rather than "Six *pair* of scissors" or "Six scissors."

When the instrument is part of a compound noun, its singular form is preferable: "We ordered the blue *scissor*-sharpener." "We want *tong* prongs that will hold."

PALINDROME

See **PHILOLOGY**

PALTRY, PETTY, TRIVIAL

How Small Can You Be?

The word *trivial* refers to the insignificant or the slight, especially when compared to something important. The ancestor of *trivial* is *trivialis*, which also begot *trivium*, a word of great importance in education during medieval days. The *trivium* consisted of grammar, logic, and rhetoric—cornerstones even in today's study of the liberal arts. Both *trivium* and *trivial* have within them the literal sense of *tri*, "three," and *via*, "way or

215

road." The modern meaning of *trivial*, "commonplace" or "unimportant," evolved from the belief that people were likely to gather at crossroads to pass the time of day or gossip, that is, to talk about unimportant matters—*trivia* or *trifles*. *Trivia* is a plural form only: "*Trivia* are always bothersome in a serious conversation." *Trivial*, unlike its synonyms *petty* and *paltry*, is less derisive.

Petty is defined as "small" or "mean." It implies unimportance or narrow-mindedness, even contempt or ridicule: petty complaints, petty arguments. The word *paltry* stemmed from the Scandinavian *paltrie*, meaning "trash," which in turn had been derived from *paltor*, "rags." Clearly trash and rags have little or no value; describing someone or something as paltry, therefore, is disparaging, if not outright scornful. The person is considered contemptible; the thing, worthless.

PARAMOUNT

See TANTAMOUNT

PARENTHESES

See PUNCTUATION—PARENTHESES AND BRACKETS

PART, PORTION, SHARE

Slices of Life

Part, *share*, and *portion* refer to something less than the whole. *Part* is a general word, meaning "a fraction of a whole." To put it differently, whatever is less than the whole is a part: a part of the loot; a part of the time; a part of a report. *Part* and *portion* are often interchanged, but in a strict sense a *portion* is "a part allotted or assigned to a particular person or purpose." It is, therefore, a specific part, an allotment, a share: "The Art Museum is to receive a *portion* of the Hermann estate." "Each person will be given his *portion* of the dessert after coffee has been served."

Share, like *portion*, refers to an allotment, but even more than *portion* it emphasizes the receiver rather than the giver. It is the receiver's portion: a fair share of the profits; an accurate share of the winnings; an equal share of the pie. "What is fair is to share and share alike"—in which *share* serves as a verb.

A verb related to *part* and *share* is *partake*. It has two uses, both of which sound stuffy. Neither is recommended. When it refers to meals, it idiomatically takes *of*, not *in*: "We are pleased to *partake of* this sumptuous dinner." The sense of the other is "to participate in," "to take part in." Then it may take either *in* or *of*: "The children wish to partake *of* [or *in*] all the camp activities."

PARTY

See **PEOPLE, PERSONS**

PASSED, PAST

A Word in Passing

No one confuses the meanings of *passed* and *past*. A person who writes "My neighbor *past* me on the street without a greeting" has simply misspelled a word.

A mnemonic aid to help avoid this mix-up is hard to come by. Possibly, remembering that what is *past* might be *last* may help because the rhyming words have a similar spelling. When past action is indicated, the past tense of the verb *to pass* is called for—*passed*: "He *passed* his test." "The bill was *passed* by the House." A wag may put it together and say, "We are happy that his *past* has long *passed* into oblivion."

Past serves as several parts of speech, but not as a verb. In "We met him this *past* week," it is an adjective; in "He strolled *past*," an adverb; in "It is now *past* closing time," a preposition; and in "Shades of her *past* keep following her," a noun.

PATRON, PATRONIZE

Patrons and Matrons

A *patron*, according to its Latin ancestor *patronus*, is a protector. He may, for example, protect an orphan, an artist, or a charitable organization as a guardian or supporter. Many museums and colleges rely on these benefactors for financial support: "The Rockefellers have been *patrons* of many public institutions." Dr. Samuel Johnson took a dim view of patrons. He defined the word *patron* as "a wretch who supports with insolence, and is paid with flattery," a feeling that has for a long time been tempered (except perhaps in nightclubs and expensive restaurants, where it sounds pretentious and suggests the presence of a fawning proprietor).

The verb *to patronize* has developed several meanings. One, "to do business with," is generally accepted. Purists still argue, however, with growing futility, that it should be used only in its original sense of "to foster or support." In another figurative sense, it is used of someone (usually in its adjective form) who treats others with condescension, as in "The owner's *patronizing* manner irritated the employees." The paradox is that although merchants want their stores patronized, they themselves do not wish to be patronized.

PENETRATE, PERMEATE, PERVADE

Very Penetrating

Penetrate is sometimes incorrectly used for *pervade*. Although both words may apply to the same effects, they are hardly synonyms. For example, "The odor of roses *pervaded* the arbor and storeroom" means that the odor was everywhere throughout the arbor and storeroom. But saying that the odor of gas *penetrated* the offices suggests that it got through to them.

Penetrate means "to enter into; to pierce." Its literal sense is to enter the interior of something, to make way into another body, as a dagger penetrates flesh or as oil penetrates wood: "A magnum slug can *penetrate* the block of a car." Figuratively the sense of *penetrate* is to comprehend, to pierce with the mind: "His insight enabled him to *penetrate* the very core of the problem."

Derivatively *pervade* means "to go or walk through." It indicates an influence, idea, or emotion that has diffused throughout: "The director's personality *pervades* the movie set." "A feeling of uneasiness *pervades* the entire community." *Pervade* is most suitably used with abstractions: "With Reagan's election, a noticeable optimism *pervaded* Wall Street." "A wondrous silence *pervades* the forest."

A related word is *permeate*. Definitions given it by dictionaries are "to diffuse through or penetrate something," as ink permeates cheesecloth or cigar smoke permeates clothing; "to pass through the pores or interstices, without causing rupture or displacement of parts," as water permeates sand or a filtering stone; and "to pervade." Unlike *pervade*, however, which is usually found with abstractions, *permeate* is preferably used in a concrete sense.

PEOPLE, PERSONS

People Who Need People

Whether one should say "Three *people* were sitting on the bench" or "Three *persons*" is a matter of style. In formal writing a small numeral should not precede the word *people*. *Three persons* is the better way to express it. If the number increases substantially, *persons* becomes *people*, even in formal usage: "Two million *people* went to the polls yesterday." *People* is always used with round numbers, whether large or small: "About 100 *people* attended." But if the number is exact, *people* reverts to *persons*: "There were 101 *persons* present."

Large indefinite numbers of persons are referred to as *the people*. The term originally applied to tribes and nations; now it frequently suggests other groupings such as a mass of ordinary people or those of a particular culture. It also refers to the electorate: "He was elected overwhelmingly by the *people*." But if the size of the group is presumably small, *persons* is preferred: "The crime was committed by *persons* unknown."

Many people must dislike using the word *persons*, judged by their frequent substitutes for it. If not *people*, it may be *individuals*, even though the term is inappropriate. Ordinarily a person is called an *individual* only when disdain is intended, as in "We know those *individuals* who are acting like teenagers." Originally *individual* was an adjective, and in the minds of some writers this is still its only proper function: "We can reach our goal only through *individual* efforts." "Let us now consider the *individual* chapters." Today it is properly used as a noun to represent a person (a particular being) in contrast to a class or body such as an agency or a corporation or the state ("The rights of *individuals* as well as the rights of society must be respected") or to distinguish the single or particular organism from the species.

Another common substitute for *person* is *party*: "There sits the *party* we were discussing." Except in a legal context, in which a person is designated as the party in an action, *party* is not properly interchangeable with *person*. It is wrongly used in "I know a *party* who has a Chevrolet for sale" and in "We think highly of the *party* applying for the job." Only in telephone lingo does *party* hold a respectable position. No operator worthy of her headset would dare say, "Here's your person."

PER

Purr, Per, Purr

Per is a Latin word borrowed into English, primarily as a business term. Its original meaning, "through," is still current, but as a commercialism its sense has been extended to include the ideas "by means of" and "on account of." Business correspondence reads better, however, if a sentence such as "We shipped the motors on April 25 *per* your instructions" is recast "*in accordance with* your instructions" or "Roberts shipped it *per* first-class mail" is reworded "*by* first-class mail." And just as *as per your directions* or *orders* is inappropriate in formal style, so is *as per usual* (which may have come from the French *comme par ordinaire*).

Per should not displace *a* or *an* in such phrases as *55 miles per hour, twice per year*, or *$4.50 per dozen*. Only when *per* is used with another Latin word—*per diem, per annum, per capita*—is the Latin form desirable.

PERCENTAGE, PROPORTION

Playing the Percentages

Since the word *percentage* is a noun that means "a portion of the whole," it must be used with a qualifying word (usually *large, small, high,* or *low*) to indicate a relationship between numbers: "The *percentage* of the student body on scholarship remains *small*." "A *large percentage* of the leaves have been collected." However, when *percentage* can sensibly be replaced by a simpler word (*most* or *many* for a large percentage; *few* for a small percentage), it is recommended: "*Many* (instead of *A large percentage*) of our guests have left." *Percentage* sounds jargonistic.

A comparably limited word is *proportion*. Its sense is "part." When it expresses the relationship of one size, quantity, and so forth, to another, it also should be qualified. For example, "A *proportion of* the employees reported sick" and "A *proportion of* the material was defective" need *large* or *small*. Better yet, rather than *a large* (or *small*) *proportion of,* is *many* (employees) and *most* (of the material).

Both these terms—*percentage* and *proportion*—are colloquial favorites. The commonly heard "He plays well a *percentage* of the time" should be rephrased, even in ordinary speech, "He plays well *a part* (or *some*) of the time." Rewording is also recommended in "No one can see the *percentage* in studying dead languages," which uses *percentage* to mean "advantage," and in "A *proportion* of the books are missing," in which *proportion* is being substituted for *few* or *some*.

Although both *per cent* and *percentage* mean "rate per hundred," *per cent*, unlike *percentage*, is not modified by general terms. Since it is specific, it must be used with numbers, preferably figures: *4 per cent. Per cent* is generally written as in this sentence, with two words. *The Style Manual* of the United States Government Printing Office recommends a single word: *percent.* (Although *per cent* is an abbreviation of *per centum*, it takes no period because it has been anglicized.) Fractions are written *6.5 per cent* or *one half of 1 per cent.* In tabular matter the symbol % is always used.

In contradistinction to *per cent*, a number used with *percentage* is spelled out: twelve percentage points. *Percentage* should not be wrongfully displaced in a sentence such as "Interest rates skyrocketed last month from 15 per cent to 20 per cent, an increase of 5 *per cent*." The increase was five *percentage* points. The increase in the rate was 33.3 *per cent*.

When an *of* phrase follows either *per cent* or *percentage*, a succeeding verb is singular or plural depending on the number of the object of the preposition. For example, "Forty per cent of the delegation *is* here (the object of the *of* phrase is the singular *delegation*), but "Forty per cent of the delegates *are* here" (the object of the of phrase, *delegates*, is plural).

PERPETRATE

See **COMMIT, PERPETRATE**

PERPLEX

See CONFUSION, DEGREES OF

PERSONS

See PEOPLE, PERSONS

PERSUADE

See CONVINCE, PERSUADE

PETTY

See PALTRY, PETTY, TRIVIAL

PHASE

See FAZE, PHASE

PHILOLOGY

Words About Words

When talking about words, one can spend much time describing the terms applied to words without being wordy.

A *palindrome*, from Greek *palin*, "again," and *dramein*, "to run," is a word, phrase, or sentence that runs back again, that is, it reads the same backward as forward, like *Mom* and *Dad* or the first words ever spoken, "Madam, I'm Adam," or the remark attributed to Napoleon after his banishment: "Able was I ere I saw Elba."

An *acronym* is a pronounceable word formed from the initial letters of a name or title: UNESCO from *United Nations Educational, Scientific, and Cultural Organization*; WAC, from *Women's Army Corps*; WAR, from *Women Against Rape*. Acronyms are almost always written in capital letters.

An *acrostic* is an arrangement of words in a series of lines or verses; but its initial letters form a name, motto, or sentence.

A word puzzle in which a person transposes the letters of a word or a sentence to form a new one is an *anagram*, literally "a new writing," from the Greek *ana*, "anew," and *gramma*, "write": *rebate* and *beater; spat* and *pats; edit* and *tied.*

Then there is *etymology* (Greek *etymos*, "true," and *logy*, "knowledge" or "science"), the study of the origin or history of words; *phraseology*, the arrangement of words; and *morphology*, the study of word structure. And the best for last—*philology*—the study of written records, chiefly to establish authenticity or originality. Its roots refer to love of learning and literature. A *philologist*, therefore (*philo* in Greek means "loving"), is a word lover.

PHYSIOGNOMY

See **FACE**

PLATITUDES

See **TRITE EXPRESSIONS**

PLEBISCITE, REFERENDUM

Don't Rock the Vote

A *plebiscite* is a vote by the people on a public proposal concerning a measure, program, or law. Used as a direct poll, a plebiscite registers public opinion without the usual political biases interfering. An incumbent government, for example, may seek a plebiscite to legitimate its power by allowing the people to affirm or repudiate its right to speak and act in their name. According to its Latin root, a *plebiscite* is a decree by the *plebes*, the common people.

A *referendum* is also a vote by the electorate, but on a measure that has been proposed or has already been passed by a legislative body. It is often concerned with the raising and spending of public funds. A proposal approved by either a plebiscite or a referendum is usually enacted into law.

PLENTY

Horn of Plenty

The word *plenty* can cause plenty of trouble. "Helen ate plenty" and "Jane is plenty big," for example, are inept expressions, not cured by frequent repetition. They need recasting or at least a replacing of *plenty* with *plentifully*. In suitable contexts other adverbs may be considered: *amply, copiously, profusely*. Another choice, but one not in common usage, is *bountifully*, which means "in an abundant degree" or "generously."

The noun *plenty*, meaning "a full supply," requires a following *of—plenty of*: plenty of money; plenty of room; plenty of nothing. Its adjective forms are *plentiful* and *plenteous*: "There is a *plentiful* (or *plenteous*) supply of foolscap in the drawer." "The corn is *plentiful* (or *plenteous*)." *Plentiful* is preferred.

The number of the verb preceding or following *plenty* is governed by context: "Although there *were* plenty of reasons advanced, there certainly *was* not plenty of thought behind them."

PLURALS

We're in for a Bad Spell

Good spellers have either a knack for spelling or a handy dictionary—more often the latter. Since the spelling of many English words follows no set rules, and phonetics seldom help, one cannot learn accurate spelling through logical patterns.

The spelling of plurals presents special difficulties. Most plurals are formed by adding *-s* to the singular, but many are not: *wife, wives; child, children; goose, geese; basis, bases; ox, oxen.*

As a further complication, the plurals and the singulars of some nouns—especially certain nationalities and animal names—are spelled exactly the same; *deer, vermin, fowl, sheep, moose, swine, Japanese, Chinese, Burmese, Vietnamese, Portuguese;* also *sweepstakes, corps, politics, series, chassis, gallows, shambles, falls, straits,* and *molasses.* Moreover, some nouns, although singular in meaning, are not always singular in form; others are always plural and have no singular form. In the singular class are such words as *comics, milk, news, music, information, whereabouts, hydraulics, measles,* and *statistics* (as a science). In the vast plural group are *tongs, environs, goods, riches, thanks, grounds, tidings, auspices, trousers, proceeds, winnings, scissors, hysterics, barracks, belongings, credentials, headquarters,* and *statistics* (referring to facts). The number of a verb used with any of these or similar words must, of course, correspond to the number of the noun; for example, "His politics *is* (not *are*) all wrong" and "The spectacles *are* (not *is*) on the table."

All this is perplexing enough, but some words are "exceptions to the exceptions," forming their plurals in an unexpect-edly simple way, by adding -*s* to a singular form. These words, such as *mongooses, still lifes,* or *talismans,* look out of place with a plural ending: "We are holding two *talismans.*" Others have been dignified with two forms, both in good usage—*elfs* and *elves, hoofs* and *hooves, scarfs* and *scarves, staffs* and *staves.* Still others have two plural forms, each having a different meaning: *indexes* (of a book) and *indices* (in mathematics); *antennas* (of radios) and *antennae* (of insects).

Foreign names that have become English are best made plural by adding *s* or *es. Formulas,* for example, is to be preferred to *formulae,* and *geniuses* to *genii.*

Clearly plurals cause a singular number of problems.

Numbers Compound Problems

Nouns have number—the property that distinguishes the singular from the plural. Ordinarily the plural is formed by adding *s; es* is used when an *s* alone cannot be pronounced as part of the final syllable. Examples of the latter are *classes, kisses,* and *quizzes.*

Plurals of compound nouns are usually formed by the ad-dition of *s* to the more or the most important word. The plural, for instance, of *assistant attorney general* is *assistant attorneys general,* since they are *attorneys,* not *generals.* And so with *notaries* public, *aides*-de-camp, major *generals, sergeants* at arms, *brothers*-in-law, *editors* in chief, and *points* of view.

When the nouns are of equal importance, they are both pluralized (*men employees, women athletes*), but only the last word is made plural if none of the words is significant: forget-me-*nots,* jack-in-the *pulpits,* put-me-*downs.*

Some plurals have the force of a singular (*gallows, measles, news, means, acoustics, politics*), and some singular nouns have a plural sense (*a dozen* boxes, *a thousand* copies). Words stating amount take a singular verb even though the amount is more than one: "Five minutes *is* (Five dollars *is,* Five feet *is,* Five pounds *is*) more than I wanted." The singular form is also used when a number and a noun are combined to form a compound adjective: *a ten-minute* discussion, *a two-week* vacation, *a 100-acre* farm, but "The discussion lasted *ten minutes*"; "He went on a vacation for *two weeks*"; "It is a farm of *100 acres.*"

Nouns whose sense suggests a fullness add an *s* at the end: three cupfuls, four bucketfuls. "Three *cupfuls* of tea" means that the cup was filled three times. "Six *cups full* of tea" refers to separate cups of tea—that is, six cups, each full of tea.

PLUS

Simple Arithmetic

When *plus* is part of a phrase, as in "That sum, *plus* interest, amounts to five hundred and twenty dollars," it does not combine with the subject or influence the verb. The construction is considered parenthetical and is treated as though it were nonexistent: "That sum . . . amounts to."

Although *plus* is occasionally used as a noun or an adjective, it most frequently serves in arithmetical contexts as a preposition, meaning "increased by" or "along with," as in "Two *plus* four equals six." The subject *two* is treated as a singular, and the singular verb *equals* agrees with it. In "Their holdings *plus* our finances *make* a good combination," both the true subject *holdings* and the verb it governs are plural. The number given a verb following *plus* is determined by the number of the subject.

Particular writers do not use *plus* as a coordinate conjunction. It therefore should not displace *and* in "Ruth is a knowledgeable nurse *plus* a pleasant and attractive person" or in "Tom *plus* his three sisters came early." Additionally, *plus* when used as a noun or adjective (as in "It was a big *plus* in our lives" and in "We're happy for the *plus* factor") is highly informal.

In colloquial speech, *minus* is used facetiously to mean "without" or "having lost," as in "No one recognized absentminded Herman at his wedding. He came *minus* his toupee."

The *s* in *plus* and *minus* is not doubled when their plurals are formed: *pluses* and *minuses*.

POLITE

See CIVIL, POLITE

PORTION

See PART, PORTION, SHARE

POSH

See LUXURIANT, LUXURIOUS

POSSESSIVES

Proper Possessions

Everyone knows that the forming of plurals of nouns (except for the exceptions) follows two simple rules: one, to add *s* to a singular noun if it does not already end in *s*; the other, to add *es* to one that does. Equally known is that the plural of proper nouns is made in the same way: Miller, Millers; Hess, Hesses. The possessive case of proper nouns or proper adjectives, like those of common nouns—boy's, boys'; student's, students'—is formed by the addition of an apostrophe and an *s*; "It is Mr. Goldman's motorboat." A plural proper name is made possessive by adding an apostrophe after the pluralizing *s*—the Millers' house; the Hesses' yacht.

A sign that identifies the inhabitants of a house should be in the possessive plural if a family lives there (The Smiths' House, The Bennetts' House) and not in the singular (not The Smith's House). If no apostrophe is used (The Smith House), the house, presumably, is occupied by one person or is a historical landmark—The Benedict Arnold House.

Persons operating a joint ownership under two names use an apostrophe only after the last one: Casell and Funk's Bookstore; Johnson & Johnson's Bandages. But each name is apostrophized if ownership is separately held: Rundel's and Clark's shoe stores; the credit association's and their customers' records.

Compound nouns, such as *lieutenant general, editor in chief*, or *chamber of commerce*, are made possessive plurals by first making the more or the most important word plural and then adding an apostrophe to the last element. In the examples, the plural forms would be *lieutenant generals, editors in chief*, and *chambers of commerce*, and with the apostrophe added, *lieutenant generals'* bivouacs, the *editors in chief's* policies, the *chambers of commerce's* headquarters. A common error to guard against is in reference to sisters- or brothers-in-law. It is not *the three sister-in-laws' houses*, but deferring to this tongue twister, *the three sisters-in-law's houses*.

A question sometimes asked is whether the nonessential

appositive following a noun or the noun itself should be made possessive. The answer—the appositive: "We heard Dr. Rappaport, the senior *cardiologist's*, report." Those preferring apostrophes must be consistent. They should apply them even to such designations as *Jr.* and *II*, as in "The class saw the tape of Robert T. Browne, *Jr.'s*, work." But an *of* phrase reads better: "The class saw a tape *of the work of* Robert T. Browne, Jr."

Doubly Possessed

The sentence "That invidious remark of my aunt's should be ignored" contains two possessive forms, an *of* phrase and a possessive noun. Both the phrase and the apostrophized *s* signify possession. Hence the construction in which they are used is appropriately called a double possessive.

This double possessive, or genitive, is an idiom of long and respectable standing. Its formula is common with pronouns (that novel dance step of *his*, a peculiar lisp of *hers*), but it is also applicable to both proper and common nouns to distinguish one or more possessions from several like possessions. For example, "Don is a friend of my cousin's" implies that my cousin has other friends. That he has other friends, according to the statement, can be substantiated by substituting "among" for "of" and completing the phrase: "Don is a friend among my cousin's friends." Without the second possessive ("Don is a friend of my cousin"), no such implication is made, and the *among* test will fail. If what is possessed is not restricted to a specific number or group belonging to the possessor, the double possessive is inapplicable. For instance, although "*The comments* (in general) *of the speaker* were controversial" is correctly put, *the comments of the speaker's* is not. But as to a specific comment, one may say, "*That comment* (or *A comment*) *of the speaker's* was controversial." As a further example, "Those paintings (specific ones) of his uncle's are invaluable," but "The paintings (generally speaking) of his uncle are priceless."

Some sentences would be ambiguous without the double possessive. "I have a picture of Gulbenkian's" means that I am in possession of one of his art treasures. But "I have a picture of Gulbenkian" refers to a photograph or some other likeness of him. And what if the sentence were to say, "Here is Gulbenkian's picture?" Out of context, one would not know which picture was meant.

Is It Wise To Pluralize?

Should Shakespeare have said, "Cowards die many times before their *death*" or before their *deaths*? Is it right to say "The teacher knew all the students by their first name" or must it be "by their first names?" Or is it simply a matter of personal preference?

A general rule governing plurals is that, when possible, they be used consistently throughout the sentence. For instance, in "Collect *the books*, rebind *each one*, and then store *them* by color," the middle clause is best rephrased "rebind them," making all three objects plural: collect *books*, rebind *them*, store *them*.

But when a plural possessive (*their, our, your*) modifies a noun, it is not always clear whether the noun should be singular or plural. In some cases a writer must be led solely by his own judgment. For example, it is correct to say either "Many people expressed their *opinion* on the subject" or "their *opinions* on the subject," or "We will analyze the statements according to their *meaning*" or "their *meanings*."

The English language, in this matter of nouns modified by plural possessives, is in a state of flux; no firm rule applies in every case. It is possible, however, to formulate a general rule: When the noun following a plural possessive is concrete, a plural noun is required; when it is abstract—that is, it represents a shared feeling or emotion—a singular noun is better; and when it hovers a little over each side, it becomes a matter of choice. To illustrate: "The two senators from Ohio changed their *seats*" (concrete, plural); "The two senators from Ohio changed their *ideology*" (abstract, singular); "The two senators from Ohio changed their *mind* (or *minds*)" (in between, either one will do).

PRACTICALLY, VIRTUALLY

A Near Miss

Dictionaries define *practically* as "in a practical manner" or "for all practical purposes." Something that can be used practically has been designed for actual use and is efficient and workable. In informal usage *practically* has come to mean "very nearly" or "almost": "My wife was *practically* asleep when the baby started to cry." This extension has won general acceptance. *Practically* also appears in the common phrase *practically speaking*, which serves to introduce a summarizing thought.

Virtually means "in essence" or "in effect," as in "During the President's illness the Vice President was *virtually* the Chief Executive." In everyday usage *virtually*, like *practically*, has acquired the meaning "nearly" or "almost."

In sentences such as "This is *practically* an open and shut .case" (in which *practically* stands for "in effect"), *virtually*, with its sense of "in essence," is better. *Practically* is preferable when hypothetical or theoretical contrasts are being made: "Theoretically, a nationwide free medical service is desirable; *practically*, it is impossible." In most other instances it is virtually or practically impossible to distinguish between these two words. Of course, one who uses *almost* or *nearly* instead, for all practical purposes, virtually eliminates the problem.

PRACTICE

See CUSTOM, HABIT, PRACTICE

PRÉCIS

See SUMMARY **and** RELATED WORDS

PREPOSITIONS ENDING SENTENCES

A Prepositional Proposition

Few, if any, of today's writers agree with the facetious statement "A preposition is an improper word to end a sentence with." That chestnut is no longer taken seriously—yet it is not untrue; it is simply not the whole truth.

The formal rule that a preposition should precede the word it links to another part of the sentence is well established. Also unarguable is the premise that a sentence should not end with an awkward or superfluous preposition, as in "Where is he at?" or "Where shall I deliver it to?" Certainly as a matter of writing style, prepositions, since they are weak words, are generally interred within a sentence. But if a preposition at the end of a sentence provides strength or if such placement has been established by idiom, the phraseology should not be inverted merely to bury the preposition. If that were done, the sentence would lose its impact and its flavor—surely its euphony. For example, "Janie has a problem to work on," "Thomas has no one to turn to," and "What did McArdle write about?" are expressed in natural word order. Diehards, nevertheless, would rearrange those sentences: "Janie has a problem on which to work," "Thomas has no one to whom to turn," and "About what did McArdle write?" All grammatically correct—but unnatural and awkward.

It is safe to say that one should feel free to end a sentence with a preposition when idiom or rhythm demands it. Robert Louis Stevenson wrote, ". . . a reflexion exceedingly just in itself but which I failed to profit by." And Winston Churchill, when chided for ending a sentence with a preposition, reportedly answered: "I agree. It is a practice up with which I cannot put." When it came to precise diction, the Prime Minister was a man you could depend on.

PRESAGE, PROPHESY

What's the Forecast?

The word *presage* refers primarily to dire prophecies portending ill or evil, as in "The wind *presages* a terrible storm" or "A black cat crossing a road *presages* bad luck." Its original definition, "to perceive beforehand," contained no element of ominousness. Certainly something foretold need not be dangerous or of sad consequence. A student's high school record, for example, might presage a successful college career; or a light breeze, a lovely day. Today the sense of *presage*, nevertheless, is to predict or foretell in the sense of a warning or a presentiment. Its closest synonyms, *forebode* and *portend*, are verbs bound to conjure up gloomy images.

The verb *prophesy* ("to foretell") is a neutral word in that it does not imply the nature of the prediction—favorable or unfavorable. Its synonyms, though they bear shades of differences, are *predict, prognosticate, foretell,* and *forecast.* Oddly, English seems to possess no verb applicable solely to the making of favorable predictions. *Augur* often conveys this sense, but it is usually accompanied by "well," as in "The drop in the prime rate *augurs well* for the stock market." In ancient days an augur was an official diviner of Rome. He foretold events by the flight of birds.

The noun meaning "prediction" is *prophecy*, spelled with a *c*; its verb form, *prophesy*, is spelled with an *s*. That one-letter difference alters the pronunciation too: the noun ends in *see*; the verb, in *sigh*.

PRESCRIBE, PROSCRIBE

Home Remedies

The look-alikes *prescribe* and *proscribe* are sometimes confused, even though they are antonymous. To *prescribe* is to direct that something be done; to *proscribe* is to outlaw it. The former has a positive connotation; the latter, a negative.

The most common definitions of *prescribe* are "to designate" and "to order." It designates when it lays down a guide to be followed, as in "The Spanish teacher *prescribed* a daily session with the audiocassettes." It orders when it directs what is to be used as a remedy. This use of *prescribe* appears most often in medical advice: "The doctor *prescribed* one vitamin-C tablet daily."

The word that means to denounce or condemn is *proscribe*. What is proscribed is prohibited, usually because it is dangerous or exceedingly annoying. The Civil Aeronautics Board has proscribed cigar smoking in airplanes. Allowing dogs to run loose is proscribed in many communities. *Banish* and *prohibit* are common synonyms for *proscribe*. The noun *proscription* has a corresponding sense.

It may be said that a doctor prescribes what is helpful but proscribes what is hazardous.

PRESENT

See GIVE, PRESENT

PRESENTLY

See FORTHWITH, PRESENTLY

PRESTIGIOUS

Presto! It's Gone

Few students would object to attending a prestigious school, and few diners would mind sitting next to a prestigious person. *Prestigious*, which means "having an illustrious name or reputation," refers to a person esteemed for his superior performance or powerful position.

But some authorities disapprove of its use in that sense, contending that rather than something praiseworthy, *prestigious* suggests legerdemain or trickery. They argue, further, that its extended common meaning is especially unnecessary because it can easily be conveyed by many other suitable adjectives, such as *reputable, renowned, illustrious, admirable, notable,* and *famous.*

Although these objections were possibly valid years ago, they have little force today. True, *prestigious* has many synonyms, with varying connotations. And also true is that from its noun form, *prestige,* evolved the term for a sleight of hand artist—a prestidigitator (*preste* [presto!], "quick" or "nimble," and the Latin *digitus*, "finger"). But *prestigious* has long outgrown its original meaning; in fact, its sense has been slightly changed.

PRESUME

See ASSUME, PRESUME

PREVAIL

See OBTAIN, PREVAIL

PREVARICATOR

See EQUIVOCATOR, LIAR, PREVARICATOR

PRICE

See COST, PRICE, VALUE, WORTH

PRINCIPAL, PRINCIPLE

A Principal Objection

Among the most commonly confused homonyms, *principal* and *principle* are in the forefront. *Principal* is either an adjective (meaning "the most important") or a noun (meaning "chief figure," "leader," or "headmaster of a school") except in the financial world, where it means "the main body, or capital, of an estate; an invested capital that bears interest; a sum owed as a debt." The word *principle* is a noun only; it means "a governing rule" or "a standard of conduct" or "a fundamental truth."

One way to distinguish their spellings is to remember that when *principal* is used as an adjective, it is spelled like the word adjective, with an *a*; or its ending may be related to other adjectives ending in -*al*: classical, prejudicial, social. *Principle* may be associated with *rule*. Those words are synonymous and both end in *le*.

PROCEED

Proceed with Caution

Proceed means "to come or go forth." Logically, its only sense is "advancing." One cannot proceed backwards, the way a ship backs into her berth or the way a car moves when in reverse. It is incorrect, therefore, to say that the students, after their recess, should proceed *back* to their classrooms. *Proceed* points one way: forward. It derives from the Latin *pro*, meaning "before or forward," and *cedo*, "move."

The tone of *proceed* is heavy. In everyday sentences it is best replaced by the lighter words *go, travel*, or *move*. In "After lunch we *proceeded* to Tarrytown," for example, *left for* is better, and in "Little Jimmy *proceeded* from one candy store to another," *went from* is what he did. In formal writing, *proceed* is found in dignified, weighty pronouncements: "The funeral cortege *proceeded* slowly." "The Senate will now *proceed* into the chamber."

In some constructions the use of *proceed* is entirely unnecessary, as in "After breakfast we *proceeded* to open the boxes" and in "The president *proceeded* to open the meeting promptly at eight." Those sentences would gain in grace and economy if they read, "After breakfast we opened the boxes" and "The president opened the meeting. . . ." *Proceeded to open*, whether boxes or a meeting, means and says no more than *opened*.

PROHIBIT

See FORBID, PROHIBIT

PROLETARIAT

See BOURGEOIS, PROLETARIAT

PROPHESY

See PRESAGE, PROPHESY

PROPORTION

See PERCENTAGE, PROPORTION

PROSCRIBE

See PRESCRIBE, PROSCRIBE

PROVEN, PROVIDING

Pro's Ain't Poetry

The question is whether two *pro* words, *providing* for *provided* and *proven* for *proved*, are acceptable in formal writing. Although these substitutes are widely used, they have been deplored by many authorities.

Provided is the past participle of the verb *to provide*, which means "to furnish or supply." It is also a conjunction meaning "on the condition that" or "if." Some writers occasionally replace *provided* with *providing*, considering them conjunctions of equal acceptability. This equating is a needless corruption of a useful present participle. In "The mayor praised the Old Age Home for *providing* hot meals daily," *providing* means "supplying." But in "The outdoor class will convene *providing* the weather is good," it does not mean "supplying"; the sentence should therefore be reworded, "The outdoor class will convene *provided*. . . ."

Strictly speaking, even *provided* in the sense of "on the condition that" is not quite correct. The complete expression is *provided that*. But, except when demanded by the most formal style, *that* is usually omitted unless needed to avoid confusion:

"They agreed to attend *provided* their children were invited." No *that*, no confusion.

In spite of what has been said about these "pro" words, a mere possibility, a supposition, or a simple condition is best introduced by *if*: "We will serve dinner *if* (rather than *provided*) Mr. James comes early enough."

The question with *prove* is whether to recognize two past participles—*proved* and *proven*—or just one: "He has *proved* himself right." "The defendant has been *proven* guilty."

Proven derives from a Scottish word used in legal parlance. It has never been accepted into standard English by diehards. They contend that the only correct form is *proved*. Current writers, however, are almost evenly divided on that point. And there are some differences of opinion even among those who disagree. Many approve of *proven* only as an attributive adjective before a noun—a *proven* theory, a *proven* success. Some use *proven* when it aids sentence rhythm; others support it at all times. Each writer, therefore, must make his own decision. Ordinarily it is best to use *proved* in actual verb usage and *proven* when it serves as an adjective.

PROVINCIALISMS

See COLLOQUIALISMS

PUNCTUATION

Apostrophe

A Word Made with Shortening

The chief function of the apostrophe is to indicate possession. For animate beings, this is done by attaching the *'s* genitive to a noun (the bird's beak, the captain's chair, the hostess's uniform). With nouns representing things, an *of* phrase is regularly used (the pages of a book, the petals of a flower, the legs of the table). Idiom has established exceptions to this rule applying to nouns of time (a three weeks' vacation), nouns of value (three dollars' worth), and nouns of abstraction (for pity's sake).

The apostrophe is also used to mark the plurals of letters, figures, and words used as words rather than for meaning (three *m*'s, five *4*'s, two *that*'s) and contractions of words (*don't, isn't*).

Many contractions involve the negative *not*—*wouldn't, aren't, doesn't*. Since the apostrophe stands in the place of the missing letter, those words shortened by two letters have two places where an apostrophe might be used. For example, *can't* might have been written *ca'n't* and *shan't sha'n't*. But only one apostrophe is used. Although abbreviations normally are followed by a period, if an apostrophe is used in an abbreviated word that has both the first and the last letter, the trend is to omit the period (*cont'd* rather than *cont'd.*; *ass'n* rather than *ass'n.*). If a period is preferred, then the apostrophe should be omitted (*contd.*; *assn.*). The first style looks better.

Till and *round* are not contractions but separate words. They therefore take no apostrophe—"We'll wait *till* the boys come home, but we may have to wait *round the clock.*" Clipped words that have been accepted into the language as complete words are no longer apostrophized: *phone, cello, plane, exam, gym.* But *o'clock*, a standardized shortening of "of the clock," is spelled as given.

Colon and Dash

Proper Introductions

The colon is an introductory mark of punctuation in that it introduces what follows while marking a discontinuity of a grammatical construction. It signals the end of a statement and the beginning of something else—another statement, a list of details, a quotation, or an explanation.

A few constructions mislead some writers into employing a colon where none belongs. For example, a colon should not be used to separate a verb from its complement ("The treasurer purchased: ledger sheets, ringbinders, and rubberbands") or a preposition from its object ("Mr. Ginley likes to read about: agronomy, astronomy, and political science"). It is also incorrect to use a colon after a verb except the verb *follow*. The verb most often followed by a colon—which therefore requires particular watchfulness—is *be*, as in "The suggestions made are: think it through, make preliminary notes, and then write in earnest."

As a matter of style, when a colon is used in conjunction with quotation marks, it is placed after the quotes ("The sign said 'Out of Bounds': however, we didn't believe it").

Dashes, when employed sensibly, contribute an emotional emphasis lacking in commas. But if overused, they become meaningless clutter. In its most ordinary use a dash marks a sudden break in thought; it indicates an interruption of the normal progress of a sentence, as in "His fourth operation—his first was ten years ago—turned out to be his last" or in "If we all attend—and there's no reason not to—we'll win the election."

Dashes are also used to explain or summarize what precedes or follows: "Beauty, serenity, security—this is what we sought." "The searching in newspapers, the endless waiting in real estate offices, the beating of the bushes, so to speak—all this has ended; we have finally found an apartment."

Some sentences are clearer with dashes than with commas, as are sentences with compound descriptions. An example is "The McNair book—lucid, provocative, comprehensive—is a masterpiece" rather than "The McNair book, lucid, provocative, comprehensive, is a masterpiece." In multiple appositives commas can even be misleading: "Three doctors, Dr. Wall, Dr. Spalding, and Dr. Boridin, conferred at length" could be misconstrued as referring to six doctors. With dashes ("Three doctors—Dr. Wall, Dr. Spalding, and Dr. Boridin—conferred at length"), the possibility of confusion is removed.

A dash and colon do not belong together in a salutation. And neither mark of punctuation should be substituted for the other. A colon, since it is a mark of anticipation, promising that something will come, usually a list or explanation, is regularly employed when the words *follow* or *following* are expressed or implied: "The following is a list of our officers: . . ." or "A list of our officers follows: Robert Simmons, Anne Morris, Ellen Trower, and Raymond Strassbourg." A dash also acts to introduce material, but that material most likely is a summarizing statement, emphasizing what preceded: "Dieting, gardening, running—these are the subjects that invariably make the best-sellers' list."

The usual dash is called an em dash. A typist sets it by striking the hyphen sign twice, with no spacing before, between, or after the mark. The smallest dash, although seldom so called, is the hyphen. The dash whose length is in between that of a hyphen and an em dash is the en dash. The en dash is used with dates (1979–1981) or a combination of letters and figures (See 4–B).

Commas

Commas: Yes, No, or Maybe

Many years ago writers used commas generously in the belief that punctuating every prepositional phrase made their writing clearer. But all they got for their efforts were comma-cluttered sentences: "In the spring, Jeremiah used to walk, with his dog, along country lanes, during the daytime, when weather permitted." Obviously today's speedreaders would not approve of those commas.

Despite the trend to eliminate them, lowly commas cannot always be dispensed with; in fact, sometimes they alone can help eliminate possible confusion. The adjoining of numbers or names raises a case in point: "In 1937, 5065 people left Paris to resettle in foreign countries." "Of the five, one went home early." "According to Johnson, Adams is their best researcher." Without commas these items would run together and be un-intelligible—"In 1937 5065 people ..."; "Of the five one went ..."; "According to Johnson Adams is their best researcher." Certainly Pope's famous quotation "Whatever is, is right" needs its comma (even though it separates the subject and the predicate) as does "Now who comes, comes too late."

A Comma-bination

Whether to use commas between adjectives qualifying the same word depends on the type of adjectives involved. If they are coordinate adjectives, that is, of equal value, commas should separate them. For example, in "His costume consisted of an old, tattered coat and a torn, misshapen, brown hat," the comma between *old* and *tattered* indicates that each adjective bears the same relationship to the noun *coat*. The same reasoning can be applied to the commas after *torn* and *misshapen*. Those adjectives independently modify the following noun.

Noncoordinate adjectives carry unequal weight and are therefore not punctuated. The test is whether the first adjective modifies the combination of the second adjective and the noun. If so, no commas are used. For example, in "Tabby was a big black cat," *big* refers to a "black cat." The two words function as a unit, and *big* modifies it. In "The principal's wife is often seen in a green silk dress," *silk dress* is an adjective-noun combination modified by *green*.

One can determine whether adjectives in a series are coordinate by mentally inserting *and* between them. If they rest comfortably, a comma is needed: "His costume consisted of an old *and* tattered coat." Coordinate adjectives can also follow each other naturally in reverse: "His costume consisted of an *old, tattered* (or *tattered, old*) coat." Further, coordinate adjectives, if used as predicate adjectives, will not appreciably change the meaning of the sentence: "The coat in his costume was old *and* tattered." Noncoordinate adjectives are not so flexible. "Tabby was a big *and* black cat" and "Tabby was a black, big (adjectives reversed) cat" misstate the sense and are completely unidiomatic.

A Pause for Clarity

The omission of the so-called serial comma before the conjunction *and* or *or* in a series consisting of three or more elements (such as *red, white, and blue* or *beg, borrow, or steal*) can affect clarity. The sentence "We received books colored green, yellow, purple, tan and black" does not make clear whether the color of the last book was a combination of tan and black or whether one book was tan and another black. Inserting a comma before *and* would eliminate any doubt that one book was tan and the other black. In "In the abandoned barn Jimmy found his father's camera, a desk containing many heirlooms and a stray cat," a serial comma would signify that the cat was not hiding in the desk.

Some editors of periodicals and newspapers omit the serial comma, perhaps to save space, even though doing so frequently causes confusion. For example, they would report that the addition to the school consists of an auditorium, a large writing room equipped with shelves for reading material and a commodious principal's office, which may be interpreted to mean that in the writing room are shelves for reading material and for a commodious principal's office.

Clearly serial commas make matters clearer.

Say It Your Way

Some common expressions, such as *nevertheless, therefore,* or *of course,* are more emphatic if not punctuated, that is, if not set off by commas. Commas make them parenthetic. (The one position in which commas are usually required is after introductory expressions. For example, "*Nevertheless,* we think George should go." "*Therefore,* it is clear that George should go." "*Of course,* George should go.")

When these terms are placed within the sentence, the punctuation is optional with the writer. One may say, "The project was funded, *accordingly,* by private sources" or, with greater emphasis, "The project was *accordingly* funded. . . ." "*Likewise,* Thomas plays the harpischord" or "Thomas *likewise* plays the harpischord." *Frankly,* we think it should be ignored" or "We *frankly* think it should be ignored." Other expressions that lend themselves to optional treatment are *furthermore, consequently,* and *certainly.*

Such words as *indeed* or *instead* are best not punctuated. Those writers who prefer pauses would in all likelihood use them anyway: "Indeed, George will not go; instead, Ralph will leave at once." But most writers would skip them: "Indeed George will not go; instead Ralph will leave at once" (no commas). If the sentence read, "George indeed will not go; Ralph instead will leave at once," in which *indeed* and *instead* are used internally, almost no one would punctuate.

When a contrasting element is introduced by *not, never,* or *seldom* (but not *not only*), the negative expression is set off by a comma or commas, as may be needed: "Johnson specified brown file cabinets, *not* red ones." "Because he referred to a snow ski, *not* a water ski, everyone got a good laugh." "It was always done in the spring, *never* later."

One or Many

Commas set a one-of-a-kind member of a family apart from a group. "My dog, Baffa, is lost," for example, implies that I have only one dog. The sentence says two things: that my dog is lost and that his name is Baffa. The appositive, since it is set off by commas, conveys information that may be omitted without impairing the sentence sense. If I had more than one dog, the sentence would be written without commas. "My dog Baffa is lost" means that I have several dogs, of which Baffa is one. As another example, "Mrs. Marshall's son, who lives in Brussels, came to visit her," refers to her only son. The clause "who lives in Brussels," is merely descriptive detail. Without the commas ("Mrs. Marshall's son who lives in Brussels came to visit her"), the restrictive clause identifies the son meant, implying that she has more sons. In effect, the sentence says that of Mrs. Marshall's sons, the one who lives in Brussels came to visit her.

Because It's Not

A sentence that begins with a main clause containing the word *not* and continues with a subordinate clause beginning with *because* can be puzzling. A comma is needed to clarify the sentence. For example, "Treverino *did not* race today because he had a sore heel" may mean (1) that his sore heel took him out of the race or (2) that he did not run, not because he had a sore heel, but for some other reason (perhaps he had been disqualified or had not arrived in time to start). A comma before *because* makes the first sense unmistakable: "Treverino did not race today, because he had a sore heel." The second sense— that he did not race for a reason other than having a sore heel— would need either "Treverino did not race today, but not because . . . ." or "It was not because Treverino had a sore heel that he did not race today."

Hyphens

Softly, Softly, Little Hyphen

A common error in hyphening appears in "It is a widely-known fact" and "Conti Inc. is a closely-held corporation." Since *widely* and *closely* are clearly identifiable as adverbs, they need no hyphens. In fact, an adverb ending in *-ly* should never be hyphened. In the following sentences, therefore, hyphens are correctly omitted: "Alfredo has a *tastefully furnished* office." "It is a *generally accepted* belief that Geoffrey intends to leave." "This is a *privately owned* company."

Possibly *-ly* adverbs are mistakenly hyphened on the analogy of composite adjectives, known as unit modifiers. These adjectives are hyphened when they and a participle are brought together to form a one-thought modifier, as in "Layton is known for his *high-spirited* attitude" or "It is a *broad-based* tax." This rule applies even though the adjective ends in -ly: "The new professor is a *scholarly-looking* person." "Everyone agrees that it is a *heavenly-smelling* aroma." A question that sometimes arises, since -*ly* adverbs are not hyphened whereas -*ly* adjectives are, is how to distinguish one from the other. The answer is found in derivation. Adverbs ending in -*ly* derive from adjectives: *bashful, bashfully; kind, kindly; rare, rarely; soft, softly.* Adjectives ending in -*ly* stem principally from nouns: *brotherly, costly, lovely, manly, orderly* ("Lewis is a *fatherly*-looking dean" and "Sadie Thompson is a *motherly*-looking woman"). *Fatherly* and *motherly* come from the nouns *father* and *mother.*

(For other rules on the use of hyphens, see **COMPOUND WORDS.**)

Parentheses and Brackets

Parentheses Can't Stand Straight

Parentheses are primarily used to enclose incidental or supplementary information not vital to the sentence. In this function they serve nearly the same purpose as dashes, but with considerably less emphasis. When parentheses are used properly, the information within them can be omitted without altering the meaning or structure of the sentence: "The brochure for our summer vacation (it will be mailed soon) furnishes all the details."

The initial letter within the parentheses is capitalized only if it begins with a proper noun: "We met the new teacher (John L. Anderson is his name) under trying circumstances." No period is used within the parentheses unless the whole sentence stands by itself and is not a part of another sentence: "The principal finally established order. (A report on student misconduct is enclosed.)" An exclamation point or question mark, if appropriate, follows the last word within the parentheses, as in "Not only do we expect a large turnout (can we count on you?), but we also plan to keep everyone happy." A comma is never placed before the first parenthesis. If one is needed, it follows the closing parenthesis, as in the preceding example.

Other uses of parentheses are almost mechanical; they raise no problems. Parentheses enclose numbers or symbols in a series—(1) (B) (i); confirm figures given in words—"He wants five hundred (500) dollars"; surround fragments—"He said he comes from Wilmington. (Delaware?)"

Brackets (called square brackets in Great Britain) enclose additions, corrections, or explanations in written material made by someone other than the author: "The discovery was made by Leaf Eriksson [he means Leif]." A bracketed *sic,* which is Latin for "as" or "thus," may be used instead to indicate that an error was reproduced as written: "The discovery was made by Leaf [sic] Eriksson." Brackets are also used as secondary parentheses, parentheses within parentheses: "The species no longer exists (see R. T. Fruendlich, *Living in Australia* [Los Angeles: The West Coast Press, 1962], pp. 80–94)."

Semicolon

It Is Half a Colon

Although it is sometimes said that a comma is the bane of a writer's life, the semicolon, too, is often troublesome. The pause occasioned by a semicolon is longer than that of a comma but shorter than that of a period. Convention has, to a great extent, established the proper uses of the semicolon; its employment, therefore, is all but automatic.

A semicolon is required between two distinct parts of a compound sentence if the connecting word between the clauses has been omitted: "Enrico thought he could pass his courses without studying; (but) he knows better now." If *but* had been used, a comma would have been the proper punctuation mark. Or the sentence could have been divided, with or without the *but,* so that each segment ended with a period.

A semicolon is best used between clauses of a compound sentence joined by a conjunction if the clauses themselves are subdivided by commas: "The mechanic, who had been working on the job for at least two hours, seized his head almost convulsively; and then he toppled over."

A conjunctive adverb (*moreover, therefore, however, consequently, nevertheless*) is preceded by a semicolon (and followed by a comma) when used between independent clauses: "The bell has rung; therefore, we must go now." The same rule applies even when the second clause is elliptical. "The battle had been a long one; however, a victorious one" (*it had been* following *however* is understood). A trend to omit the comma after the conjunctive adverb is gaining momentum. But it is a policy generally not adhered to except after one-syllable adverbs (*thus, hence, so*) and the two-syllable *also*: "It was a rainy day; hence few members attended the meeting."

Semicolons, for the sake of clarity, should separate enumerations or complex items in a series. This is especially so when internal punctuation is used: "The vote was as follows: Atlanta, 4; Memphis, 6; Miami, 7; New Orleans, 11." "My uncle said that he planned to leave early; that if all went well, he would arrive in Chicago at nine o'clock; and that he would spend no more than two days there."

Expressions such as *namely, that is,* or *for example* may be preceded by a semicolon if a separation greater than that marked by a comma is desired. "They raised objections to many things; namely, the place, the date, the hour, and the orchestra." If *namely* is omitted, a colon or a dash may replace the semicolon.

Two cautions when using the semicolon: no hyphen is used in the word *semicolon,* and quotation marks precede it ("The sign said 'Closed'; however, we snooped about").

PUPIL, STUDENT, SCHOLAR

There's Also the Drop-out

The terms *pupil, student,* and *scholar* are distinguished by the kind of school each one attends. A *pupil* attends an elementary school; a *student,* a secondary school or college; and a *scholar,* on the highest level, a college or university.

Pupil comes from the Latin *pupus,* which originally meant "boy." Its sense has now been extended to include both sexes. Even animals attending school, from seeing-eye dogs to pet lap dogs, are called *pupils,* albeit facetiously. The word, however, ordinarily applies to a child under the direct supervision of a teacher and pertains to "someone being taught in the lower grades."

A *student* is one who studies. The English word comes directly from the Latin *studens,* which means "applying oneself to" or "striving after."

The most unlikely, yet the literal, meaning of *scholar* is "one who has leisure." The word derived from the Greek *scholazein,* "to have leisure." Of course, in ancient days those who sought to cultivate philosophy and the arts, or wanted to engage in other academic pursuits, could not be concerned with mundane activities. They needed the time, the leisure, to contemplate, study, and discuss.

Today scholars are learned or erudite persons who are pursuing, or who have pursued, advanced study. They are mature students devoted to a specialization. At one time, the term *scholar* signified a holder of a scholarship—a still valid but obsolescent use of the word. (A *scholarship* is a partial or total payment for a student's tuition.) But its original figurative sense continues, referring to the quality of a student's work: "Edith's thesis reflects fine *scholarship*: it is well researched and intelligently written. A *fellowship* is a "scholarship" awarded to a graduate student.

PURPORT

The Annual Purport

The verb *purport* means "to profess to be"; the noun *purport,* "the meaning or significance conveyed or professed." The verb is pronounced puhr-*port*; the noun, *puhr*-port.

As a verb, *purport* is used most effectively to express a noncommittal attitude or to raise a slight doubt. In the sentence "This book purports to describe the daily lives of prisoners of war," *purport* suggests that this is not what the book actually does. The noun *purport,* if a negative connotation is not intended, is best replaced by a word like *gist, substance,* or *drift.* For example, *gist* is to be preferred, in "Fortunately, the lisper gave the *purport* of his message in a few words."

The verb *purport* should not be used in the passive voice. In "That poem *is purported to be* from the pen of Robert Frost" (possibly *purported to be* was confused with *was supposed to be,* an established phrase that says almost the same thing), the active voice is needed: "The poem *purports* to be. . . ."

A different kind of error appears in "He *purports* to have studied at the Sorbonne," for the subject of *purport* may be only a thing, not a person: "This document *purports* to clarify your rights as a tenant." A person *claims*; a thing *purports*: "She claims she left on time." An exception to the rule permits the use of a personal subject when the verb "to be" follows *purport*: "He *purports* to be a playwright."

PUZZLE

See CONFUSION, DEGREES OF, and ENIGMA, PUZZLE, RIDDLE

Q

QUAINT

See ODD, QUAINT, QUEER

QUARTER

See HALF, QUARTER and FRACTIONS

QUEER

See ODD, QUAINT, QUEER

QUITE

See JUST, QUITE

R

RACIAL TERMS

A Boering Subject

Afrikaans, a language developed by the seventeenth-century Dutch, is spoken by *Afrikaners,* white people of Boer descent. Most Boers, pronounced *boors,* are found in the Republic of South Africa.

The term for a native of South Africa is *Negro.* Many natives prefer to be called *natives,* however. Still others prefer to be known as *Africans.*

A *Negro* is "a member of the Negroid ethnic division of the human species." This is an accurate racial term, although some members of the race dislike it. It is no more disparaging in itself to be called a Negro than it is a native. (In the United States Negroes are now called *blacks.*) A *Caucasian* is "a member of the Caucasoid ethnic division." The anthropological term for the third major racial division is *Mongoloid,* people who resemble, in some way, the Mongols. This racial stock includes not only the Chinese and the Japanese, but also the Malaysians, the Eskimos, and the American Indians.

RACK, WRACK

All Racked Up

The words *rack* and *wrack* have *racked* (or is it *wracked?*) the minds of many a person. Since the days of Middle English *rack* has meant a framework, either an inviting one (such as a holder for fodder above a manger) or a repellent one (such as an apparatus for torture). From its latter association—with punishment and torture—the sense of *rack* has been extended to embrace the idea of stretching, straining, or spreading out in a tense, if not torturous, way. In this sense it is used as a verb: "He *racked* his memory for a clue to her identity."

The meaning of *wrack,* a variant spelling of *rack,* according to some etymologists, is "wreck," which has led to the phrase

249

"wrack and ruin," referring to pieces of wrecked ships that have been washed ashore. As a verb, *wrack* may be equated with *ruin* or *destroy*.

Nerve-racking should be spelled without a *w*, for it connotes straining, perhaps so severe as to be agonizing, but it does not suggest destruction or wreckage. Clearly the proper word in the first sentence of this article is *racked*, since thought merely strains (it does not destroy) one's mind. The cliché *to rack one's brains* similarly means to strain the thinking processes; *to wrack one's brains* would ruin them.

The past tense of the verb *wrack* is not *wreaked*, but *wracked*: "The tornado *wracked* the farm buildings." To *wreak* means to vent anger or to inflict vengeance or punishment, as in "The Huns *wreaked* their vengeance upon the inhabitants of the conquered territory by *wracking* their homes."

RAISE, RISE—SET, SIT

Verbal Elevators

The use of *rise* and *raise* and *sit* and *set* are governed by similar rules. Basically, their distinctions lie in whether or not they take a direct object.

Rise and *sit* are intransitive verbs, that is, they are complete in themselves without an object: "A gentleman should *rise* when a lady enters the room." "The elevator *rises* quickly." Here the sense of *rise* is "to get up from a lying or sitting position" or "to move upward." In "Carol McAuliffe likes to *sit* down before lecturing" and in "We are happy to *sit* in the park on a sunny day," *sit* means "to be seated."

Raise and *set*, since they take direct objects, are transitive verbs. Transitive *raise* in this usage means "to move upward," as in "The patient *raised* her right arm" and in "The maid *raised* the window." *Set* is commonly used in such expressions as "*set* a watch," "*set* a price," or "*set* a table."

Sit may be used transitively in some constructions. The most common of these is in this example: "Her aunt *sits* herself down the moment she enters a room." In some cases either *sit* or *set* is possible: "The hens *set* (or *sit*) on eggs." "Rise up" and "sit down" are good idiomatic expressions, but the *up* and *down* are usually unnecessary.

Both *rise* and *arise* have the sense of sitting up or standing: "The audience *rises* (or *arises*) as one." *Arise* also has an extended meaning of "to originate," "to spring up," or "to come into being," as in "New difficulties *arise* daily."

As nouns, both *raise* and *rise* mean an increase in salary. In America, one gets a *raise*; in Britain, a *rise*. To raise another point, a building that is utterly destroyed has been *razed*, not *raised* (same pronunciation). *Raze* means "to make level with the ground"; *raise*, to lift from it.

RARE, SCARCE

What Is So Rare As . . .

Although the adjectives *rare* and *scarce* are synonymous (each implies something in short supply), they enjoy distinctive usages. In its primary sense, *rare* suggests an item of special quality and great value. Inherent in it is a sense of uncommonness—that which is permanently not plentiful: "Precious stones are costly because they are *rare*." Something may be scarce yet not rare. Although cantaloupes are not rare melons, they may be scarce late in the season. Items that are scarce, unlike rarities, have no lasting value; they are merely temporarily unobtainable, as is meat during a drought or a bestseller after a sellout at the bookstore. But meat will become available once the drought has ended, and the book, once it is reprinted.

The adverb *rarely* means "seldom" or "infrequently," as in "She *rarely* goes shopping" or in "We *rarely* see them." The expression *rarely if ever* is acceptable formal usage, but not *rarely ever*. Since *rarely* establishes the time element, the added *ever* (which means "at any time") is superfluous. One may properly say, "We *rarely if ever* see them" or, more simply, "We *rarely* see them," but not "We *rarely ever* see them."

RAVAGE, RAVISH

The Savage Ravage

The sentence "The nomads ravaged everything in Celicia, including the women" is only partly correct. A town, a building, or an army camp might be ravaged, that is, plundered or destroyed. But since people cannot ravage people, the nomads could not ravage the women, although they might have ravished them. *Ravish* means "abduct" or "rape." A person who is ravishing, however, is probably not committing rape. *Ravishing,* as an adjective, is used today to mean "inspiring joy or delight." A beautiful woman may aptly be described as ravishing.

The expression *cry havoc* seems unrelated to *ravage* and *ravish,* but there is a distant connection. Some people imagine that the phrase means "to complain unnecessarily." The chronic complainer, they would say, should stop crying havoc. But this use of *havoc* is incorrect. In ancient days to *cry havoc* (or, as then spelled *havocke*) was to issue an order releasing soldiers for rape and plunder. The expression received its immortality, thanks to Shakespeare, through the words of Mark Antony: "Caesar's spirit . . . shall . . . cry havocke and let slip the Dogges of warre." Today the word, although suggesting an exceedingly unpleasant happening, has outgrown its gruesome connotation; *havoc* now means "general destruction or devastation," usually the result of a catastrophe: "The hurricane brought *havoc* to South Florida."

RE-

Radishes Repeat, Too

One can repeat only what has been previously said or done. Thus, although a repetition may occur once (as when a person repeats an oath) or be continual (as is the ringing of a telephone), the number of repetitions is always one fewer than the total number of acts. For example, a play repeated four times has been performed five times altogether.

Not all words bearing the sense of *repeat* are prefixed by *re-*. *Iterate,* for example, means "to state again." With the *re-* affixed—*reiterate*—it means "to iterate again." *Iterate* implies a single exact repetition; *reiterate,* at least in current usage, suggests the saying or doing of something over and over so frequently as to make the repetition wearying. It is redundant to use *again* with *iterate* or *reiterate,* although some writers occasionally do so for emphasis.

Many *re-* words have lost their derivative meaning of "doing or saying again." One is *rehearse,* as in "to *rehearse* one's speech" or "to *rehearse* a part in a play," which means to practice privately what is to be performed publicly. Even the initial practice performance is called a *rehearsal* despite its etymological meaning "to harrow again." Verbs such as *regret, relate, remedy, relieve,* or *reject* similarly refer to initial acts.

REACTION

Reactions to Responses

A *response* is an answer. It may be spoken or written, or even a gesture. For example, a nod of the head may signal yes; a shrug of the shoulders, maybe.

A popular synonym for *response,* of which purists disapprove, is *reaction,* an especial favorite of journalists. Its technical meaning, "to display some form of energy in response to a stimulus," does not logically fit into figurative English. Only a staunch behaviorist would contend that man, like a chemical, reacts in this sense. Preferably, unless used for an action generated directly by a stimulus—an electric shock, a drug, a slap in the face—*reaction* is a term best restricted to science.

If employed in general contexts, it should be used only of a response that is immediate and more or less automatic, as in "What was your *reaction* when you won the Irish Sweepstakes?" or in "The chairman's angry denunciation of the committee met with a surly *reaction.*" But if time has elapsed since an interview or event, a response to it would be reflective and could therefore not be considered a reaction. In "Please let me have your reaction in a few days," clearly *reaction* is a poor choice. More suitable words would be *opinion, feeling, conclusion, attitude, response, judgment,* or *thought.* Or, if recast, perhaps the direct "Please tell me in a few days what you think."

REAL, REALLY

It's Real Enough

The adjective *real* means "true, actual, genuine." It is an unsuitable colloquialism for "very" or "very much." In "She is *real* hungry," *very* is called for, as is *very much* (or *greatly*) in "Guarino was *real* upset."

Saying "Mrs. Moore has *real* discomfort" poses another kind of problem. If the intent behind the word *real* is to emphasize *discomfort,* then *great* is needed. If the purpose is to indicate that the discomfort is actual, not supposed, *real* is used correctly. But in no instance should *real* be substituted for *really.* "My aunt is *really* ill," not "My aunt is *real* ill."

On the other hand, in at least one instance the correct use of *real* is regularly displaced in informal language by the word *regular.* And *real* and *regular* are not synonymous. This occurs in such sentences as "Mr. Coyne is a *regular* booze-hound" or in "Jean Hathaway is a *regular* scholar." In both sentences *real* would serve better. In the second, the word *thorough* would be even better.

Really is sometimes used unnecessarily to bolster a point: "The keeping of American personnel in Iran during a period of crisis was *really* a mistake." Immature writers may think that *really* makes their writing more emphatic, but *really* is as useless as *actually* in "I *actually* believe it." And that is *really* so.

REASON

Because Is No Reason

The commonly heard expression *the reason is because* is redundant, since the idea of *because* is already contained in *reason.* *Reason* means "the fact given as the motive or cause of an act or condition." It explains or justifies the effect produced. One may say, "Sitting too long under the sun is the cause of many illnesses" or "The reason for many illnesses is too much exposure to the sun," but not "*The reason* for many illnesses *is because* one sits too long under the sun." No sentence can logically accommodate both *reason* and *because.*

A sentence containing both these elements is corrected by omitting *because* and substituting *the reason is that* (*that,* a relative pronoun, introduces a noun clause) or by using *because* (a subordinate conjunction, which introduces an adverbial clause) and omitting *the reason is.* For example, "The reason he did not receive the invoice *is that* it was misdirected" or "He did not receive the invoice *because* it was misdirected." The usual remedy is to change *because* to *that.*

More to be criticized is *the reason is due to* and *the reason is on account of.* They are as repetitive as *the reason is because* and even wordier. The following exemplifies correct usage: "His failure was due to (not 'The reason for his failure was due to' or 'The reason for his failure was on account of') carelessness."

A sister expression, *the reason why,* although deplored by purists, is a generally accepted colloquialism. The phrase is often used unnecessarily, however, for either *the reason* or *why* can be omitted with no loss in sense. In "*The reason why* he didn't know is that he failed to look," for example, *why* is superfluous; and, with a little juxtaposing, in "We know *the reason why* he failed to look," *the reason* serves no purpose: "We know *why* he failed to look."

Lord Tennyson immortalized the phrase *reason why* in his "Charge of the Light Brigade." But *reason* was there used as a verb: "Theirs not to reason why, / Theirs but to do and die."

REDUNDANCIES

Some Words Say Nothing

The following redundancies are not made any more palatable by their commonness.

Customary practice combines *practice,* which means "customary action," and the therefore superfluous *customary.*

Continue to remain, as in "We hope they *continue to remain* on their jobs," can continue without *to remain.*

Since *herewith* means "with this" or "enclosed in this," it is unnecessary to say *enclosed herewith* or *attached herewith.* Nothing is lost without *herewith* except verbiage: "Our latest price list is *enclosed.*" "*Attached* (or *Here*) is the brochure you wanted."

The expression *up above* ("The shoe department is *up above* on the fourth floor") needs no *up.* And someone told to go *down below* knows that *below* is *down* and that *down* is *below.*

Each in its respective way says no more than *each in its way.*

The *or* in the correlative conjunction *either . . . or* can function without support. In "Branton must either cash his securities or *else* face dire consequences," *else* should be omitted.

A meeting that was discontinued was canceled, not canceled *out.*

REFERENDUM

See PLEBISCITE, REFERENDUM

RENT

See HIRE, LEASE, RENT

REPEL, REPULSE

All Repellents Are Not in Aerosols

Repel and *repulse* are interchangeable when they mean "to force back," "resist," or "beat off." An intruder or a commando raid, for example, may be either *repelled* or *repulsed,* although *repulse,* a more forceful word, is preferred when physical violence is involved.

Because people associate *repulse* with *repulsive,* errors appear in such sentences as "The campers were *repulsed* by the prospect of cooking their own food." But the words are not so close as they sound. To be repulsed is to be rebuffed or snubbed. To find something repulsive (that is, to be disgusted or offended, as the campers were) is not to be repulsed but to be repelled. This sense of *repel* is "to cause aversion, to so disgust as to turn one away," as in "His peculiar mannerisms *repelled* me." A suitor who has been spurned by a woman he still loves has been repulsed but not repelled, whereas a waiter who sees a guest eating like a farm animal is repelled, not repulsed.

To come full circle, both *repellent* and *repulsive* mean arousing such distaste or aversion as to drive one away: "The mixture of odors was *repellent.*" "He has a *repulsive* way of wiping his nose."

REPLACE, SUBSTITUTE

A Substitute That Needs Replacing

One may say "Here comes my *substitute*" or "*my replacement*" with no change in sense. The nouns *substitute* and *replacement* are synonymous. Their corresponding verb forms, however, do not have precisely the same meanings. To *substitute* is "to put in place of another." To *replace* is "to take the place of," as when something new or different is made to serve or function for another. If a brown book is removed from a shelf and a green one is put in its stead, the green book has been substituted for the brown, and the brown book has been replaced by the green.

But since this distinction is of little practical effect, the verbs may be interchanged if used with their proper preposition.

The preposition that *substitute* takes is *for*. In "The board *was substituted* last year, because of the mayor's insistence, by an enlarged committee," either *substituted* should be changed to *replaced* or the sentence recast: "An enlarged committee . . . *was substituted for* the board." With *replace*, idiom permits a choice of prepositions—*by* or *with*. For example, a vase on the shelf may be replaced *by* or *with* a figurine. And if the chairman of the Admissions Committee replaces Dr. Bois *with* Bradford, Dr. Bois has been replaced *by* Bradford, who has replaced Dr. Bois *as* a member of the committee.

Replace and *supplant* have a sense in common; they both refer to the putting of someone or something in the place of another. *Supplant*, derived from the Latin *supplantare*, "to trip up one's heels" (a *planta* is the sole of the foot), has logically come to mean "to cause the downfall of." It frequently denotes an ouster of a person from a position by a usurper, but it may also refer to technical progress. For example, motor vehicles have supplanted the horse and wagon in the postal department. Central heating has supplanted fireplaces in most homes. Although someone supplanted has been replaced, *replace* has the feeling of an ordinary, usually agreeable move. *Supplant* suggests a move against a person's wishes or advantage: "Mary has *supplanted* Joyce in Henry's affections."

REPORTEDLY

See ALLEGEDLY

RESTRICTIVE CLAUSES

See THAT, WHICH

RÉSUMÉ

See SUMMARY AND RELATED WORDS

REVEAL

See DISCLOSE, REVEAL

REVERENT, SOLEMN

A Solemn Matter

Reverend means "deserving of respect or worthy to be revered." It is an honorific adjective when addressing a clergyman, but it may apply to anyone or anything deserving reverence: "The Lincoln Memorial is one of America's most reverend symbols." In this sense *reverend* is a synonym for *revered.*

Both *reverent* and *reverend* derive from the Latin *reverens,* "fearing" or "respecting." Now defined as "feeling, exhibiting, or characterized by reverence," it implies respect tinged with awe: "There was a *reverent* silence in the auditorium when the Nobel Prize winner entered." "Dr. Hall is a *reverent* disciple of Sigmund Freud." It might be said that a person is *reverent* (deeply respectful) in the presence of the *reverend* (one who deserves reverence).

Solemnity is not necessarily inherent in feelings that are *reverend* or *reverent. Solemn* has many meanings, among which only "marked or observed with religious rites" would be a companion to those words. Occasions other than religious ones may also be solemn, that is, performed with full ceremony, as is the investiture of a university chancellor. With regard to individuals, *solemn* primarily suggests an earnest and thoughtful attitude. One's face, voice, or mood may be solemn, meaning "serious and sober," or even "gloomy and disheartening." Situations or events are solemn if grave and somberly impressive.

REVERSAL, REVERSION

Put It in Reverse!

Reversal is the corresponding noun of the verb *reverse.* Its literal meaning is "a turning back." In ordinary usage *reverse* means "to turn completely about in position or direction." *Reversal*—the act of reversing—is a change to an opposite or contrary position. It may pertain to a physical change ("Her *reversal* of the order of entries made the bibliography more confusing") or to a change of opinion, judgment, or policy ("The doctor's second opinion was a *reversal* of his former one").

Reversion is the noun form of *revert,* meaning "to go back." Like *reversal,* the word *reversion* denotes "a turning back" but in the sense of change to a former state or to more primitive behavior rather than to an opposite or contrary position. More specifically, it is a "turning back" to childish or uncivilized conduct or to a former way of life, such as a young man's reversion to financial dependence on his parents, a rehabilitated criminal's reversion to crime, or an ex-addict's reversion to drugs. In law, *reversion*, according to Black's *Dictionary*, is "the returning of an estate to the grantor or his heirs after the interest granted expires." In biology, it applies to atavistic characteristics, the recurrence of ancestral types.

RIDDLE

See **ENIGMA, PUZZLE, RIDDLE**

RIGHT, WRONG

The Difference Between Right and Wrong

Wrong is an adjective: "He made a *wrong* turn." It is also an adverb: "The words were spelled *wrong.*" Used before a verb, the correct adverbial form is *wrongly:* "The words were *wrongly* spelled." As a verbal modifier following a verb, either *wrong* or *wrongly* is permissible, though *wrong* is preferred.

Just as both *wrong* and *wrongly* are adverb forms, so are their antonyms, *right* and *rightly. Right* means "straight or directly": "After work, he will go *right* to the meeting." *Rightly* means "properly" or "justifiably": "The doctor *rightly* refused to discuss his patient's condition."

In strict formal English *right* should not be equated with the verb "to deserve" nor be used as a noun meaning "just cause to expect." One should say "Allen *deserves* (or *rightly* expects to receive) the trophy" rather than "Allen has a *right* to that trophy."

RITZY

See **LUXURIANT, LUXURIOUS**

ROBBER

See **BURGLAR, ROBBER, THIEF**

RUDIMENTARY, VESTIGIAL

Rudimentary, My Dear Watson

The words *vestigial* and *rudimentary* are not synonymous. They are, in fact, nearly opposite in meaning. Whereas *vestigial* pertains to a remnant of something that has passed and no longer exists, *rudimentary* refers to an incipient development, something just beginning. The word comes from the Latin *rudis,* which means "rough or raw" and "inexperienced or untrained." What is rudimentary, therefore, is still so incompletely formed as to be thought of as crude or undeveloped, like a rudimentary drawing or a rudimentary knowledge of science.

Some degenerate bodily structures are called vestigial— the so-called floating rib, for example, or the appendix, or nipples in male animals. What is *vestigial* has little or no utility; it merely is visible evidence of something that at an earlier stage performed a useful function.

S

SALARY

See **NEPOTISM, SALARY, SINECURE**

SCARCE

See **RARE, SCARCE**

SCARCELY

See **HARDLY**

SCHOLAR

See **PUPIL, SCHOLAR, STUDENT**

-SELF

Get Hold of Yourself

"Let us think about *ourselves.*" Adding *self* or *selves* to the genitive form of a personal pronoun in the first and second persons and to the accusative case in the third person makes it either reflexive or intensive. The forms of these pronouns are identical—*myself, yourself, ourselves, himself*; only their uses differ.

Reflexive pronouns are employed when the identity of the subject and object is the same. They are called reflexive because the subject of the verb is also its object; for example, "He hurt *himself*" (direct object), "She bought *herself* two pairs of shoes" (indirect object), "The chain was twisted back on *itself*" (object of a preposition).

Not infrequently the reflexive pronoun is mistakenly used as the second member of a compound subject or object. Sentences like "My wife and *myself* are pleased to invite you to

261

dinner" need correcting, since the subject of a sentence must be in the nominative case: "My wife and *I* are pleased . . ." Likewise, in "The supervisor made the secretaries and *ourselves* wait for over an hour," the objective case is required: ". . . the secretaries and *us*."

Intensive pronouns are actually reflexive forms construed as pronouns in apposition to emphasize the "doer": "The captain *himself* told me." "The prisoners *themselves* refused to leave." "You *yourself* ought to know better." The position of the pronoun is immaterial as long as it functions clearly: "He *himself* wired the whole house" or "He wired the whole house *himself*." Preferably an intensive is placed next to its antecedent.

What must be guarded against is the tendency to punctuate these pronouns. "She, *herself*, did it" needs no commas.

Some idiomatic phrases are formed with reflexive pronouns preceded by a preposition. These expressions are not applicable in all constructions. For example, it is correct to say, "He wrote it *by himself*" because *by himself* is an idiomatic unit meaning "alone or apart from others." But it is incorrect to say, "It was written *by himself*," since *by* is here used as a simple preposition, which requires the objective case—in this instance *him*.

SEMI-

See BI-, SEMI-

SEMICOLON

See PUNCTUATION—SEMICOLON

SENTENCE TYPES

Sentences for Life

Every sentence—simple, compound, or complex—has at least one clause, a group of related words that contains a subject and a predicate. Even a one-word command qualifies. Its subject is implied. "Stop!" really says "*You* stop!" What is implied in "Go" is "*You* may go."

A simple sentence consists of a single clause. It can stand

by itself because it is complete—truly independent—with a final mark of punctuation at the end: "He took his family to dinner." A compound sentence contains two or more independent clauses joined by a coordinating conjunction (*and, or, but, nor*) and no subordinate clause: "He is going, *and* I am planning to go, too." Complex sentences consist of an independent clause (also called a principal or main clause) and one or more subordinate, or dependent, clauses. Although a subordinate clause contains a subject and a predicate, as do all clauses, it cannot stand alone. To complete its meaning, it needs to be attached to the main clause. If the subordinate clause is deleted, what remains is an independent clause. For example, removing the subordinate clause in "The band was marching as I was being seated" leaves the simple sentence: "The band was marching." Subordinate clauses are introduced by subordinating conjunctions (such as "*if* I go"; "*when* it rains"; "*because* I'm older") and relative pronouns (such as *who, which,* or *that*).

The most common sentence is one that makes a statement. It is labeled loose or periodic, depending on the arrangement of its words. A loose sentence follows normal order (subject, predicate, object), such as the simple *declarative* sentence "I found the book." A periodic sentence withholds its meaning until the end or near the end. Only those sentences that are invertible can be expressed this way. For example, "I looked here, I looked there, but guess where I found it—under my feet." The effect of withholding the meaning is to create suspense; the reader continues in expectation: "Though Beethoven composed music all his life, during his last ten years when he wrote some of his greatest works he heard not a note, for he was totally deaf."

Sentences of different lengths, because their pace changes, add interest. Especially if a short sentence is occasionally interspersed. Even a fragment. Some sentences should begin with adverbs or adverbial clauses ("Generally it is done early in the year." "Though late in the season, it should be done promptly"). Others with an infinitive ("To scale Mt. Everest is the goal of almost every mountain climber"), a prepositional phrase ("During this period the schools have an intersession"), or a gerund ("Swimming is the best exercise"). Variety is bound to spice up one's writing.

SET, SIT

See RISE, RAISE—SET, SIT

SEXISM

S/he

Webster partially defines the word *he* as "one whose sex is unknown or immaterial . . . 'he that hath ears to hear, let him hear'; used as a nominative case form in general statements . . . to include females, fictitious persons . . . and several persons collectively." However, the supporters of the recent movement for equality of the sexes have thrown this use of the pronoun into disfavor because they consider *he* acceptable only when it refers to a male. Since writers have traditionally used *he* or *his* if either the sex of the antecedent was unknown or if both sexes were being referred to, avoiding sexism in language, without disturbing the integrity of the written word, has become a distressing problem.

One way to avoid sexism in language is by writing in the plural. Rather than "A doctor must keep himself clean; otherwise, he will lose his patients' respect," a sentence may read, "Doctors must keep *themselves* clean; otherwise, *they*. . . ." This subterfuge cannot be used in all cases, however. If *each,* for example, is the subject of the sentence, a singular pronoun is needed, and the problem must then be confronted. "Each is entitled to *their* own view" is ungrammatical and "Each is entitled to *his* or *her* own view" is graceless. Most writers would use *his.*

Words that patronize women, such as poetess, Negress, or usherette, are easily replaceable by more suitable terms. What is more pressing and more controversial is the use of everyday words like Congressman and chairman. Many persons of both sexes do not accept Congresswoman, and they deplore the word *chairperson.* Calling the person who presides at a meeting "the chair" is even sillier.

This matter of sexism is so controversial that no one has suggested a solution satisfactory to all factions. The easiest thing is to avoid words that patronize women. And yet a person who drops a tray in an airplane and hollers for a stewardess probably is not trying to be offensive, although other words, say, attendant, have no sex connotation.

SHALL, WILL

Should You?

The schoolhouse rule that *shall* and *should* express futurity or condition in the first person and *will* and *would* in the second and third persons apparently was made to be broken; it is very rarely observed. Ordinarily *will* is used in all three persons to express the simple future: "I think he will go, and I think I will go, too" (rather than the precisely correct "I shall go, too"). The rule has so many legitimate exceptions that correct usage seems simply a matter of current usage. For example, *shall* and *should,* regardless of person, are used in *that* clauses after the verbs *intend, demand, desire, order,* and the like: "Marchand *intends that we shall* have a good reception." "The company *demands that the customers shall* return every item."

According to strict formal style, the auxiliary verb in interrogations is the one that is idiomatic in the expected reply. For example, "*Shall* you be comfortable alone tonight?" (I *shall* be.) "*Will* you finish your chores by this evening?" (I *will* finish.) "*Shall* you go?" (I *shall* go.) The speaker puts himself in the place of the one he is addressing and uses *shall* or *will* accordingly.

Rhetorical questions that indicate the speaker's doubt or concern are all phrased with *shall,* regardless of the person: "When lawyers argue among themselves, who *shall* stop them?" "What *shall* I do?"

In laws, motions, resolutions, and directives—all of which signify control by an authority— the use of *shall* (or *should*) is customary: "No unauthorized person *shall* be permitted access to the records." "A subcommittee *shall* be organized within six weeks to review fiscal policies."

The so-called *if* clauses take *should* in all three persons to express condition or supposition: "If *I* (or *he*) *should* need more books, Miss Grash will certainly supply them."

In current usage *will* appears more than 200 times to each *shall.* The American people have a strong will.

SHAMBLES

After the Grandchildren Leave

Whether the word *shambles* may describe any scene of great disorder is a matter of dispute. Some word-usage authorities say yes; others, no. But the widespread acceptance of that sense makes it unlikely that *shambles* will ever be dislodged as a synonym for *disarray*.

The term *shamble* comes from the ancient word *scamellus*, "a small bench." It originally referred to a butcher's bench on which meat was cut and later displayed. By extension, the plural *shambles* became a synonym for slaughterhouse and was later broadened to cover any scene of carnage or bloodshed. Further progression has given it a current meaning of "great destruction," "complete ruin," or "wreckage"—ideas that do not necessarily encompass butchery.

Strictly speaking, *shambles* should refer only to an abattoir and not to mere clutter or turmoil. Its popular meaning, however, is so deeply entrenched that trying to turn back the linguistic hands of time is futile. Shambles is definitely how the house looks after the grandchildren leave.

SHARE

See PART, PORTION, SHARE

SHORTFALL, WINDFALL

It's Not an Ill Wind

In medieval times branches blown down from trees could be kept by the finder and used for firewood. This was called a *windfall*. In modern days the term has been enlarged to cover any unexpected gain or advantage: "Inheriting his uncle's wealth was a *windfall* that helped launch his career." "The newspaper morgue produced a *windfall* of leads." It is redundant to say "It was an unexpected *windfall*" because implied in *windfall* is the sense of the unexpected. After all, one cannot foretell when the wind will blow with such force as to cause something to loosen and fall.

A *shortfall* is defined as "an act or an instance of falling short, or the amount by which something falls short." In everyday language a *shortfall* is a shortage. A bank account with a deficit shows a shortfall.

SHOULD

See OUGHT, SHOULD

SIGHT, SPECTACLE

Seeing Is Believing

The word *sight* refers to vision or to something seen. A *spectacle* is also something seen: "As we turned the bend, we caught *sight* of the fair grounds—what a *spectacle!*"

Although occasionally interchanged, *sight* and *spectacle* have developed some distinctive usages. For one thing, *sight* is often employed deprecatingly ("What a *sight* my mother-in-law was in that frowsy dress") as is *spectacle* in the sense of showiness ("making a *spectacle* of oneself"). But neither term need be pejorative; for example, "The Barnum and Bailey Circus is a colorful, noisy, and exciting *spectacle*" and "Mt. Fuji in Japan is truly a magnificent *sight.*"

The phrase *a sight for sore eyes,* although hackneyed, is usually pleasantly received as a warm greeting. Its sense, of course, is that a pleasant sight can help heal one's sore eyes. Another *sight* expression, *sight unseen*—referring to the purchase of something that has not been seen—is also good idiom, even though it may be poor judgment.

SIMILAR

How Similar Can They Be?

Things that are similar have a general likeness or resemblance, or have a quality in common. A person's condition of health may be similar to another person's. A student's point of view may be similar to that of his teacher. A boy's clothing may be similar to his brother's.

When the adjective *similar* follows a linking verb, it modifies the subject of the sentence: "This *story seems similar* to one he wrote last week." But with other verbs (as in "This story *reads similar* to the one he wrote last week" and "That washing machine *operates similar* to mine"), the adverb *similarly* is required because it modifies the working verbs *reads* and *operates*.

Similar and *same* are not exact synonyms. Whereas *similar* refers to that which is almost identical, *same* means "identical in every respect." *Similar,* therefore, does not belong in the following sentences: "Prescott's uncle died in a plane crash, and his son met a similar fate (should be *the same fate*) a year later." "Three patients were waiting for Dr. Mirachi and a similar number (should be *the same number*) for Dr. Anzaldo."

It makes no sense to say *exactly similar,* although *exactly the same* is good idiom to emphasize that the identicalness matches in all respects. Ordinarily the phrase *similar to* can be economically replaced by *like:* "Their apartment is *like* our apartment."

SIMILES

See FIGURES OF SPEECH

SIMULTANEOUS

See COINCIDENT, SIMULTANEOUS, SYNCHRONOUS

SINCE

Since We're All Here Yet

Does *since* mean *because*? If so, are the words interchangeable? The answer is yes on both counts. However, *because* is more formal and places greater emphasis on the reason for an action. Also it serves as a subordinate conjunction. *Since* functions as several parts of speech: an adverb ("The police have been looking for him ever *since*"); a preposition ("Ettinger has been absent *since* last week"); and a conjunction ("We have moved twice *since* you last visited us").

When *since* is used temporally to indicate "from then till now," as in "The students *have been* waiting *since* nine o'clock," the principal verb is in the present perfect, not the past tense (not *were waiting*). Or, to take another example, "There *has been* (not *was*) no interference with the operation of the company *since* Sheldon *took* it over." But the tense of the verb in a clause introduced by *since* is in the past tense (*took*).

As a conjunction introducing a subordinate clause expressing cause or reason, *since* may serve for *as, because,* or *on account of*—any of which may replace *since* in these examples: "*Since* there is no one here, we may leave." "Jasper should revise his book quickly, *since* it is outdated." (However, *on account of* is wordy and *as* is weak; either *since* or *because* is preferable in formal English.) Care must be taken to avoid ambiguity in those sentences in which *since* may mean either "because" or "between then and now." For example, "*Since* the dean went away, the secretaries have been preparing all the rosters" may be construed either way.

Because in these uses takes no comma; *since,* when meaning "because," needs one: "We are leaving now *because* the hour is late," but "We are leaving now, *since* the hour is late."

Since and *ago* do not go together. In "It was about five years *ago since* we met," *ago* should be omitted: "It was about five years *since* we met." Coupling these words is like the effect of the Greek river Meander, which, as Ovid said, seemed to meet itself. The word *ago* makes one think from the present to the past, whereas *since* emphasizes a past time, bringing the mind up to the present. *Ago,* on the other hand, takes *that*: "It was about five years *ago that* he first went into business." Another uncompanionable pair is *since* and *until*. In "The farmer with the broken leg has not plowed *since* November *until* March," *between* November *and* March and the past tense of the verb (*did not plow*) are required.

SINECURE

See **NEPOTISM, SALARY, SINECURE**

SINGULAR NOUNS THAT APPEAR PLURAL

One of a Kind

Mumps and *measles,* despite their plural form, are singular nouns and therefore take singular verbs: "*Measles is* a disease contracted by many children." "*Mumps is* an infection of the salivary glands." It follows that the pronoun referring to either one is singular: "Ernestine has had the *mumps* for several days. She should be recovering from *it* soon."

Although the larva of certain tapeworms is called a *measle*, one does not speak of a measle with reference to the childhood disease. It is *measles*, or more properly expressed, *a case of measles*. As with other nouns of this kind, neither *a* nor a numeral may immediately precede it. It is wrong to say "There were four measles on our block" instead of *four cases of measles*.

Many other nouns ending in *s* are singular, but retain the same form when used as plurals. Only the number of the verb changes. For example, "The Shah's *riches is* unbelievable," but "Their *riches are* untold." "Rudi's annual *savings increases* regularly by 5 per cent," but "The partners' annual *savings increase* by more than 5 per cent." "One's *morals is* a very personal matter," but "During wartime, men's *morals seem* to deteriorate quickly." Some dictionaries regard these words only as plurals; others regard all or some of them as singular. In formal language both *savings* and *riches* should be treated as plurals.

(Words ending in *-ics* are discussed under -IC, -ICS.)

SITUATION

See OVERALL, SITUATION

SKEPTIC

Antiskeptic Solutions

About 2,400 years ago, a Greek philosopher, Pyrrho of Elis, taught his followers to view the world with detachment—to doubt systematically—on the theory that ultimate knowledge was unattainable and that even physical senses were unreliable. Those adopting this thoughtful, inquiring philosophy were called Skeptics, from *skeptikos*, "to look at something carefully" or "to consider." As time passed, the meaning of *skeptic* was applied more widely to anyone who instinctively or habitually doubted, questioned, or disagreed with generally accepted conclusions.

Although a skeptic is someone who questions the truth or genuineness of something, a cross-section of skeptics would be those who abstain from making value judgments in certain fields—particularly the metaphysical, moral, and religious. Skeptics would, for example, question, without denying outright, the theory of immortality or someone's conviction of immutable standards of what is right or wrong.

Whereas a skeptic is simply unconvinced, a *disbeliever* has reached a firm conclusion of unbelief. One may say, for example, "Roberts is *skeptical* about the mayor's assurance that he will not violate the charter" or "Anderson's innate *skepticism* warred continually with his deep piety," but "Lehman greeted his cousin's bizarre story with frank *disbelief*" or "Although a cleric's son, Miller is a firm *disbeliever* in the existence of God."

As applied to religion, *skeptic* and *agnostic* are similar terms. An agnostic, one who does not know (Greek *a*, "no" and *gnosis*, "knowledge"), believes that since nothing is known or can be known about the existence of a god, its existence cannot be proved or disproved. Coined in 1869 by the noted biologist Thomas Henry Huxley to describe those—including himself—who considered the ultimate nature of things unknowable, *agnostic* has become a common word to distinguish the questioners from the nonbelievers, the atheists, those who deny the existence of God. The word *atheist* derives from the Greek *atheos*, meaning "godless."

SLANDER

See LIBEL, SLANDER

SLOTHFUL

See IDLE, INDOLENT, LAZY, SLOTHFUL

SO

So To Speak

So is a pesky word, for it is so often misused—as it is in this sentence.

The adverb *so* means "to this extent." It is employed in negative comparisons of persons or things of unequal size, quality, or quantity: "It was *not so* humid yesterday *as* it is today." "Tulsa is *not so* large *as* St. Louis." *So* may also qualify such terms as *hardly, rarely,* or *scarcely*—words that merely imply a negative: "The treatise was *hardly so* well written *as* we were led to believe." "He is scarcely *so* vigorous *as* his father." "Sparrows are *rarely so* numerous here *as* bluejays." Affirmative statements—those comparing persons or things that are equal or that approximate each other—use *as . . . as*: "It is *as* humid today *as* it was yesterday." "Roland is *as* tall *as* Winston."

Some reputable writers ignore these conventions and use *as . . . as* in all statements of comparison, whether affirmative or negative. "This orange is *as* large *as* that one, but this apple is *not as* large *as* the one in your hand." Nevertheless, *so . . . as*, at least in formal usage, is to be preferred in comparisons of unequal elements.

In questions, too, these *so . . . as* and *as. . . as* constructions have distinctive uses, since different inferences can be drawn from each one. For example, "Is Professor Martin *so old as* his colleague?" implies that the questioner knows the colleague's age and desires to make a comparison. But in "Is Professor Martin *as old as* his colleague?" no such inference is justified. The question simply asks whether their ages are similar.

So is best not used as an intensive, as in "She is *so* tired," unless followed by a completing clause: "She is *so* tired *that* she ought to go to bed at once." Otherwise, *very* should replace it: "She is *very* tired."

One more *so* merits consideration—the one that introduces clauses expressing purpose or result. That *so* is followed by *that* or *as to*. For example, "He signed up for biology *so* he could spend more time with Janet" should be reworded ". . . *so that* he could spend more time with Janet," and "The teacher closed the windows *so* the students could hear better" reworded ". . . *so that* the students" or "*so as to enable* the students to hear better."

SO FAR AS

See AS FAR AS

SO THAT

So It Came to That

Whether the connective *so that* takes punctuation depends on the phrase it introduces. The general rule is that when *so that* introduces a clause of purpose, what follows is essential to the sense of the sentence; therefore, no comma separates the elements. In this use, *so that* is the equivalent of *in order that*: "Aunt Matilda went home early *so that* she could feed her parakeet." "The polls remained open an hour longer *so that* everyone would have a chance to vote."

When *so that* introduces a result clause, a preceding comma is unnecessary ("We were *so* far away *that* we could see nothing"), but it may be used if the *so that* clause is believed to be unessential ("Mr. Halstead had spent many years as a gamekeeper, *so that* he was familiar with the animals' habits"). In this sense, *so that* is the equivalent of the conjunctive adverbs *therefore* or *consequently*.

Despite the foregoing prescription on the use of commas, no comma precedes the clause when a *so that* connective is separated by intervening words, for those words are an integral part of the sentence: "Our agent is *so* well regarded *that* he is being considered for a promotion." "The mechanism is *so* enormous and complicated *that* to understand it takes years of study."

SOLECISMS

See **TYPES OF ERRORS**

SOLEMN

See **REVERENT, SOLEMN**

SOLID, STOLID

Deceptively Solid

The words *solid* and *stolid*, when referring to people, should not be confused. Each word describes someone in its own way.

Solid suggests that a person is "substantial, upstanding, dependable." One who enjoys a reputation for probity and financial integrity is considered a solid citizen. By many community standards, *solid* is equated with sober-minded and sensible. Expressions such as the solid phalanx of labor, the solid South, or the solid minority vote use the word somewhat differently. Here it indicates unanimity among a group of people—hence cohesion, the producing of "a solid mass."

Stolid means "impassive, having or showing little emotion." Originally it had an unflattering sense, signifying one who was emotionless or impassive from dullness or stupidity. The word comes from the Latin *stolidus,* which means "stupid." Impassivity does not necessarily reflect mental inability, however; it may, in fact, reflect admirable self-control and reserve. A stolid person may be a solid citizen.

A synonym of *stolid* is *stoical,* defined as "indifferent to, or unaffected by, pleasure or pain; impassive." The word refers to the Stoic school of philosophy, whose members used to gather in Athens on a *stoa* (the word for *porch* in Greek) to learn from their leader, Zeno. He taught that all happenings stemmed from a divine will and that wise men, therefore, should free themselves of emotions by practicing indifference to both pleasure and pain.

SOME

Some Do and Some Don't

Someone may say, and correctly so, that some people always make some errors with *some* words. For example, "*Some* of us get what *they* deserve" should be rephrased: "*Some* of us get what *we* deserve." Similarly, in "*Some* of us get *their* deserts," *our* should replace *their.*

Some is a word of many uses. Most commonly it serves as an adjective of indefinite number, as in "We saw *some* robins yesterday" or in "The librarian bought *some* new shelving for the library." It is also an indefinite pronoun: "We have many, and he has *some,* too." If used to mean "remarkable or surprising" ("He turned out to be *some* singer" or "My Champion is *some* horse"), it is poor English. And saying "The patient has improved *some,*" instead of *somewhat,* is even worse.

Many compounds are formed with *some*: the nouns *somewhat* and *somewhere* ("Ralph is *somewhat* of a magician." "He left for *somewhere* in Nebraska"); the pronouns *someone, somebody, something* ("*Someone* is knocking at the door"); and the adverbs *somehow, someway, somewhat,* and *somewhere* ("His grammar is *somewhat* improved; it is not surprising that he is getting *somewhere* at last").

Somewheres is substandard. Only the singular *somewhere* is correct: "We thought we had seen them *somewhere.*" No *where* compound (*nowhere, anywhere, everywhere*) uses a terminal *s*. Substituting *someplace* for the vulgate *somewheres* raises the level of writing somewhat. But since *someplace* is a colloquial term, it is not appropriate in written English.

Someway is preferred to *someways*. *Sometimes* (adverbs with a plural form are a rarity) means "at several indefinite times," as in "*Sometimes* he writes in his study till midnight." *Someone* is a one-word pronoun when it is the equivalent of *somebody* ("*Someone* [or *Somebody*] has opened the door"), but it is spelled as two words when the *one* is stressed ("If *some one* person is given the responsibility, the project will begin sooner").

One-word *something* is either a noun or an indefinite pronoun; the words *some things* consist of an adjective and a noun. "There may be *something* to discuss now and *some things* to rearrange later." *Something* when used adverbially is colloquial. In "She is *something* like her teacher," *somewhat* is called for. And saying "He cried *something* awful" is awful. *Something awful* is slang.

When to use *some time,* an adjective and noun, and when to use *sometime,* a one-word adverb, may be a source of confusion. As two words, the phrase means either "an amount of time," as in "We usually spend *some time* (direct object of the verb) each summer at the Cape," or "at a particular time," as in "He will return at *some time* in the future (object of a preposition). The one-word adverb *sometime* means either "an indefinite time" ("Our family invites you to visit us *sometime*") or "at a point in time" ("I met him in City Hall *sometime* last month").

Whether the phrase or the single word is called for can be determined by omitting the expression from the sentence. If there is no loss in meaning, as is so in "The meeting should be held (*sometime*) in November," the one-word adverb *may* be used. If the sense is affected, two words *must* be used. For example, without *some time* the following sentence would be nonsensical: "Unless you put *some time* aside to take care of your lawn, you'll have serious trouble."

This test also applies to *someday* and *some day.* In "For the family reunion, my grandmother will choose *some day* suitable to everyone," *some day* is an essential part of the sentence; but *someday* is not in "We say *au revoir* in the hope of seeing you again *someday.*"

-SOME

This Will Ful Some

Words ending in -some do not suggest an unspecified number, degree, or quantity as some does when used as a pronoun, adjective, or adverb. The suffix -some, except in its collective sense with numerals (as in threesome or foursome), indicates a tendency. For example, a quarrelsome person has a tendency to quarrel, and a matter that is burdensome has a tendency to burden.

Many words that end in -some do not refer to a disposition or inclination at all. Handsome, for instance, which originally meant what was wrought by the hand of man, means "pleasing to the eye." Wholesome has within it both holy and healthy. And then there are noisome and fulsome.

Noisome means "offensive" or "disgusting" and pertains chiefly to unpleasant and disagreeable odors. It in no way relates to sound and is not a synonym of noisy. The following is an example of correct usage: "The odor of the escaping gas was noisome and unbearable."

The odd thing about fulsome is that it is often used incorrectly as a complimentary term. The phrases fulsome praise and fulsome oratory are not commendatory, no matter how well intentioned the speaker might have been. The ful- in fulsome may deceive one into thinking that the word means "generous." It does not. Nor does it mean "full or overabundant." It means "offensively excessive," and describes what is so extravagant and so overdone as to seem insincere. What is fulsome, therefore, is objectionable or perhaps even offensive to a person of taste: "No one enjoys McConnell's fulsome monologs."

SPECIE, SPECIES

Money—the Endangered Specie

"The rarest specie of baboon has spots on its forehead" is incorrectly stated. The specie of the realm—specie meaning "money in the shape of coin"—might be rare, but among animals the spotted baboon is a rare species.

The word species, an equivalent of kind, is the basic scientific category used to classify animals and plants. It matters not whether one organism or many are meant because species has one form for both singular and plural: "This species of bluejay *is* seldom seen so far north." "*These species* of plants *grow* in the tropics."

The collective noun *specie*, however, is a singular form only: "One might be paid in *specie* or might collect the ancient *specie* of both Japan and Thailand." It is improper to precede *specie* with *a* or a numeral.

Specious is a word that looks deceptively like *specie* and *species*. It means "seemingly true, but actually not so." What is specious is fallaciously plausible, as in "It was a *specious* argument."

SPECTACLE

See SIGHT, SPECTACLE

SPELLING

Look It Up

The distinction of winning a spelling bee may be important to orthographers. But the distinction of spelling correctly in ordinary correspondence or in other writings is nonexistent. Everyone is expected to spell every word correctly. The only comment made concerning spelling applies to a misspelling. With spelling, therefore, a person cannot win; he can only lose.

(In addition to the problems discussed below, see PLU-RALS.)

The Exception Is the Rule

One of the most confusing combinations to manage in spelling is the *ie-ei* diphthong. Their governing rules not only are imprecise but filled with exceptions. The usual spelling is *ie*: *niece, relieve, efficient, friend, believe, piece, field, view*. After the letter *c*, however, the combination is often reversed: *receive, deceive, conceive*. But there are exceptions. Words pronounced with a long a (*ā*) also use *ei* even though not preceded by *c*: *weigh, freight, eight, neighbor*. The exceptions continue to mount. Although not preceded by the letter *c* and not pronounced with a long *a*, certain words use *ei* anyway: *either, seize, height, leisure, forfeit, weird, foreign*. Even the rule that *ei* normally follows a *c* has exceptions: *species, financier, conscience, omniscient, science*—all are spelled with *cie*.

A jingle designed as a memory device for this particular problem is in the *Harper's Handbook*:

Write *i* before *e*
Except after *c*,
Or when sounded like *a*
As in *neighbor* and *weigh*
Either, neither, leisure, seize,
Are exceptions; watch for these

He Knew It to a T

The past tense and past participle of many English words offer a choice of endings—either *t* or *ed*, as in *leapt* and *leaped* or in *smelt* and *smelled*. Other such words are *spilled, spilt; spoiled, spoilt; dreamed, dreamt; kneeled, knelt;* and *bereaved, bereft*. The preferable form is the one ending in *-ed*: *learned* rather than *learnt*.

When a suffix beginning with a vowel is added to a monosyllabic word ending in *t*, the *t* is doubled if it is preceded by a single vowel: *batting, putting, cutting* (but not *rusting*, since the vowel does not immediately precede the *t*). Doubling the *t* prevents the word from being confused with similarly spelled words. For example, the past tense of *fat* is *fatted*. Without the double *t*, the word would be *fated*, which has an entirely different meaning. Those words that have two vowels preceding the *t* do not observe the rule: *sweeter, boating, greeted*.

Polysyllabic words are treated in the same way if the accent is on the last syllable: *commit, committed; befit, befitted*. But not otherwise. The past tense of *benefit*, for example, is *benefited*, with one *t*.

The *t* remains silent in many words. This is so in *often, Christmas, fasten, listen,* and *mortgage*.

SPURIOUS

See **ARTIFICIAL**

STALACTITE, STALAGMITE

Icy Fingers

Laymen seldom use the geological terms *stalactite* and *stalagmite*. But when they do, they may not be certain which is which. Of one thing they are certain: these formations are found in caves.

A *stalactite* is an icicle-shaped mineral deposit that develops from water dripping from the roof of a cave; it grows downward. A *stalagmite,* formed in the same way, is a cone-shaped deposit on a cave floor that grows upward, sometimes beneath a stalactite.

The terms can easily be distinguished by associating the *c* in *stalactite* with the *c* in ceiling, from which the formation hangs. Similarly, the *g* in stalagmite reminds one of the *g* in ground, from which a stalagmite rises.

When stalactites and stalagmites meet, they become single columns. These pillars are as yet unnamed. Perhaps they should be called *stalactagmites.*

STANZA, VERSE

It Gets Verse All the Time

Verse is commonly confused with *stanza.* A *verse* is a single line of a poem or other metrical composition. The word derives from the Latin *versus,* "furrow," the noun form of *vertere,* "to turn." The idea is that a verse is a line that leads into the next and then to the next to the end of the poem, just as a plow turns a furrow and returns to dig another and another to the end of a field.

A *stanza* is a series of metrical lines—it is a succession, in other words, of verses. For example, Tennyson's "Crossing the Bar" contains four stanzas, of which "Sunset and evening star" is the first line or verse. In everyday language *verse* is used interchangeably not only with *stanza* but also with *poem.* Although some dictionaries equate the meanings of these words, in formal language the distinctions between them should be preserved. Calling a poem a *verse,* unless no possibility for confusion exists, needlessly forces the reader to decipher what is meant.

The verb indicating "to change from prose into poetry" is *versify*: "People with a flair for words and a feeling for rhyme like to *versify.*" An adjective form, *versed,* means "knowledgeable" or "skilled," as in "The priest is well *versed* in medieval music."

STEREOTYPE

See TRITE EXPRESSIONS

STOLID

See SOLID, STOLID

STRATEGY, TACTICS

Tic-Tac-Tics

Strategy has to do with an overall plan; *tactics*, with the specific means by which the plan is implemented, the method for advancing the objective. In warfare, strategy refers to the planning of campaigns: "General Brown's *strategy* is superb— everyone does exactly what he is told." Outside the military, *strategy* is a scheme for attaining a goal: "Arnold's *strategy* in dealing with his employer is highly successful." In military usage, *tactics*—a plural word, since it refers to maneuvers—is "the art of disposing troops in single battles": "High officers must learn the *tactics* of military strategy." *Stratagem* has two *a*'s; *strategy*, one.

STUDENT

See PUPIL, SCHOLAR, STUDENT

SUB ROSA

See FOREIGN WORDS

SUBJECT–VERB AGREEMENT

See COMPOUND SUBJECT; -IC, ICS; INDEFINITE PRONOUNS; PAIR WORDS; SINGULAR NOUNS THAT APPEAR PLURAL

SUBJUNCTIVE MOOD

An Uncertain Mood

The subjunctive mood has three tenses, and each has its mark of distinction. The *present subjunctive* indicates that the statement is concerned with an idea rather than a fact. It is introduced by *that* and is constructed in one of two ways: (1) the verb *be* used directly with a subject ("He asked *that* he *be* permitted to leave") and (2) a third person singular without the *s* ("The teacher recommended strongly *that* everyone *study* [not *studies*] for the coming exam." "We demanded *that* he *come* [not *comes*] with us").

The *past subjunctive* indicates uncertainty. It may even imply the impossible or refer to what is contrary to present fact. Its form is identical to that of the past indicative, but rather than referring to past time, it expresses a present or future happening by using an *if*-clause: "*If* I *agreed* with you, I would be a dolt" (unlikely). "*If* the boss *took* a rocket to the moon this minute, we would all be happy to run the business" (impossible). "*If* I *were* king, I would rule wisely" (contrary to fact). An exception to this formula is that a past subjunctive following the verb *wish* uses a *that*-clause: "We all wish *that* the war *were* over." "Sydney wishes *that* he *understood* the problem." (See also **IF CLAUSES**.)

The *past perfect subjunctive* is the only one of the three subjunctive forms that refers to time, and that is past time. The past condition that it expresses is not factual but, quite oppositely, is contrary to fact; that is, it indicates something that did not happen. This construction is formed with the auxiliary verb *had* and a past participle—had gone, had known, had eaten. The *had* construction distinguishes the form from the others: "If Rosalie *had known*, she would have come early" (the subjunctive implies that Rosalie did not know). "*Had* Jack seen the figures, he would not have bought the business" (Jack did not see the figures).

It should be noted that while the past perfect subjunctive may be expressed with only the auxiliary verb *had* and a past participle ("*Had* Peters *been* there, McGowen would have seen him"), it may also be introduced by such conditioned terms as *if, although, suppose,* or *unless* ("*If* Peters *had been* there . . .").

In addition to the subjunctive forms of the verbs, the mood may also be expressed by certain auxiliary verbs, such as *ought, must, might,* or *would*, which have a subjunctive meaning: "This *may* happen (conceivable). "*Should* he ignore his duty, he will be punished" (unlikely). "Jimmie *could* have been a good president" (contrary to fact).

SUBSTITUTE

See REPLACE, SUBSTITUTE

SUCCEED

See FOLLOW, SUCCEED

SUCCESSIVE

See CONSECUTIVE, SUCCESSIVE

SUCCINCT

See CONCISE, SUCCINCT

SUCH, SUCH AS

Such Nonsense

May one say, correctly, "*Of such* I want no part"? Not in the opinion of most authorities. In that example, *such* is acting as a pronoun, a part of speech to which it does not belong, even though the Bible says ". . . *of such* is the kingdom of God."

As a replacement for a personal pronoun—*it* or *them*—*such* is strongly disapproved by all grammarians. Either *it* or *them* is called for in "If you want *such*, let us know." Equally objectionable is the use of *such* as an indefinite pronoun for *all, one,* or *any* ("He is a good neighbor, and I treat him as *such*" [*one*]) or as a demonstrative pronoun for *this, that, these,* or *those* ("What could Randell do to stop *such?*" [*that* or *that practice*]).

The phrase *such a* presents a different kind of problem. The *a* should be omitted when a general sense is meant. For example, in "Prepare *such* studies as will be helpful" or "Put it to *such* use," nothing in particular is specified. In these cases *such* modifies a plural word or one used in an abstract sense, hence no *a*. However, when a single thing is referred to, then the *a* is needed: "Prepare *such a* study as the one we just finished." The rule is to use *such a* if the item has been particularized; that is, the *a* would be needed if *such* were omitted. As a further example, in "Wear *such* clothing as is suitable for the tropics," the idea is general; but it is specific in "Tonight wear *such a* suit as you're wearing now."

The phrase *no such a* is never correct because the *a* does not belong in a negative construction ("There is *no such* thing," not *no such a* thing). The *a* is also superfluous before *any, other,* or *one*; *such* alone should serve as the modifier: any *such* item, at one *such* location, another *such* happening.

Such as It Should Be

The conjunction *such as*, which introduces examples, is governed by the following rules. First, a series of words or phrases following *such as*, which points to selected items, should not in turn be followed by "and the like," "and so forth," "and so on," "and others," or any other all-inclusive expression. These phrases simply repeat the sense of *such as*. In "The finest newspapers are published in the large cities, *such as* New York, Los Angeles, Chicago, and so forth," *and* should precede Chicago and *and so forth* should be deleted.

Second, nouns, not prepositional phrases, follow *such as*. For example, in "These trees grow in temperate states, *such as* in Florida, Louisiana, and New Mexico," the *in* after *such as* does not belong. The sentence should be reworded, ". . . temperate states, *such as* Florida, Louisiana, and New Mexico."

Third, a comma is placed before *such as* when the material it introduces is not a part of the primary thought expressed: "He wore bizarre accouterments, *such as* Indian headdresses, brocade obis, and snowshoes." Since the information *such as* introduces is merely explanatory or illustrative, the entire phrase may be omitted with no loss in sense. Defining information, on the other hand, is so essential to meaning that without it the sentence would become nonsensical; hence it is not set off by commas. In "Presidents *such as Truman* are hard to find," omitting the phrase *such as Truman* would make the sentence absurd. A comma is never placed immediately after *such as*.

When *such* is an antecedent, serving as an adjective before a noun, *as* is its proper companion. This means that other combinations with *such—such . . . which, such . . . where, such . . . when, such . . . that*—should be avoided. In the following sentences, therefore, *as* should replace *who, which,* and *that*: "This seminar is designed for *such* physicians *who* (*as*) plan to study gynecology." "The club's Grounds Committee objects to *such* playing conditions *which* (*as*) exist in the farthest greens." "Horace will render *such* assistance *that* (*as*) the circumstances allow."

A final caution. In "At the fairgrounds we saw acrobats, aviators, ballplayers, and *such*," *such*, meaning "and the like," is substandard.

SUFFICIENT

See ENOUGH, SUFFICIENT

SUFFIXES

See AFFIXES

SUIT, SUITE

Suited to a T

The words *suit* and *suite* derive from the French *suivre*, "to follow." Despite their common ancestor, the words have established their own individual uses, and neither, by itself, is completely informative. Their meanings are clear only in an explanatory context. As a noun, *suit* may refer to a suit of clothes, the wooing of a woman, a legal procedure, or a set into which playing cards are divided. Among the various meanings of *suite* are certain musical compositions, connected rooms or offices, and sets of furniture.

It is considered gauche to employ one of these terms where the other belongs. Some usage authorities recommend that because *suit* is so often misused for *suite* regarding a set of furniture, the best way to avoid that misusage is to ignore those words and use *set* instead: "Today we bought a *set* of furniture for our patio." *Suite* is pronounced "sweet."

SUMMARY AND RELATED WORDS

Briefs Are More Revealing

A *summary* is "a condensation of the substance of a work."

It is a concise statement containing the premise of a subject as well as its conclusions: "His fine *summary* of the course gave us new insights." The briefest possible summary of the essential points of a work is called an *epitome* (Greek *epi*, "upon," *temnein*, "to cut"); hence to cut short. More often than not, *epitome* is wrongly used to mean "high point."

An *abridgment* is a shortening of a large work, such as a book or treatise, by selecting the most important portions. Its synonym, *digest*, is regarded as an informal term except in the legal profession. *Précis* means "a statement of the gist." It is an abstract, and is more suitably used of small works—a passage, a chapter, or a report. A *synopsis* is a summary presented as an outline or a list of headings, sometimes of a work in progress or of a text to be presented in the future. It is, according to its Greek forebear (*syn*, "together"; *opsis*, "view") a general view, a viewing all together (as in "From the *synopsis* presented, we gather he will not address the risks of gene-splicing"). *Compendium* refers to a brief compilation, a summary. Its adjective form *compendious* is more common.

The French-spelled *résumé*, "a summing up or recapitulation," is best used to denote a summary of pertinent experiences submitted with a job application.

Curriculum vitae, which literally means "the running course of one's life," is a stiffer expression than *résumé*. The latter remains the preferred word for a brief listing of one's experience and education.

Each of these words has a distinctive plural form: *summaries*; *epitomes*; *précis* (the same form as its singular); *synopses*; *compendiums* or *compendia*; *résumés*; *curricula vitae*.

SUPERLATIVES

Can You Top This?

To express the highest or the lowest, the best or the worst, a superlative form of comparison is used. (See COMPARISONS.)

Some words are superlatives, not because they are used for comparisons, but because they represent the ultimate. They cannot be made more or less; they simply are incapable of being compared or qualified. For example, *essential* and *perfect* are either *essential* and *perfect* or not, since nothing can be more important than that which is essential or more faultless than that which is perfect. These are absolute terms, so-called because they are indivisible; that is, they do not exist in degrees. Some other "absolutes" are *impossible, round, empty, matchless, excellent, equal, true, fatal, universal, final,* and the word *absolute* itself. An empty can in a group of cans, for instance, is not the emptiest—an empty can cannot become more empty. Something square or round, as the case may be, cannot be made squarer or rounder, and cannot, therefore, be the squarest or the roundest. Since *unique* means one of a kind, nothing can be more unique or the most unique. A superlative cannot be intensified; it already is the highest or lowest of its kind.

Some absolute expressions are nevertheless subject to a special kind of comparison. They may be modified by words indicating degrees of approximation; for example, *nearly* perfect, *almost* equal, or *a little more* round. These qualifiers are gradations to an ultimate. The variations, however, cannot apply to all absolutes. It would be nonsensical to say that something is deader, as children sometimes say, or more dead than the others. In fact, the comparative form *more* by itself may not qualify any of these words. Such phrases as *more equal, more round,* or *more circular* are not grammatically feasible. One notable exception is the Constitution's "to form *a more perfect Union.*" Although less than perfect, the phrase has spawned a government that is nearly so.

SUPPLANT

See **REPLACE, SUBSTITUTE**

SURPRISE

See **ASTONISH, SURPRISE**

SWEAT

A Sweater Is Warm

Is the past tense of *sweat* "sweat" or "sweated"? Either is correct, but there are preferences dependent on usage and locality. In the United States, *sweat* predominates; in Great Britain, *sweated*: "We were told that she *sweat* (or *sweated*) the fever out of her system." Used transitively, as when the sense is "to produce by hard work," *sweated* is correct in both countries: "The horses *sweated* their burdens along the rough road."

The saying "Animals sweat, gentlemen perspire, and ladies glow" is a euphemistic play on words. *Sweat* consists of droplets of moisture excreted through the pores. In its most common use—applied to persons—it is too indelicate for the genteel; they use *perspire*. However, *sweat* is inoffensive when employed figuratively. For example, "The walls of our kitchen are *sweating*" and "My son is *sweating* out his examinations" are acceptable in all societies, even in one that glows.

SYLLEPSIS

See **TYPES OF ERRORS**

SYMBOL

See **EMBLEM, SYMBOL**

SYNCHRONOUS

See **COINCIDENT, SIMULTANEOUS, SYNCHRONOUS**

SYNOPSIS

See **SUMMARY AND RELATED WORDS**

SYNTHETIC

See **ARTIFICIAL**

SYSTEMATIC, SYSTEMIC

Get It Out of Your System

Systematic and *systemic* are not interchangeable terms. The first is used generally; the second, only in physiology and pathology.

Systematic implies following a method to reduce a complex procedure to a system: "Lorenzo drew up a *systematic* plan to incorporate three units within three years." An ordered system, such as a complete scheme, outline, or classification, is said to be systematically arranged: "The Soviet leaders presented a *systematic* economic program, divided into five-year blocks."

Systemic is defined as "pertaining to a system or systems," but more usually it denotes something that affects the entire body. Hence its common use in sciences pertaining to diseases and living organisms: systemic death; systemic wilting in plants.

The verbs *systemize* and *systematize* mean "to reduce to a system." Since they are exact synonyms, either may properly be used to suggest arranging in an order or according to a system: "The chief clerk decided to *systemize* (or *systematize*) the storage bins." "This library would operate more effectively if someone were to *systemize* (or *systematize*) the catalogs." *Systematize* is the more common term.

TACTICS

See **STRATEGY, TACTICS**

TANDEM

Just a Little Behind

Tandem was originally a Latin word used to denote time. It meant "at last" or "finally." This temporal sense has now evolved into one of space, meaning "at length," as of two horses harnessed one behind the other or a bicycle with one seat behind the other, a bicycle built for two.

The sense of *tandem* should not, however, be further extended to signify any *two* or *two together,* as in "These books should be read in *tandem*" or "The motorcycle with a side car attached allows the officers to ride in *tandem*." It is correctly used only of such things as railroad cars, pieces of machinery, or animals arranged front to back, or head to tail: "The royal coach was drawn by matching grays, in *tandem*."

TANTAMOUNT

Tanta Mount

The word *tantamount* evolved from the Latin *tantus,* "so much," and *ad montem,* "to the mountain." These parts acquired a meaning of "amount to so much (as)," or "the same as," or "equal to." Today *tantamount* means "equivalent to" in almost anything—value, significance, effect. Primarily used of abstractions rather than material things, it is frequently applied to acts and remarks: "Comstock's gratuitous comment is *tantamount* to an insult." Because of its overuse, *tantamount* is no longer regarded as a desirable term. Further, it bogs down some sentences that, without it, would gain in economy. The phrase "is tantamount to" is easily replaced by *means* or *amounts to*: "The nod of his head *means* (rather than *is tantamount to*) approval."

Strangely, *paramount* is often confused with *tantamount*. Although the words resemble each other phonetically, they are unalike in meaning. The definition of *paramount* is "superior to all others, highest, chief"; its closest synonym is *supreme*. Like *tantamount, paramount* had an engaging ancestor. It derived from the Old French *par amont,* "at the top of." The last syllable of both *tantamount* and *paramount* is still used of some mountains: Mount Everest; Mount Fuji.

TENSE

See VERB TENSES

TÊTE-À-TÊTE

See FOREIGN WORDS

THAN

More than You Know

Many people would agree that *than* is incorrectly used in "He *hardly* went outside *than* it started to rain." *Hardly,* of course, should be followed by *when,* not by *than.* But *than* leads to other pitfalls, some of which are less obvious. For example, in "Almost three times as many voters are under thirty-five years of age *than* are over thirty-five," *than* is mistakenly used for *as.*

One of the most common and controversial uses of *than* is in a sentence like "Bob is taller *than* me." Although some authorities approve of this usage, most do not. Strictly speaking, *than,* when used to make comparisons, is a comparative conjunction and must be followed by a word in the nominative case, as in "Bob is taller *than I*" because the meaning is that "Bob is taller than I am tall." In formal writing this is the only accepted construction.

In some sentences of this type an extra word or words should be expended for the sake of clarity. "I like Susie better than Jane" presents two possible meanings: "I like Susie better than I like Jane" and "I like Susie better than Jane does."

Repeating the verb would clarify the meaning. But in those sentences in which the sense is clear, elaboration is unnecessary. For example, no one is likely to misconstrue this sentence: "The American people liked Reagan better than Carter."

THAT

That Is Wrong Because

That is frequently used colloquially to replace *because* in an elliptical answer to a question. A reply to "Why are the gasoline stations closed?" may be "Perhaps *that* it's Sunday," whereas it should have been either "The reason is that it's Sunday" or, more simply, "Perhaps because it's Sunday."

That is also made to serve as an adverb where it cannot function as one. In "Did you think he was tall" "No, I didn't think he was *that* tall," and in "Is the heat bothering you?" "No, it's not *that* warm," the *that*'s are wrongly employed for *very* or *so*.

The use of *that* after a comparison is a common error. In "The sooner *that* he does it, the better for us all," the *that* should be omitted: "The sooner (no *that*) he does it. . . ."

Using two *that*'s where only one belongs is another common error of surplusage. In "Some spectators think *that* if their cheers are louder than the opponents' *that* it will help their team win," the second *that* should be excised. The rule is that the conjunction *that* should not be repeated within a single clause. This despite the fact that the word *that* can be used many times successively. According to an old teacher's tale, criticism had been made of a *that* in a composition, but "it was shown that *that that* that that pupil used was correct."

THAT, THIS

Be Not Afraid of This

When *this* serves as an adjective (*this book, this melon, this shirt*), it qualifies the following noun, which in general is something close at hand. Something farther away is modified by *that*—"that boy at the end of the line."

When *this* and *that* as demonstrative pronouns are used to point out a specific object, something that can be seen ("*This* is my house, and *that* is my uncle's"), their meaning is clear. But when they are used in reference to a preceding general idea in a clause or sentence, particular care must be taken to avoid ambiguity. This usage, with the proviso just stated, is considered correct by most grammarians. In "I love this country; *that* is all I have to say," and in "A broken door, furniture all askew, drawers pulled open—*this* is what we found in our summer home," *that* and *this* obviously refer to a general statement which is easily understood. But in "The architect changed the blueprints to eliminate two side doors. *This* was a disastrous move to make," the question is to what does the *this* refer—the changing of the blueprints or the elimination of the two side doors.

If the writer is uncertain whether the preceding general statement is sufficiently explicit and unmistakable to serve as an antecedent for *that* or *this,* the safest thing to do is to convert the pronoun into a demonstrative adjective ("this event," "this theory," "this idea") to identify the previous thought. This is the way to avoid *this* problem.

THAT, WHICH

Which Was That?

Two of the most misused words in the English language are the relative pronouns *that* and *which*. Although they introduce different kinds of information and take different punctuation, they are sometimes inadvertently interchanged.

That is used of persons, animals, or things; *which*, only of animals or things. One may say, "He is the man *that* we saw" or, if preferred, ". . . *whom* we saw," but not ". . . *which* we saw." Except in formal writing, however, it is best to omit these words altogether if they are not the subject of a clause: "He is the man (no *that,* no *whom*) we saw yesterday." (The choice between *who* and *that,* when referring to persons, is that *who* preferably designates the individual or distinguishes each member of a group ["He is the man *who* won"], whereas *that* identifies the group or class itself ["Anyone *that* trains hard can win"].)

Clauses essential to the sense of a sentence (called restrictive clauses) are introduced by *that*. In "This is the house that we just purchased," *that we just purchased* identifies the house involved, the pronoun *that* restricting the application of the word *house* to the one house. A restrictive clause cannot be removed without impairing the intended meaning. For example, in "A magnet that has lost its power is useless," removing the *that* clause ("A magnet . . . is useless") makes the sentence absurd.

Nonrestrictive clauses—those that describe their antecedents—are introduced by *which*. These clauses are parenthetical, merely expanding the meaning of a preceding word or phrase, and may therefore be omitted without harm. For example, in "The Montgomery Villa, which was built in 1912, was sold last week," the *which* clause is merely descriptive. Its inclusion is not essential to the sense of the sentence. And neither is the *which* clause in "The Sixth Avenue bus, which is never on time, is running late again."

Nonrestrictive clauses are set off by commas; restrictive clauses are not. Failing to punctuate properly, or confusing *that* and *which,* may even convey a wrong message. For example, the sentence "The barn, *which* has a sloping roof, needs repair" says that there is only one barn—and it has a sloping roof. But "The barn *that* has a sloping roof needs repair" implies the existence of more than one barn. The *that* clause identifies the one that needs the repair.

When two restrictive clauses are near each other, and one is an adjective clause describing an antecedent, the relative pronoun *which* should arbitrarily introduce the clause to avoid the unpleasant repetition of *that*. In the following sentences, both *that*'s are ordinarily required; the recast examples contain the substituted arbitrary *which* (introducing the adjective clause). "He was so explicit *that* there was nothing *that* could be misconstrued" (nothing *which* could be misconstrued). "The mayor announced *that* Judge Webster would receive the community award *that* is presented annually" (award *which* is presented annually). "The principal's expression was the kind *that* said *that* the teacher should refrain from interrupting" (kind *which* said). Unlike the punctuation ordinarily used with nonrestrictive *which* clauses, no punctuation mark precedes an arbitrary *which*.

Recurrent *that*'s are also objectionable when one introduces a clause that is subordinate to the other. In "Enzo said that if the weather is clear tomorrow *that* he will go sailing," the second *that* is superfluous. Further, although it is not incorrect to say "Freddie said *that* he will leave soon," the *that* is unnecessary and stylistically inept.

Omitting a necessary *that,* however, can be a more serious syntactical offense than using a superfluous one. This is so when a time element follows the verb. There a *that* is required to indicate whether the time referred to applies to what appears before or after the verb. For example, in "Major Williams announced this evening the army would move out," a question is whether "this evening" applies to the announcement or to the moving out. A *that* is needed after "evening" to remove the ambiguity: "Major Williams announced this evening *that* the army would move out."

If a *that* is used in a sentence with two parallel clauses, for the sake of clarity both clauses should be introduced by *that.* In some constructions omitting the initial *that* may not affect the flow or sense of the first clause, but the first *that* is needed anyway to balance the one introducing the second clause. For example, in "The engineer hollered the building is on fire and that everyone should leave at once," a *that* should be inserted between *hollered* and *the.*

THERE IS, THERE ARE

See EXPLETIVES

THIEF

See BURGLAR, ROBBER, THIEF

THIS

See THAT, THIS

THOUGH

See ALTHOUGH, THOUGH

TIME EXPRESSIONS

What a Time!

Although almost anyone can tell time correctly, not everyone always writes it correctly. In formal writing, hours are expressed in words: at two o'clock in the afternoon; almost three-thirty in the morning. In informal writing, figures and abbreviations are customary (2 P.M., 3:30 P.M.). Words should not accompany them (not two P.M., not half past 3), nor should *o'clock* be used with the abbreviations (not 2 o'clock P.M.).

A.M. stands for *ante meridiem* (which means "before noon") and P.M., *post meridiem* (which means "after noon"). *Noon* is expressed 12 M (*meridies*); and midnight, 12 P.M. Preferably, to avoid confusion, one should be called 12 noon and the other 12 midnight.

Saying 9 A.M. in the morning is redundant, since A.M. and *morning* mean the same thing. Likewise, P.M. is repetitious if used with either "afternoon" or "evening." A reference to yesterday might read "10 A.M. yesterday" or, more formally, "ten o'clock yesterday morning." Hours and minutes are separated by a colon; but if only the hour is given, the ciphers are unnecessary—9 P.M. rather than 9:00 P.M., but 9:30 A.M.

In typescript, A.M. and P.M. may be set either in capital or in lowercase letters, with no space between them. The lowercase letters are neater: *a.m., p.m.* Since periods of time are not punctuated (they are considered a single unit), no commas appear in the following sentence: "It took him 3 hours 12 minutes 9 seconds to complete the task."

A Short Time

Instance means "example," as in "There you see an *instance* of how Helen wastes money." An *instant* is a moment of time: "He decided in an *instant*."

The connotation of *instant* is a short time. Unlike the word *minute,* which is a precise interval of time, *instant* denotes a trifling, unmeasurable, imperceptible moment. One who has been told to wait a minute should relax as the seconds tick away, for there will be sixty of them. But "I will be with you in an *instant*" keeps one alert, for the waiting period is expected to end almost immediately. The same thing may be said of *second.* "He'll be here in a *second*" implies a momentary appearance. As a practical, everyday matter, no time can be shorter than a second.

It is wiser to use the word *moment* when a short but indeterminate interval is intended. A *moment* may be an infinitesimal part of time, or it may be as long as, say, a minute. But considering what is involved, it is bound to be a comparatively brief period.

Sometimes the word *time* itself needs the support of other words. For example, "What time did you say we should meet?" although standard English, is best rephrased, "*At* what time. . . ." On the other hand, both *at no time* and *at any time* need the preposition *at* even in informal English. Those locutions enjoy no leeway. Some *time* phrases need a preceding *the,* but others do not. One may say, "We will do it *next time* as we did it *last time,*" but not "We will do it first time." It must be "*the* first time."

TOKEN

Sign of the Times

A *token* is defined as "a sign or symbol that serves to represent a fact, an event, an emotion, or the like." It often appears in the phrases "by the same token" and "as a token of" (my esteem, my appreciation, my devotion). Some precisians object to the expression "by the same token" as a wordy, hackneyed combination. They recommend that it be replaced by *likewise, moreover,* or *furthermore.* Certainly they have brevity on their side. But in some sentences, the extra wording, despite its triteness, provides a pleasing rhythm. The expression, therefore, should not be condemned out of hand. The phrase *as a token of,* however (meaning "as an evidence of"), spoken before the giving of a gift or award, is tiresome. A wag might say, "Let's have the gift and forget the token."

Synonyms of token are *sign, emblem, representation, memento, remembrance, mark, image,* and *souvenir.* This list is not exhaustive. Naturally, the word selected must suit the context.

The verb form of *token,* which is *tokened,* is rarely used. Its common replacement is *betokened.* Both verbs mean "to give a sign or *portent* of," as in "Those clouds *betoken* a severe storm." Although a *portent* is a sign of an impending calamity, and its verb form *portend* is used for warnings of unfortunate occurrences, *betoken* has no such implication. What is betokened may be unfortunate, or it may be, by the same token, something highly favorable.

TOO

Too, Too Much

A supervisor who says "I can't recommend my secretary *too* highly" may mean that she deserves the highest recommendation or, quite oppositely, that she does not deserve much of a recommendation.

Too is an adverb used in several senses. Primarily, it means "also": "The men, *too*, will have to perform some duties." (Although *also* may begin a sentence, *too* may not. In "*Too*, this matter needs attention," *too* should be replaced by *also, besides, moreover,* or *in addition*.) A second meaning is "more than is desirable": "He seems *too* dignified for such a menial job."

This last example points up another matter. *Too* generally does not modify past participles directly. Participles that denote action (that have retained their verbal force) are modified by adverbs of quality or condition, such as *much, greatly, deeply,* or *highly*. *Too* is an adverb of degree. To put it differently, for *too* to function properly, that is, to intensify a quality or condition, it must precede another adverb, as in "*too* greatly concerned," "*too* highly spiced," or "*too* deeply entrenched." Only those past participles that have lost their verbal force (their sense of action) and are now regarded as descriptive adjectives may be modified by *too* alone; for example, *too conceited, too complicated, too reserved,* and *too tired*.

Idiomatically *too* may mean "very much": "Leo was only *too* pleased to accommodate us." What legitimates this construction is the word *only*, which must immediately precede *too*.

TRACE, VESTIGE

The Vestige Yet To Come

A *trace* is a mark or slight evidence of something past or

present. It is barely perceptible, consisting of the smallest possible amount: "A *trace* of her perfume lingered in the room." "A *trace* of gunpowder was found on his sleeve." Its adjective form, *traceable*, retains its central *e*.

The word *vestige* came from the Latin *vestigium*, "footprint or sign." Although used synonymously with *trace*, it is more restricted in meaning, denoting the last, usually slight, remains of something currently nonexistent. It is actual, visible evidence: "*Vestiges* of Mayan civilization can be found in Cozumel." "A *vestige* of a broken spade led to the discovery of the missing tomb."

Trace, more general in application than *vestige*, may refer to the tangible remains or simply to a discernible effect of a now indiscernible thing: "Neither ships nor divers could find a *trace* of the sunken vessel."

TREACHERY, TREASON

Too Treacherous To Discuss

Both *treachery* and *treason* denote betrayal or violation of trust or confidence. *Treachery* has the more general meaning, suggesting disloyalty to a friend, colleague, or member of one's family: "The *treachery* of his adopted son broke the old man's heart."

Referring to one's country, *treachery* is the hallmark of a *traitor*. Used of things, it suggests false allurement that masks hidden dangers: the treacherous ocean current; the treacherous mountain path.

Treachery may also be treasonous. The offense of treason is the most serious violation of allegiance an American citizen can commit. It consists, according to the United States Constitution, of "laying War against them [the United States], or adhering to their Enemies, giving them aid and comfort." The treason of Benedict Arnold during the American Revolution is a famous example. His name has since become an epithet for *traitor*.

The term *high treason* in old English law was the highest offense against the state; it was, in fact, an offense against the sovereign. *Petit treason* was the killing of a master by his servant or a husband by his wife; it was considered the murder of a superior. *Treason* has two equally acceptable and interchangeable adjective forms: *treasonous* and *treasonable.*

TRITE EXPRESSIONS

It's Trite True

Everyone's language would improve if clichés would, like a morning mist, just fade away. How tiring it is to hear "I have news for you"; "It is a necessary evil"; "Now it's a whole new ball game"; "It is a fate worse than death"; "Thanks for nothing"; or "He's wild like a March hare." The last suggests how some readers feel about these hackneyed expressions. A discriminating writer or speaker avoids them.

Cliché and *stereotype* are synonymous terms. Their sense is "something repeated without variation." A *cliché* is a trite expression, so frequently repeated as to be devoid of evocative powers. It derives from the French *clicher,* which means "to stereotype." In application, however, these words differ. Technically, to *stereotype* is "to cast from a mold," "to use over and over." In a related sense, a stereotype is a printing plate made from a mold of type. But it is primarily an oversimplified idea or image that people adopt as representative of a diverse group of individuals. Thus we have a stereotype of a Southern belle or of a Harvard lawyer.

The gists of the adjectives *trite, hackneyed,* and *cliché* are similar: all refer to once effective ideas or statements gone stale. *Trite* derives from the Latin *tritus,* "rubbed" or "worn out." What is trite, therefore, has worn thin; it has become so familiar that it no longer stimulates thought. A *hackney* originally was "an ambling horse for ladies to ride on"; later, it came to describe any horse with a coach for hire. These horses eventually wore out from long and continual use. Figuratively, then, *hackney,* in the sense of "an overworked and worn-out horse," applies to any phrase once novel but now banal.

A *commonplace* is an ordinary, hackneyed, obvious remark, a stock comment, such as "All men are born to die" or "The sun is bound to shine again." At one time, those were notable sayings, but because of frequent repetition they have lost their freshness and are now as stale as three-day-old bread.

Coined from a French word meaning "flat," a *platitude* is

a dull, trite comment, like "You have to take the good with the bad." The statement is particularly disturbing because the speaker imagines it to be novel and profound. Usually the remark is greeted in a fitting manner—with silence or disdain. *Platitudes* are also called, appropriately enough, *bromides*.

A *truism* is a pronouncement of a self-evident truth; for example, "A mute person cannot speak." Such unquestionably true statements are never contested, since they are, of course, incontrovertible. In fact, one may wonder why they were voiced in the first place.

TRIUMPHAL, TRIUMPHANT

The Arch of Triumph

Unless the right dictionary is consulted, one could be misled on the proper use of *triumphal* and *triumphant*. Some lexicographers incorrectly consider them synonyms.

Triumphal originally described the solemn entrance into Rome of a general returning from a victory. The word, therefore, means "pertaining to or celebrating a triumph." In today's usage, *triumphal* refers to a commemoration or reception on the account of any triumph, not just military. Triumphal festivities may follow an election, a graduation from high school, or even a basketball game. Its use, however, is restricted to events and activities such as processions; a person cannot be triumphal.

The word *triumphant* suggests victory or a rejoicing in success, a feeling of triumph. It is synonymous with victorious, exultant, and successful: "The *triumphant* candidate was lifted aloft by his enthusiastic followers." "The students surrounded their *triumphant* football team." Although *triumphant* may be applied to the success itself, it usually refers to successful persons.

The word *trump* has the same ancestor, the Latin *triumphus*. In card games, trump is the superior unit; it outranks all other suits during the play of the hand, and thus assures victory or *triumph* over the other cards.

Trump is also seen in the figurative expression *trump card,* which signifies a telling argument or a decisive act. The trump card, whether in a game of cards, a legal argument, or a business transaction, is the clincher. "The oil-producing nations seem to be holding all the trump cards!"

TRIVIAL

See **PALTRY, PETTY, TRIVIAL**

TRUISMS

See **TRITE EXPRESSIONS**

TRUTH

The Truth of the Matter

Truth has many definitions depending on whether the sense involved is an abstraction or an actuality. In the former class are those matters regarded as spiritual reality. In terms of the quality of statements, acts, or feelings, *truth* may be defined as "that which corresponds with, or adheres to, reality and avoids error or falsehood." Generally one may define *truth* as something accepted as true or known with certainty, a fact. It is correct to say "Mrs. Hall wondered about the *truth* of Reginald's story (it was not proved to her complete satisfaction), even though he bore a reputation for veracity."

The term *veracity* implies devotion to the truth and applies to persons or to the statements made by them. Whereas what is true pertains to a fact, *veracity* suggests an unfailing observance of truth. It may be considered habitual truthfulness. A person, therefore, does not have a reputation for truth but for veracity. The adjective form of *veracity* is *veracious*.

A related but rarely used word—*verisimilitude*—must be spelled with care. The common error is omitting the first *i*. The word can be traced to the Latin *verisimilis*, which means "like the truth" or "probable." Its English definition is "the quality or state of being probable," that is, having the appearance of truth. Most often *verisimilitude* refers to the quality of an artistic or literary representation that is so lifelike or true to human experience as to cause one to accept it as such: "The effect of light rather than its *verisimilitude* was the most important aspect for the Impressionists."

TYPES OF ERRORS

Say It Right

The principal errors in grammar or in the use of words are labeled *barbarisms, improprieties,* or *solecisms.*

A *barbarism* is an irregularly formed word that has not been accepted into good usage: *someways* for *some way; irregardless* for *regardless.*

An *impropriety* is a word used in an incorrect sense or, more simply stated, an improper use of a word or expression: *learn* for *teach; affect* for *effect.*

A *solecism* is a grammatical error. It is, of course, an impropriety, too; but rather than the mere misuse of a word, it is a deviation from approved idiomatic usage: *these sort* for *this sort; between you and I* for *between you and me; different than* for *different from.*

A *syllepsis* ("a taking together") is the use of one verb in different senses with two objects, sometimes deliberately employed to afford humor: "He kicked the mule and his bad habits." "Cator destroyed the balloon and his son's chance for winning the race."

A less usual kind of syllepsis is the *zeugma* ("a yoke"). It is the faulty joining of a word with others to serve two senses when only one is correct: "The judge sentenced him to a prison term of two years and a fine of five hundred dollars." "He regularly ate for breakfast a slice of toast, a cup of coffee, and a fat cigar."

TYRO

See AMATEUR

$\mathcal{U}$

UN-

See IN-, UN-

UNCOMPARABLE

See INCOMPARABLE, UNCOMPARABLE

UNDERHANDED

Throw It Underhand

The question is whether *underhand* or *underhanded,* both meaning "deceitful, crafty, clandestine," is the better form. The original word was the shorter *underhand.* The longer *underhanded* evolved later, but it has overtaken *underhand* in today's general usage: "Crosson is *underhanded* in his dealings with the public."

Nevertheless, some authorities resist this usage, accepting only its classic meaning, "insufficiently provided with hands, or workers." Although that definition is still current, *underhanded* now not only is interchangeable with *underhand* (in the sense of sly, unfair, or secret) but is even the favored form. (*Shorthanded* has taken over the older meaning of *underhanded* and has become the term to indicate an unsufficient work force.)

The advantage of *underhanded* is that it is the base for the adverb and noun forms—*underhandedly* and *underhandedness.* Using *underhanded* as the adjective brings these words in line.

UNDER WAY

See NAUTICAL TERMS

UNINTERESTED

See DISINTERESTED, UNINTERESTED

UNIVERSAL

See COMMON, GENERAL, UNIVERSAL

UNLESS AND UNTIL

See IF AND WHEN, UNLESS AND UNTIL

UP

On the Up and Up

Up serves in combination with many verbs to form a sense different from that of the sum of their parts. The distinctions in meaning between "I shall dress for the meeting" and "I shall *dress up* for the meeting" and between "Speak, son" and "*Speak up*, son" are quite apparent. Likewise, in *get up, come up, dig up,* and *bring up, up* contributes an element of meaning. Nevertheless, many of these verb-adverb combinations, though widely and usefully employed, are "officially" rated as colloquialisms. Strict formal writing refuses their admittance, requiring instead single verbs like *rise* or *arise* for *get up.*

Of course, when *up* is unnecessary, it belongs nowhere, not even in informal usage. For instance, it is meaningless in "Let's *divide up* the profits" and in "Anna will *make up* the bed." It is redundant in *end up, finish up, hurry up, join up,* and *pay up.* It does not belong in "His son *signed up* with the Marines," and it is surplusage in "The minister *opened up* the sermon with a parable." *Up* is also up to no good in "*up until* the time of." Since *till* or *until* means "up to that point," *up until* actually says *up up to,* which sounds like a drill sergeant's bark.

On the other hand, although *up to now* is impermissible in serious writing, *up to date,* meaning "current" (as in "Bring the books *up to date*" or in "This is an *up-to-date* record") is acceptable on the highest levels.

Ordinarily *up* should immediately follow its verb to avoid clumsy wording and misinterpretation. For instance, there is a marked difference in criminality between "That man held the teller up" (the teller was a midget) and "That man held up the teller" (the teller was the gunman's victim).

USAGE, USE, UTILIZE

Get Used to It

It is poor English to say "To do the job quickly, we *utilized* all the help we could get" instead of "we *used* all the help." It is worse English to say "When the need for its *usage* declines, we will have more oil available."

Use is the ordinary word for the act of employing or putting into service: "That which serves well has been put to good *use*." "Machinery wears out after many years' *use*." In the last two sentences *usage* would be incorrect. As an everyday term *usage* means the customary way of doing things or a manner of use. One might therefore say, "Judging by the looks of these books, I think they have had hard *usage*." But *use* would not be wrongly used there either. In specialized matters of language, *usage* suggests adopted practice, referring to a standard of use evolved from word frequency and patterns. A word properly employed may be said to be in good use or good usage.

Another word containing the sense of use is *utilize*. It denotes a practical and profitable use. Something utilized has been made useful. In "We never thought that we could *utilize* our old inventory," the implication is that something dead has come advantageously alive. A person who makes do with a poor substitute is utilizing what is available: "The children are *utilizing* their mother's outdated hats for the Halloween party." Ordinarily *utilize*, with its pretentious sound, is best confined to its narrow strictures and employed only when *use* will not serve—which is seldom.

A near synonym of *utilize* is *exploit*. It derives from the Old French *esploit*, meaning "revenue or profit," a meaning not particularly dissimilar to its present one, "to utilize fully." What has been used profitably has been exploited. The thought expressed in "Howard *exploited* his knowledge of archeology by writing and lecturing" is that Howard used his knowledge to his practical benefit. A less appealing sense of *exploit* that has evolved is "to make selfish or unethical use of": "It was said that the railroad developers *exploited* the workers unconscionably." In its noun form, *exploit* means "feat or achievement"— usually one that is adventurous or heroic.

USED TO

What Used To Be

No one has trouble with the ordinary expression *used to,* when it refers to a regular practice or habit at some unspecified time in the past. One says, "We *used to* fish every Sunday when we were kids" or "Our family *used to* visit my aunt in Minneapolis." In this sense *used to* is an auxiliary verb to the infinitive that follows. But when its meaning is "accustomed to," a participle must follow, as in "During the war the Senate became *used to holding* night sessions."

Uneasiness develops, however, when a past negative form of *used to* is called for. The correct combination of words is *used not to* or *did not use to.* On a formal level, one may say, for example, either "The professor *used not to* mind the untidiness of the classroom" or "Francis did *not use to* criticize very much." The obstacle to overcome is the urge to say, "Francis did not *used* to criticize very much."

The forms used in interrogative sentences, primarily negative interrogatives, sound even stranger. A normal question is, "Did he *use* to work at Budd's?" Adding a negative element then makes the sentence read: "Didn't he *use* to work at Budd's?" But this ordinary construction is not accepted in the strictest formal style, which requires *"Used he not to* work at Budd's?"—a contorted assemblage of words hard to justify to the untrained ear. Though graceless, the phraseology is nevertheless correct. An easy way to sidestep it is by substituting *formerly* or *once.* "Did he *once* (or *formerly*) work at Budd's?" In all fairness to the expression *didn't he use to,* such a strong trend has developed in its favor that only a pedant would dare criticize it.

USUAL

See **FREQUENTLY, OFTEN, USUAL**

$\mathcal{V}$

VACANT

See EMPTY, VACANT

VACILLATE

See HESITATE, VACILLATE, WAVER

VALUE

See COST, PRICE, VALUE, WORTH

VERACITY

See TRUTH

VERB FORMATION FROM NOUNS

See BACK FORMATIONS; NOUNS AS VERBS & ADJECTIVES

VERB-SUBJECT AGREEMENT

See COMPOUND SUBJECT; -IC, -ICS; INDEFINITE PRONOUNS; PAIR WORDS; SINGULAR NOUNS THAT APPEAR PLURAL

VERB TENSES

The Present Follows the Past

Changing tenses in the middle of a sentence is ordinarily as inadvisable as changing horses in midstream. When an independent clause contains a verb in the past tense, a dependent clause also needs a past tense to maintain continuity of thought. The following sentences exemplify this principle: "The applicant said his name *was* Arnold Lucker and that he *lived* (not *lives*) in Dunmore." "The chemist *explained* what the new formula *meant* (not *means*)." "Margaret *wondered* aloud whether the decisions *were* (not *are*) just." An exception to this rule is found in expressions of universal or timeless truths—so-called permanent truths—that are as true in the present as they were in the past. These expressions, when set out in a dependent clause, are placed in the present tense even though they follow a principal verb in the past tense: "We were *taught* that *Hamlet is* (not *was*) Shakespeare's greatest tragedy." "The class *learned* today that water *freezes* (not *froze*) at 32°F." "Who first *proved* that the world *is* (not *was*) round?"

The permanent truth rule applies only to dependent clauses. Therefore, a sentence having only one verb, although expressing a timeless truth, cannot qualify: "Runnymede *was* (not *is*) the birthplace of the Magna Carta." "George Washington *was* (not *is*) the father of our country."

Verbs That Past Twice

Weave, wove, and *woven* are the principal parts of the verb *to weave.* In the sense of interlacing threads, *wove* is the common past tense and *woven* the past participle: "The company *wove* many baskets to sell during the Easter holiday; some were hand *woven* by the blind." When reference is made to threading in and out of traffic, moving from side to side, or following a widening circle, *weaved,* not *wove,* is the customary form: "The ambulance *weaved* swiftly through the traffic." "The right wing *weaved* through the opposition and slipped the puck past the goalie."

Dive also has two past tense forms. The one recognized in formal style is *dived,* yet only a pedant would say, "They *dived* for the ball." Common usage, borrowed from the lingo of sports announcers, calls for *dove.*

Opinion is divided on the past-tense form of *kneel. Knelt* predominates, but *kneeled* is equally correct. And then there is *knit,* with its two forms: *knit* and *knitted.* Adjectivally, either word is correct—a knit scarf, a knitted scarf; as a verb, however, only *knit* may be employed in an abstract sense ("Their common problem *knit* them into a life-lasting friendship").

Another variant past tense with a special use is *winded* for *wind,* as in "to wind a rope." In normal usage it is *wound,* but in nautical language it is *winded* (as in "Charles *winded* carefully both the hawser and the mainsheet").

Variant past tenses of many other verbs are interchangeable: *dreamed* and *dreamt; sank* and *sunk; thrived* and *throve.* The first one of each pair is preferred in the United States; the second, in Great Britain.

VERBAL

See ORAL, VERBAL

VERISIMILITUDE

See TRUTH

VERSE

See STANZA, VERSE

VERY

Intensive Care

Possibly the most frequently abused adverb in the English language is *very.* Many people are unable to say that something is *good, warm,* or *sour.* It must be *very good, very warm,* or *very sour.* These people are uncertain whether, without *very,* the idea can come across. And so they use it whenever possible.

Yet omitting *very* often improves, even strengthens, style, for *very* adds nothing but verbiage while foreclosing the use of more accurate terms. It may be said that *very* is generally a *very* (?) *good* word to forget. According to Shaw, a teacher once told his students to delete the word *very* whenever it appeared and to substitute *damn* for it—and then to delete the profanity.

Sometimes, however, and this at first sounds contradictory, *very* is an important auxiliary in some grammatical constructions. This is so with the adverb *likely.* When *likely* means "probably," it needs a qualifying word, which may be *very, most,* or *quite.* Ordinarily the one used is *very.* The sentence "The game will likely be held on Thursday," for example, should be rephrased: "The game will *very likely* be held on Thursday." In the sense used, *likely* may not travel by itself: *very* makes a perfect escort.

As a modifier of a participle, *very* raises another problem. May it serve alone? Or does it require the company of *much* or some other adverb? From a strictly grammatical point of view, *very* may not modify a past participle. Since it is an intensive (that is, an adverb of degree), it may modify only an adverb of quality. For example, "We were very concerned by his absence" needs rephrasing: "We were *very much concerned*" or, perhaps, "We were *very greatly concerned.*" "The effect was very enhanced" also needs changing: "The effect was *very much enhanced.*"

What complicates the matter further is that some past participles have lost their verbal force and are now treated as pure adjectives. As such, they take *very* by itself. "He is *very upset*" and "We are *very tired*" are therefore correct as given, as is "She was *very disappointed.*"

The distinctions in these uses are subtle. Whether a participle may be treated as an adjective is not easy to determine, for the guidelines are far from precise. The rule generally followed is to regard the word as an adjective if it suggests a quality or condition, as do *determined, annoyed,* and *dignified,* but as a verb if it indicates action, as do *disturbed, emphasized,* and *excited.*

Prudent writers refrain from using *very* when the status of a participle is uncertain. They lose nothing but an unnecessary word.

VESTIGE

See TRACE, VESTIGE

VESTIGIAL

See RUDIMENTARY, VESTIGIAL

VIA

But Is It Via-ble?

Via is the Latin word for way, road, or path. In English, it is used as a preposition to signify a relationship to a place, such as a highway or route that passes through a city: "You can drive from New York to Baltimore *via* Philadelphia." "We are flying to Paris *via* London." The term is particularly applicable to travel and shipping routes.

The common error with *via* is extending it to mean "through the agency of" or "by means of." Since it does not refer to a means of transportation, saying "We traveled *via* plane and train" is informal at best, as is "The news reached the treasurer *via* the controller." In the first example *by* should replace *via,* and in the second, *through.* The United States Post Office has unfortunately sanctioned the extended sense of *via* with the phrase "via airmail," now imprinted on the front of airmail envelopes.

VIRTUALLY

See **PRACTICALLY, VIRTUALLY**

VISAGE

See **FACE**

VITAL

See **ESSENTIAL, INDISPENSABLE, VITAL**

VIS-À-VIS

See **FOREIGN WORDS**

VOCIFEROUS, VORACIOUS

Loudmouth

The sentence "Professor Clarke is a vociferous reader" exemplifies a common but incorrect usage of the word *vociferous.* The word intended was *voracious,* which, from the Latin *vorare,* "to devour," means "having an insatiable appetite." The professor, figuratively, devours books and other reading material. Originally pertaining only to the gluttonous eating of food, the meaning of *voracious* has been extended to encompass other forms of hunger, such as hunger for achievement or success, as in "He has a *voracious* desire for more honors." Words related to voracious are *insatiable, gluttonous, ravenous,* and *rapacious*; each, however, signifies a different kind of prodigious appetite.

If Professor Clarke were a vociferous reader, he would probably be thrown out of the library. *Vociferous* means "characterized by loudness and vehemence." Synonyms of *vociferous* point to the nature of the word: *boisterous, strident, loudmouthed.*

VOICE

Hear the Voice of the Verb

The voice of a verb, which is either active or passive, is the way the verb speaks about the subject. When the subject is the agent of the verb—the performer of the action expressed by the verb—the verb is said to be in the active voice (as in "Janie *loves* Herbert"). If the action is reversed ("Herbert *is loved* by Janie"), so that the subject of the verb is the receiver of the action, the voice of the verb is passive.

Only a transitive verb can be in either form: active ("The secretary *signed* the reports") or passive ("The reports *were signed* by the secretary"). Transitive verbs take a direct object; intransitive verbs do not. An intransitive verb expresses an action that stops within itself, as in "He spoke loudly" or in "Vavra has been dancing for hours." To determine voice, therefore, one must decide whether the verb is transitive or intransitive or, to put it differently, whether the action expressed by the verb needs an object to complete its meaning.

VORACIOUS

See **VOCIFEROUS, VORACIOUS**

W

WANE, WAX

The Wane in Spain

If something waxes, it gradually becomes larger, more numerous, stronger, or more intense. If it wanes, it decreases gradually in size, amount, intensity, or degree. The words *wax* and *wane* are usually employed independently of each other except in reference to the phases of the moon, which "wax and wane."

Wane is normally used without modifiers, as in "His enthusiasm *waned*." But *wax* cannot stand alone; one does not say, for example, "His enthusiasm *waxed*," to suggest that it grew stronger. The sentence needs rephrasing, "His enthusiasm *waxed strong*," for by convention *wax* is used in the sense of "growing or becoming as specified" ("He *waxed eloquent*." "It *is waxing late*"). Since *wax* is a linking verb, it takes an adjective, as in the previous examples, not an adverb. It is therefore incorrect to say, "Mrs. Tyler was *waxing joyfully* at her son's wedding," unless she was busily polishing his furniture.

WANT

See LACK, NEED, WANT

WAVER

See HESITATE, VACILLATE, WAVER

WAX

See WANE, WAX

WAY, WAYS

You've Come a Long Ways, Baby

Habits die slowly. In January school children say, "We have a long *ways* to go before summer," and in June, "The ballfield is a short *ways* past the house." Though forgivable in childhood, using *ways* for *way* in adulthood is less pardonable. The singular noun *way*, when referring to distance in general, is the only acceptable form. And it always needs a preceding *a, this,* or *that*: *a* way; *this* or *that* way.

The adverbial use of the noun *way* is permissible in such constructions as "Look this *way*, please" and in "Let's do it my *way*," in which *way* manifests direction or manner. It is colloquial, however, when substituted for *away*, as in "The school is *way* across the park" or in "*Way* back in the good old days when a nickel was a nickel, that's what a cup of coffee cost." Further, *way* is sometimes superfluous—the preceding sentence would be just as informative without it—"Back in the good old days. . . ."

The plural form *ways* has two proper uses: to indicate more than one way (as in "How do I love thee? Let me count the *ways*") and the structure on which ships are built (as in "Everyone cheered when the ship slid down the *ways*").

Direction may be shown in some nouns by attaching the suffix *-ways*: *edgeways, sideways, endways*. It is the equivalent of *-wise*: *endways* or *endwise, lengthways* or *lengthwise*.

Whether *anyway* and *someway* may correctly end in *s* is a matter of dispute among authorities. Generally the *s* should be omitted, especially since some dictionaries continue to label *anyways* and *someways* nonstandard or colloquial. *Anyway* and *someway* are adverbs meaning "nevertheless" and "in some way," respectively. When written as two words, they are used as other parts of speech. Whether to spell them as two words or one word is easily determined by substituting *a* for *any* or *some*. If the sentence using *a* makes sense, two words are needed; for example, "We have to find *a way* (or *any* or *some way*) to simplify the equation."

WEAPONRY TERMS

A Shot in the Dark

Although no one wants to be shot with either a bullet or a cartridge, only the bullet can do any serious harm, since it is the missile. A descendant of the French *boulette,* a bullet is a spherical pointed piece of lead fired from a gun, whereas a cartridge is the container for the bullets or pellets. Cartridges are normally ejected from some guns after they have been fired. Firing *rounds* means firing a series of cartridges.

Any device that shoots a projectile is a *gun.* A *gun,* therefore, may be a cannon, a firearm, or even a mine thrower. Handguns, commonly called *pistols,* are either *revolvers* or *automatics.* An *automatic* is capable of firing continuously until all the ammunition is expended. Revolvers are loaded with individual bullets; automatics, with cartridge clips.

Caliber, spelled *calibre* by the British, is the measurement of the diameter of the bore or interior tube of a gun, bullet, or shell. *Gauge* is an indirect measure of caliber, determined differently and expressed as a different unit. Figures are used to designate both caliber and gauge: .45 caliber revolver; 12-gauge shotgun. The *au* in *gauge* should not be inadvertently reversed—*gauge,* not *guage.*

WEIGHT, TERMS FOR

Weighty Matters

In a strict sense, a fat person should not be called *obese,* for more than mere overweight, *obese* means "excessively fat." The word comes from the Latin *obedere,* "to eat away" or "devour." Physicians use *obese* as a medical term for those patients whose heaviness constitutes an unhealthy condition.

The general word to describe an abundance of flesh is *fat.* People whose avoirdupois gives them a rounded appearance are called *plump,* a not uncomplimentary word in some contexts: "My friend is pleasingly *plump.*" A *stout* person, especially a man, is fleshy: "Mr. Arkwright is jolly enough but not *stout* enough to be a Santa Claus." Moreover, *stout* may not mean "fleshy" at all but rather "characterized by physical or moral bravery," as is a stout-hearted fellow, like a Canadian Mountie.

The term to designate a large and bulky body is *corpulent,* a euphemism that suggests a stoutness which is not disfiguring.

Other synonyms of *fat* include *pudgy, rotund, chubby, adipose, portly, thickset,* and *fleshy. Portly,* like *corpulent,* describes a person whose bulk does not detract from an imposing figure. *Pudgy* and *chubby* are used especially of children or of those who seem not to have outgrown their "baby fat."

The only word in this listing that poses a problem in pronunciation is the word in the first sentence: *obese.* It is pronounced oh-*bees*.

WHAT EVER, WHEN EVER, WHO EVER

Ever, Ever Land

The spelling of *-ever* words (such as *whenever* or *when ever, whatever* or *what ever,* and *whoever* or *who ever*) has been a source of controversy. The question raised is, Should they be written as one word or two words? Most grammarians agree that in an interrogative, only the two-word phrase is permissible: "*When ever* may we expect to receive them?" "*What ever* does he want?" But the second element, *-ever* (a provincialism meaning "in the world"), since it merely intensifies, need not be used at all. "*What* (*ever*) does he want?" will suffice.

Those authorities who insist that all *-ever* words be written solid, even in interrogative sentences, regard the use of two words as informal. But their opinion has not altered standard guidelines. The rule by and large is that the declarative sentence gets one word ("*Whoever* comes in first will be declared the winner") and the interrogative, two ("*Who ever* will be declared the winner in the beauty contest?").

WHEN, WHERE

Where O Where Did When Come From?

It is poor style to define a word by using the phrase *is when* or *is where. When* and *where* are generally adverbs and therefore cannot properly introduce noun clauses. It sounds juvenile to say, "A callus *is when* you have thickened skin" or "A convention *is where* people assemble." Those sentences have false predication—the predicate complement of a noun must be another noun or an equivalent, not an adverbial clause. The sentences should be recast: "A callus is thickened skin" and "A convention is an assembly of people." The expression *see where* is just as gauche in "We *see where* the Governor was reelected." *That* should replace *where*.

Similarly, *when* and *where* should not be used immediately after the word *example*. Idiom calls for *of*. The sentence "Recalling your youth, can you give an example *when* jealousy destroyed a friendship?" should be rephrased "an example *of* how your jealousy . . . ."

Where presents another problem, in that frequently it is wrongly used for *when*. *Where* should introduce an adverbial clause of place; *when*, of time. In "*Where* children quarrel, their parents are reluctant to intervene," *when* is needed. Further, *where* is neither a substitute for *that* ("The reporter observed *that* [not *where*] the House had no quorum") nor a replacement for *in which* ("This is a group *in which* [not *where*] everyone is involved").

WHEN CLAUSES

When Not To Do It

A *when* clause, like any other subordinate clause, should not appear to carry the major thought of a sentence. Its purpose is simply to fix the time of an occurrence or event stated in the independent clause. Therefore, in "The teller was thinking about his imminent engagement *when* suddenly he spied a man with a pistol leap over the cage," a restructuring is needed because the impact of the subordinate idea is greater than that of the principal statement. One way to restructure the sentence is by cutting it in two: "The teller was dreaming about his imminent engagement. Suddenly he spied a man with a pistol leap over the cage." A better way, since the first thought hardly warrants a separate sentence, is to convey it subordinately: "The teller, while dreaming about his imminent engagement, suddenly spied a man with a pistol leap over the cage." Another example of a major thought made minor is in "They began to discuss financial problems *when* Frank suggested they sell the remaining stock." The elements need reversing: "*When* they began to discuss financial problems, Frank suggested they sell the remaining stock."

If *when* begins a sentence, the clause it introduces should modify the principal verb: "*When* it comes to pass, we will leave." But in "*When* medical students acquire a little knowledge, we can understand their desire to act like doctors," the sentence needs recasting: "We can understand that *when* medical students acquire a little knowledge they want to act like doctors."

When should not be used in defining other words, as in "A report *is when* a detailed account is given" or "A hurricane *is when* a high wind blows." Nouns are to be defined in terms of other nouns: "A report is a detailed account." "A hurricane is a violent storm."

WHERE

See WHEN, WHERE

WHERE-

Why or Wherefore?

Although such pompous adverbs as *whereof*, *wherein*, and *whereon* are tolerated in formal usage, simpler words are preferable because they make the reader feel more comfortable.

The sentence "We visited the room *wherein* he was assassinated," for example, is more acceptably expressed, "We saw the room *in which* he was assassinated," or, better yet, "We saw the room *where*. . . ." Saying "The students listened attentively to their teacher's parting statement, *whereupon* they rose and left" sounds stilted—*after which* or *and then* would flow better.

Whereon is replaceable by "on which" or "on what"; *wherefrom*, by "from what" or "where" (*whence* is just as formal as *wherefrom*); *whereat*, by "at which time" or "as a result of which" (here again, *whereupon*, a synonym, is no improvement); and *whereof*, by "of what," although no one would dare change "They know not *whereof* they speak."

Wherewith, meaning "with what" or "which," has a cousin, the noun *wherewithal*, which means "the necessary means." It suggests financial ability: "He now has the *wherewithal* to begin his new business." The final syllable of *wherewithal* is *al*, not *all*, and the word has no plural form. There is no *wherewithals*.

In "O Romeo, Romeo, wherefore art thou Romeo?" *wherefore* means "why." Except in formal resolutions, such as "Wherefore the Governor declares this day a holiday," the word is seldom seen except in the phrase "the whys and wherefores," in which *wherefores* is a noun meaning "reasons" or "answers."

WHICH

See **THAT, WHICH**

WHILE

A Wily Word

The adverb *awhile* and the prepositional phrase *for a while* have identical meanings and are interchangeable. The sense is the same whether one says "Sleep *awhile*" or "Sleep *for a while*." Because of these different constructions, however, writers must distinguish between them.

While is a noun meaning "a space of time." Except for the idiom *a while ago*, it is usually preceded by a preposition: *after a while, for a while*. The one-word *awhile*, meaning "for a short time," modifies verbs. One must be careful, therefore, not to write either "We intended to watch the parade *for awhile*" or "We looked *a while* but soon tired." Those examples need their *while*'s reversed—*for a while* and *awhile*.

While as a conjunction of duration means "at the same time" or "during the time that." Colloquially it often substitutes for *but, and, on the other hand*, and *although*. In strict formal writing, however, only *although* is acceptable. In less formal writing, *while*, for the sake of variety, may replace it if doing so leads to no ambiguity: "*While* I approve of his plan, I think it's costly." What must be carefully guarded against are such ludicrous statements as "*While* he was a well-behaved youngster, he spent much of his adult life in prison" and "*While* she had her first baby in Alabama, she had her second in Kentucky."

As a verb, *while* is less common but is a useful word nonetheless. It means "to cause to pass, especially without boredom or in a pleasant manner," and is usually accompanied by *away*:

"Let us *while away* the time in our garden." Still less common is the alternative *wile*. It, too, is followed by *away*: "He *wiled away* the afternoon tending to his flowers." *Wile* has unrelated meanings. As a verb it means "to entice," as in "The spider *wiled* the fly into its parlor," and as a noun, "a trick, artifice, or stratagem."

WHO, WHOM—WHOSE, WHO'S

Who's So Wise as an Owl

Whom do you think has a problem in deciding whether to use *who* or *whom*? Teachers? Students? Telephone operators? Everyone? Probably "everyone."

Who and *whom* are most often misused in interrogatives, particularly in the omnipresent question: "Whom shall I say is calling?" What induces this error is the "interrupter" *shall I say*. The proximity of the interrogative pronoun to the nominative *I* or *you* in expressions such as "do you think," "do you suppose," or "do you believe" leads almost naturally to the objective case *whom*—hence the mistake in the opening sentence of this article. It should have been "*Who* do you think has a problem."

In declarative sentences as well, parenthetical remarks make the issue of *who* or *whom* cloudy. For instance, in "Max is a pharmacist *who* (*whom*) I think is highly ethical," *who* is called for, since it is the subject of *is*. In effect the sentence says (omitting the parenthetical "I think") "Max is a pharmacist *who is* highly ethical." The practice of mentally omitting an interrupter to straighten the grammatical seams may eliminate the quadrennial query, "Whom do you think will win the election?" Even an owl says "Who!"

Who's Who is the title of a prestigious biographical guide; "Who's Whose" are two words that are sometimes confused. *Who's* is a contraction of *who is* ("*Who's* responsible?") or *who has* ("*Who's* forgotten the picnic hamper this time?"), whereas *whose* is the possessive form of *who* or *which*. Therefore, in "Here's a man who's pride is in his home" and "Here is a man whose always thinking of his home," the pronouns must be switched to learn who's who and what's what.

(The use of *whose* in possessive reference to inanimate nouns is discussed under ANTECEDENTS.)

WIDE

See BROAD, WIDE

WILL

See SHALL, WILL

WINDFALL

See SHORTFALL, WINDFALL

-WISE

A Word to the Wise

The best advice a person can find on the use of the suffix *-wise* is in Strunk's *Elements of Style*: "There is not a noun in the language to which *-wise* cannot be added if the spirit moves one to add it. The sober writer will abstain from the use of this wild additive."

This suffix, which came from the Anglo-Saxon, means "way," "manner," or "fashion," as in "in any wise" or in "in no wise." Most often, however, it is added to a noun to form a compound word meaning "in a specific direction" (*lengthwise, edgewise*) or "in the manner of" (*clockwise, otherwise*). Both are legitimate uses. But what should be discouraged is the faddish sense of "concerning" or "with regard to" in contrived adverbs, such as *functionwise, healthwise, flavorwise, marriagewise, marketwise,* or *sanitationwise*. Those terms lack grace; they are, in fact, abominations. Some writers use these coinages under the false belief that their creations are so effective as to encompass entire concepts.

All temporary *-wise* compounds are not to be condemned out of hand, however. Those nouns that have no adjectival form may, for the sake of conciseness, be converted into an adverb by adding the suffix. But if economy is a virtue, it is not achieved in a sentence like "Pricewise, we have received no complaints from anyone." Just as brief—and simpler—is "No one has complained about our prices."

WORDINESS

Be Stingy

Even a short sentence is too long if it contains unnecessary words. Excessive wordage—superfluities—is distracting or, at the least, tiresome. Wordy or useless phrases are set in parentheses in the following sentences. "The Revenue Act is (a) baffling (and puzzling enactment)." "He bought all (of) the extra books (that) we had." The president started (out) as a mail clerk." "(Anyone who comes from the Midwest) Any Midwesterner has a distinctive drawl." "Order the book now (so that you may be sure) to be sure of getting yours." "What my uncle remembered best was (the fact that his friend was reliable) his friend's reliability."

Participles can be a word-saving device, for although they take fewer words than adjective clauses, their function is the same. The sentence "He is a student who works hard" is more economically put: "He is a hard-working student." And "Andy Peltz, who was chosen for his ability, won the instant approval of the crowd" might read: "Andy Peltz, chosen for his ability. . . ." The question to ask is, "Who needs *who*?" Usually no one.

The active voice says what the passive says but with fewer words. "Contributions were made by many members" shrinks to "Many members made contributions," and "The patient was told by the orderly to restrain himself" becomes "The orderly told the patient to restrain himself."

Negative forms are more economical than positive forms preceded by negatives. For example, in "He is not aware of what she is doing," *unaware* can substitute for *not aware*. Similarly, "William is no longer enchanted" can be replaced by "William is disenchanted" and "He is not civil" by "He is uncivil." Sometimes, however, a word couched in its negative form does not furnish the emphasis desired; at other times it might affect sentence rhythm. "The soldier was disloyal to his comrades-in-arms" has a weaker ring than "The soldier was *not loyal*. . . ." Whether to employ a negative just for the sake of economy becomes a question of judgment.

Some wordiness can be avoided by exchanging long-winded phrases for single words. For example, *in my estimation, in my opinion,* and *in my judgment* are often replaceable by "I think," "I feel," or "I believe." *As a method of* and *as a way of* go a long way to say *in* or *for.* "Gymnastics is helpful *as a method of* reducing" itself is reduceable: "Gymnastics is helpful *in* reducing." "Cooking vegetables by steam is effective *as a way of* retaining vitamins" needs only "is effective *for.*" The following replacements also economize: *from time to time,* "occasionally"; *in many instances,* "often"; *in accordance with,* "by" or "with"; *for the reason that,* "because"; *with great emphasis,* "emphatically"; *in relation to,* "about" or "to" or "toward"; *of his own free will,* "freely"; *without meaning to,* "unintentionally"; *in advance of,* "before"; *of a generous nature,* "generous"; *is in possession of,* "has"; *by no manner of means,* "in no way"; *by means of,* "by" or "with."

"Since" and "because" are good substitutes for many wordy phrases, among them *seeing as how, seeing that, because of the fact that,* and *owing to the fact that.* The phrase *the fact that* is, in fact, almost always unnecessary. *Except for the fact that* may be shortened to "except that"; *in spite of the fact that,* to "although."

Some phrases can be omitted entirely with no loss in meaning. For example, "He wants something *in the line of* a ball-bearing file cabinet" says, with the clutter removed, "He wants a ball-bearing file cabinet."

WORDS OF APPROXIMATION

Give or Take

What a difference a hyphen makes. A brochure announcing that the school has thirty odd teachers on its teaching staff had not intended to refer to an eccentric faculty. What was meant was "thirty-odd teachers." In the sense used, *odd* indicates an approximation—it means "a few more"—and it therefore may be used only with a round number and preceded by a hyphen. The sentence "New York is ninety-two-odd miles from Philadelphia," for example, should read "ninety-odd miles."

Any word of approximation, like *odd,* runs counter to the sense of an exact figure. "*Some* forty-six birds were on the fence" is another case in point. The *some* should be dropped. *About*, too, since it already is an estimate, is contradictory when it precedes an exact number. In "We saw *about* 467 students there," the number should be made round or the word *about* omitted.

It is correct to say "*About* 2,000 people were injured in the flood," or "The number of people injured in the flood was *estimated* at 2,000," but not "was *estimated* to be *about* 2,000." One guess is enough. In describing a person's age as "*about* 26 to 29 years old," *about* is redundant. In "We met *at about* 11 A.M., *about* is superfluous: at "11 A.M." is precise; "*about* 11 A.M.," approximate; "*at about* 11 A.M.," confusing.

Another confusing phrase is "around about." *Around* refers to motion; *about* to an approximation. The words are therefore not companionable and adjoining them makes for poor English. *Around* should be omitted in "We will have *around about* twenty guests for dinner." And the sentence "There are *around* fifteen books on the shelf" would read better if *around* were replaced by *about*.

Although dictionaries regard the words *approximately* and *about* as synonyms, *approximately* is a more precise term. In strict formal English *approximately* should replace *about* in "The lodge is *about* three miles from the highway." Many writers, nevertheless, prefer *about* because it is a lighter and shorter word.

WORTH

See COST, PRICE, VALUE, WORTH

WRACK

See RACK, WRACK

WRONG

See RIGHT, WRONG

XYZ

X RAY

X Rated

X is a symbol used to designate any unknown or unnamed factor, thing, or person. The term *X ray*, of German origin, was so called because its exact nature was unknown. For the technically minded, an *X ray* is an electromagnetic wave with a radiation wavelength of 0.1 to 2.0 Angstroms.

The noun *X ray* is preferably spelled as in this sentence, with a capital *X* and no hyphen. Used as a verb or adjective, the *X* followed by a hyphen is standard: "The doctor *X-rayed* Paul's jaw." "Eleanor has just become an *X-ray* technician." (A specialist in the theory and use of X rays is called a *roentgenologist* [*rehnt*-gehn-ol-uh-jist].) The discoverer of X rays was Wilhelm Konrad Roentgen, a German physicist.

The expression *cross reference* is treated similarly. As a noun, it takes no hyphen, but it needs one when serving as a verb or adjective: cross-reference pages; pages that were cross-referenced. Informally it is sometimes spelled *x-reference*.

YET

But Not Yet

Except when *yet* acts as a coordinating conjunction meaning "but" ("Ralph acts the part of a buffoon, *yet* I enjoy his antics"), it serves as a temporal adverb. In that function, reflecting time (in the sense of "up to now"), a perfect tense is needed in negative constructions. It is therefore wrongly used in "The teacher gave me a book, but *I did* not open it *yet*." The sentence should be rephrased: ". . . but I *have* not opened it *yet*." "The architect *did* not call *yet*" should also be rewritten: "The architect *has* not called *yet*."

Usually the expression *as yet* can be shortened to *yet* without

325

affecting the sense of the sentence. This is a stylistic decision. In "Caldwell has not *as yet* made his plans," the *as* is optional. When used to begin a sentence, however, it is required: "*As yet,* we have not been informed."

ZEUGMA

See **TYPES OF ERRORS**

ZOOM

Ups and Downs

In aeronautics, *zoom* means "a brief, sharp-angle climb by an aircraft." Airplanes zoom over obstacles or clear them by turning suddenly and sharply upward. Since *zoom* implies an upward movement, the word is wrongly used in reference to a downward motion. Gulls, for example, do not zoom down on their prey. They swoop. In popular usage the meaning of *zoom* has come to include a rapid move on the level. When an automobile is traveling at a high speed, it is said to be zooming along.

Index